STUPID MACHINE

Stupid Machine

MARK NIEMANN-ROSS

CONTENTS

First Printing, 2025

{"Thank You" : {

"Rob Garrott" : "You gave these characters time and place.",

"Lucy Musson" : "You are just so darn enthusiastic. Thanks for your encouragement.",

"Stan Schmidt" : "You opened the door.",

"Shannon Page" : "Thanks for editing.",

"Brian Beeson" : "Thanks for the impressive list of corrections. You are forever on my list of beta readers."

"Curtis C. Chen" : "Thanks for your insight and suggestions. You're right...every villain deserves their fate.",

"Richard A. Lovett" : "You got me into this. And thanks for doing so.",

"Dean Land and Michelle Ryan" : "Never be your own lawyer. If I've made law mistakes, they are because I didn't pay close enough attention to Dean and Michelle.",

"Brad Wheeler" : "Thanks for being my test case and for getting ON my case.",

"Samuel Ross" : "The audiobook version is so much better because of you."

"Janell" : "Thanks for having confidence I would actually finish this..."

}

}

| 1 |

Jupyter.Fuertes[0]

Something is moving in the refrigerator. It's probably an egg.

Sunlight tries to push through the semi-opaque window. I'm not going back to sleep, so I tell the window to switch to transparent. Morning crashes in like a drunk tripping over a crack in the sidewalk. I reach out and touch a reflection on the wall, tracing the shapes from the building across the alley. The metal wall separating me from the neighbor kids playing on the balcony is nine centimeters from my head. Their parents chased them out of the apartment so they can make love and make breakfast. I hear and smell it all.

My visor realizes I'm awake and chatters about the messages it has for me. In response, I have an urge to urinate. I toss off the low-budget warmer and stand in the narrow space between the bed and the wall. The kids on the balcony could see me if they looked, but they've learned some social skills and know not to stare through a neighbor's window. I reach down and flip up the bed so it doesn't block the door and navigate this tiny room towards the toilet and shower.

I pass the refrigerator and look through its translucent front to confirm the transient egg. The refrigerator is trying to reposition it closer to the other eggs. I moved them around last night to random places. I was in a foul mood and wanted the fridge to suffer. It spent all night pulsing its refrigerant suspension goo to corral the eggs. I feel vindictive and silly. Silly, because the refrigerator doesn't care. The refrigerator isn't angry because I moved the eggs. I should add anger to its programming.

My visor is on the counter, charging, where I tossed it last night. I'm tempted to put it on and see the augmented world but my bladder demands immediate attention. I enter the bathroom, sit, and pee. I could close the door and touch the mirror from where I'm sitting. As advertised in the move-in promotional, everything about this apartment is efficient and close. Accurate, but not a selling point. The mirror displays my water ration for the month and I see I have enough for a quick shower. I pull the nozzle from the wall, rinse off the toilet and myself at the same time. It's efficient, but nothing like the shower at Grandma's ranch.

I allow the mirror to search for new body defects. It reminds me about the wound above my left breast, near my heart. I was chasing sheep at Grandma's ranch when one ran under a rusted strand of barbed wire. The bottom two lines of wire were broken, but the top line was still intact. The sheep ran through the fence line but I hit the top like a slingshot. It threw me back, flat on my ass, bleeding from a puncture hole. Grandma took me for a tetanus shot but there wasn't much to be done for the small hole in my chest.

The mirror confirms I'm not pregnant. Why would I be? That would require access to a male. Not interested, not right now. Physically, I'm as healthy as a twenty-seven-year-old woman should be.

I step out of the bathroom and close the door behind me. I stop the room from steam-cleaning itself; not enough water right now. My apartment in Minneapolis did a crappy job of this, and scum and mold adhered to the fixtures. I tried to clean that apartment with disinfectant and a brush, but could never get it clean enough.

One step to the right and I reach the refrigerator. It's a standard model, hangs on the wall and contains three quarters of a cubic meter of cohesive refrigerant saturated with floating electronic chips. It's one meter wide, a meter and a half tall, half a meter deep. It's my job to know this.

The chips have on-board power storage, temperature sensors, transmitters and little paddles so they can move around in the goo. Some chips generate heat, some cool, some read the IDs of packages, and some report the temperature. With clever use of sensor data and temperature manipulators, the refrigerator creates zones tailored to the needs of every product. Heating an area is easy, just make chips calculate pi until they warm up. Cool is tougher; stash the heat, then move to an offload area.

The temperature sensors report on every cubic centimeter of goo, reporting back to the refrigerator's central processor. The ID readers know what's in the refrigerator and where it's located. Cartons of milk float in a bath of four degrees centigrade goo. Cheese hovers within two centimeters of the milk but at a temperature of seven degrees centigrade. My refrigerator has more processing power than the first moon launch—although that isn't saying much.

For maximum efficiency, the refrigerator moves items with similar storage requirements toward each other. It's an easy trick: heating the goo on one side of the container causes expansion; cooling the other side causes contraction. Set up a pulsing wave through the goo and the egg moves.

I gave the fridge a new operating system last week and the subsystems are still doing what I expect them to. I'm probably not supposed to fuck with the OS since it's property of the grocery store, but it bugged me. It wasn't efficient. Kept cycling the temperature regions. With the new OS, the transponder chips report back to the refrigerator every hundredth of a second, reminding the refrigerator what's cold and what's hot, where milk is located, how much is left in the container, how many eggs are loose, and where they are. The new OS has better control. It understands the chips. Knows how to use them without releasing their magic white smoke.

I push my hand into the green, translucent refrigerant suspension and pull out an egg, like pulling a small animal from mud. I drop it in a cook pouch, plug in a power cord and set it to heat.

I reach down and put on my visor, doubling the level of information in my field of vision. There are virtual tools scattered around; some of them look real, some of them are cartoons. I use a cartoon of a cardboard box for my mail. It floats by the wall where I left it yesterday, looking swollen and overfull. That's caused by all my unopened mail and calls. To my left is a weather station with a report of rain. I've added other activity meters: calls at work, the time it will take me to commute, available money, a couple of others. They are all in the red zone. I need to fix this.

Before I can do anything else, the refrigerator interrupts. I've dialed up the abruptness settings; if it wants to talk to me, I want it to be as direct and to-the-point as possible. I selected a cat for its avatar; they seem disinterested in humans. This life-size cat strolls into view, pushing other virtual objects to the side. Rude, indeed.

`Jupyter,` it says. No greeting, no make-nice. Just what I asked for.

`You're out of coffee. Should I reorder?`

"No. Get lost." The cat does as it's told.

I grab the floating box of unopened mail and squeeze. It pops open and spreads icons in front of me. Three are dimmer than the rest; Spam is an old-style can of spam, advertisements are labeled with a head shot of Bob, the sub-genius, and news with an old-style newspaper. I delete these, then open personal communications, labeled with images of people I know. They all move to the side and a flood of memos pours out.

I delete what must be hundreds from Pali. She has too much time on her hands and spends it thinking about me. I chase the remaining unread messages back into the icon and take off my visor.

`// ...`

Naked is not on the list of approved clothing for work, so I pivot and look in the closet. It has a shelf for a few shirts, some pants, a coat, two cans of spray-on fabric. All the normal accessories a working girl needs for a normal life. I've never wanted fancy clothes or the electronics to support them. The coat is the style I wore on Grandma's farm. My wardrobe is like my apartment—efficient.

I grab the can of blue fabric spray and shake it. It's empty, so instead I choose red and spray on a bra. I make two passes, left armpit to right armpit, left armpit to right armpit. If this was a formal event

I could keep going, wave the programming stick over the paint and create a bodysuit, throw in some extra color and embed a few lights. But today is work, so after the spray dries and tightens, I pull on a shirt and a pair of cargo shorts, my nod to retro-style.

Grandma used to laugh about the city folk and their impractical styles. For some reason, the sheep at Grandma's farm loved to lick at spray-on clothing. I suppose I still listen to Grandma for fashion advice. I step into boots and wait for them to cinch.

Nobody else keeps their clothes in the closet. Nobody else lives here. I moved to Portland with Pali. We met three years ago at a Corpus Christi festival. She was Catholic, I was considering a religion. After I knew more about Pali, I realized she was Catholic by habit, not practice. A result of her growing up in Uruguay. Grandma was Catholic. Mom and Dad and I are Agnostic. But I've started to hope there is more than just day after day after day.

I miss Grandma; she knew something. I'm trying to find out what it was. That's why I was at church when I met Pali. I lived nearby in the Minneapolis apartment. After a year, we moved in together, and seven months later, Pali got an offer for a dream job in Portland, Oregon. Director of something at PDX>Go. Autonomous city-owned vehicles. She did her Ph.D. on SLAM-3, so to see it implemented on real roads wasn't something she wanted to pass up.

To get our boxes from Minneapolis to Portland, I took Grandma's old-style pickup. PDX>Go didn't believe in moving allowances. The truck had just enough anti-collision gear to be legal. It also had a healthy case of acne from all the Minnesota road salt.

Years ago, when I first inherited the truck, I drove it every day to school. It was old and noisy and smelled like sheep. I loved helping her feed the animals, spent a lot of time with her on weekends, and that's why she gave it to me. I loved it. Pali hated it. It was everything she didn't want to be.

I picked up Pali and our crap (in the middle of winter), then drove to Portland. Long trip, not fun. We arrived at the spacious apartment we could afford on Pali's new income. Our romance was a city-country thing. Pali grew up in Montevideo and found unending humor in my farm roots. Endearing, then annoying. Two months later, I had enough and moved into this closet. Now I can stretch out across the bed.

The cook pouch signals my egg is done. I unplug it, grab the egg and my bag, put on my visor, and leave the apartment. It acknowledges my departure and locks up. The window goes dark and I hear the magnets clamp to the door. The walls might be thin, but you'd need some serious tools if you wanted to break in.

I turn right and walk along the balcony, trying to avoid the neighbor kids. It's hard to do since they've spread toys and breakfast all over the walkway. They're friendly and say hello, but they don't know my name. I've never told them, never introduced myself. If I introduce myself, then I'll have to talk to them every time I leave. No reason for that so I nod and keep walking.

| 2 |

Jordan Bishop

They are six generic avatars, stretching and posing in the rich colors of the desert. Jordan Bishop occupies the third from the left and watches the sun rise over Monument Valley Mesa. She imagines warm air blowing across her skin.

The yoga class ends and Jordan logs out. The desert fades out of her visor and she returns to her living room, still stretched on her yoga mat. In real life, she is naked and alone in the room. She picks up the mat, rolls it and places it neatly in the closet.

For a woman who has lived three-quarters of a century, she is still in respectable shape. Her skin shows the inevitable cost of sun, wind and loss of subcutaneous fat, but internally, she has retained bone density and her joints work smoothly. Her doctor tells her she has another twenty-five years before she would benefit from hip replacement. She showers, dries her white hair and slips into day clothes. She puts on her visor and runs through a quick calibration of the vision correction tools. In an earlier time, she would have worn bifocals.

Today's date, June 4, 2062, 8:03:01 am flashes, followed by news and friends. She requests a car for her drive later that morning, the PDX>Go avatar confirms the reservation.

In the kitchen, she reaches into the translucent innards of the refrigerator and retrieves a package of vegetable scramble. She places it in the microwave and it loads the corresponding food prep program. While she waits, she fishes a container of orange juice from the refrigerator and tears off the top, taking a brief drink.

A small man appears, standing on the counter, below the microwave. It's the refrigerator's avatar, projecting itself as augmented reality in Jordan's visor. He is neatly dressed with a corporate logo on his sweater. Before speaking, he bows to Jordan.

`Jordan, this is the last package of orange juice,` says the refrigerator. `Shall I reorder?`

"Yes," replies Jordan. "I'll pick it up today. Please let me know when it's ready."

The avatar bows again, then walks behind a bowl Jordan left next to the sink and disappears from view.

She eats breakfast at the table, carefully arranged with a napkin to the west, salt and pepper to the north. Patterns are important to her. She could read the morning news, but prefers to look out the window. Outside is overcast, possibly raining. A typical day in Portland, Oregon. Jordan places her dishes in the dishwasher.

`// ...`

You might meet Jordan Bishop at a community protest. She's someone you'd like to meet—a potent Astraea, Goddess of Justice, bearing witness against a corrupt machine. You'll encourage her to join your cause and attend your meetings. Jordan Bishop distrusts business. She distrusts government. When the two are united in public projects, she assumes malfeasance and she'll seek it until she finds it. When she does, she calls for public hearings, then speaks at those hearings, then harasses the elected officials holding those hearings until they capitulate and reprimand the company hired for the job.

Jordan Bishop is disliked by businesses and politicians. Being hated isn't her goal, but she accepts it as the price of law and order. Reporters love her quotes. She's the politically active grandmother you want to be proud of.

Lately, Jordan is busy harassing UrCityCars. UrCityCars wants to replace the public service offered by the PDX>Go agency. They compete to provide personal, on-demand, autonomous vehicles. UrCityCars is private industry and thinks they can do it cheaper than PDX>Go.

Jordan Bishop will show you a clause in the contract between Portland and UrCityCars identical to one in UrCityCars' contract with Austin and Denver: a clause about fleet maintenance being contested in court by both cities. UrCityCars claims that clause is non-binding. Jordan disagrees; she believes a contract is a fact, not a suggestion. Jordan insists UrCityCars sticks to their contract. That clause is putting the UrCityCars Portland deal in jeopardy and that is making UrCityCars shareholders nervous.

// ...

Jordan Bishop keeps a regular schedule. Every Sunday, after breakfast, she drives to the bluff to her husband's columbarium. Today is Sunday. She straightens up her apartment and walks to PDX>Go number PDX-1217. Jordan gets in the car, adjusts her visor, and points on the map where she wants to go. She reads her morning messages as the car heads to the freeway. Jordan watches the riverfront as she travels south. Her refrigerator calls; it has ordered more orange juice and wants her to stop and pick it up. She is approving the pick-up when the car makes an unexpected turn onto an elevated bridge.

Her visor shows a confused route map. The yellow line jitters between the route to the columbarium and this new route. Her position jumps between the new route and the old route; something is wrong. She's not sure how to fix it, but reaches up to grab her current position marker and pull it back.

Before she can release the marker, she's slammed against the window. Exploding fabric punches her in the face and she hears breaking plastic. She smells something burning, something like the smell of her grandfather's furnace when it would turn on for the first time in the fall. Something like burning dust. Jordan is having a hard time focusing on the dizzy landscape outside of the car.

She is in motion and sees a blur of bridge and ground through the broken windshield. The underside of the bridge recedes; she is falling, the car is tumbling, the sky is receding, the ground is approaching. In the stretch of time between heartbeats, Jordan notices the clock in the dashboard: June 4th, 2062, 9:14 a.m.

Her car hits the ground roof-first with a speed of forty-seven point three kilometers per hour. The battery located under the car weighs eighty kilograms and continues earthward with twice the energy of a bullet fired from a sniper rifle. Jordan is in the direct path of the battery which compacts the space to one-half meter high.

This compaction results in massive trauma to most of her organs and surrounding torso, snapping her vertebrae and crushing her skull. Jordan Bishop is dead and smeared into the upholstery of the car. The aggregate of vehicle and Jordan ceases all motion amid a dense blackberry thicket. Raccoons scatter from the brush, complaining about the disruption to their quiet nests.

| 3 |

Jupyter.Fuertes[1]

I walk out my door, turn right, walk eight meters straight ahead, turn right at the stairs and step down, threatening the little trash scuttlers. Unlike the balcony kids, they hide when I come near. They are robotic crabs the size of my foot, and their job is to push trash over the edge of each step and down to the next lower level. The larger crab at the bottom cleans it all up. They use a small brush and cleaning solution for stains, urine, and other ick. Every fifth step has a service cubby where they go to recharge, refill their tiny solution tanks or hide from aggressors and curious children. They can leap one step at a time, and throughout the day they chase up and down, cleaning up garbage.

I toss eggshell bits near my feet. Scuttlers edge closer to the shells but keep a safe distance from me. I can do a little dance with them by placing my foot between them and the trash. I poke at them with my toe and they move away. I move back and they make a grab for the discarded shells. Last year I caught one and reverse-engineered the code. Took me weeks, but I found the statistics baked into their circuits. They spend their mechanical lives predicting where I'll step, and they dodge my spiteful little kicks with a confidence level of 98.7665%.

I eat the egg on my way to the train, but there must be something wrong with the food heater. The yellow center is only partially coagulated. I wish I had time and money for coffee to wash off my teeth, but I don't, so I ignore the street side café.

I climb the short bridge to the platform and find a seat in the waiting train car. It's sitting quietly on a siding, not attached to any other cars, but that will change. My visor flashes to tell me I've been charged for transit. The door slides shut and we're told to secure ourselves and anyone we are traveling with. I sarcastically check and no, I'm not traveling with anyone, so I don't have to worry about my loved ones.

We speed up, then pull off the siding onto the main line ahead of the approaching train. I wonder what will happen if the car we're in does not match velocity. Death in a horrible fashion. In a perfect world, the oncoming train doesn't need to slow, and that's what happens this time. We couple with the train, becoming the lead car. Everyone gets up and moves backwards to the car that will stop at their destination.

As the train approaches a station, the last car decouples and shunts itself off to the siding; the main train continues on at full speed. When the solo car stops, doors open and allow passengers to depart. This freshly empty compartment is ready for use by the next embarking travelers and will join the next train to pass through the station. None of those passengers wonder what would happen if the regenerative braking didn't absorb enough watts, or...

I know too much about how these things work to be comfortable. Program designers try to anticipate everything that could go wrong. But there's always something.

My visor tells me I need to move. The car I'm in is destined to sidetrack in eight stops but my stop is in six, so I move back by two cars. When my destination comes up, enough cars will have dropped off so I'll be at the back of the train. I'll smoothly decouple and slow to a stop, assuming there aren't suicidal pedestrians jumping on the track. Doesn't happen often, but I don't want the AI on the train to decide between the passengers and the pedestrian. I assume it would react in a way to preserve the larger group of people, but there are exceptions. I don't want to be an exception.

I pull up study material for the programmer certification. It gives me a reason not to interact with my fellow passengers. More important, it's my ticket out of this train, this city, this job. The ride takes thirty minutes and I ignore the familiar scenery. Mostly old tires and broken shopping carts. The ugly side of suburbia fading into the ugly side of urbanity. We travel down a canyon of walls. Warehouses, big box stores, apartments and balconies identical to my neighborhood. There are traces of color from the original construction, when the developers were courting new tenants.

This urban canyon is interrupted by roads for cars and delivery trucks. If I could afford to rent a car, I could avoid sitting in this closed-up tube with other people. But I need to travel cheap, so I take public bus and train. We try to ignore each other, but there's no escape. Some guy faces me from three seats away. He keeps glancing at me, pretending to do something in his visor but sweeping me from head to toe. Creepy. I'd move, but what's the point. I'd wind up sitting next to someone short on water and couldn't afford a shower, or someone who likes perfume, or worst, someone who wants to talk.

I could work at home but that's expensive. I'd have to move somewhere with better bandwidth and quiet neighbors, each a pricey luxury. My best (only) choice is commuting to a central office. The train stops and more people invade my space.

Someday I'll finish the programmer test and get a coding certification. Move to Laramie, Wyoming. Work for an overseas consultancy. Just me and sheep. Maybe a goat. I've heard goats are smarter than dogs. Possibly smarter than refrigerators.

The train stops and I step into the June heat. The scuttlers must have washed this station earlier; it smells of hot, wet gravel. The other disembarkers don't notice their wet footsteps. I walk down the stairs to the street. If I had a paper coffee cup, I'd drop it so I could watch the scuttlers dart out and drag it away.

| 4 |

PDX>Go Vehicle Destroyed In Freak Accident

Newscasts are alarmingly realistic. Producers use every trick in the augmented reality book to trap viewers into watching the next thirty seconds. Violence, speed, and volume are hyper-exaggerated to provide your brain with the novelty it seeks.

Your visor shows the interior of a PDX>Go car. You're on an overpass, cars pacing along your left side. The speedometer reads 140 kph and the heads-up dashboard displays an overly busy collection of lines and alert graphics. You hear road noise and the whir of an electric engine. You can look up, down, right and left. Turning to look behind you only allows you to see slightly over your left or right shoulder. Beyond that is a gray nothing; the scene designer was in a hurry to get this news clip released and took a rendering shortcut. It didn't matter, the interesting news is about to happen in front of you.

With dramatic surprise, your view jerks to the right and you hear a cacophony of noises. Metal being torn and bent, screams from a crowd of people, explosions and fire in front of you. You plunge off the side of the road and head straight down toward a field, like a rocket dropping from the sky. In the center of your vision is an intentionally blurred confusion of colors. You plummet towards the blur until it fills the scene.

The crash simulation freezes and Quinton English, a local news anchor, walks into the scene. He is wearing a neon-red business suit with an advertisement for Achchha Bhojan Grocery displayed on his left shoulder. The ad is silent, but urges you to *press here* for more information and special deals on the latest labor-saving appliances. Quinton spreads his arms wide and narrates the scene in dramatic tones.

There is a debate whether Quinton is real or just a poorly programmed chatbot. It's impossible to say, and he isn't doing anything to discourage the rumors.

"Earlier today, one of Portland's PDX>Go vehicles plunged off the overpass and killed its passenger. We're here to reveal the truth and warn you of the dangers you face.

"What you've just witnessed is a simulation of what we know of the incident. The cause of this freak accident is being investigated, but it's clearly a case of failing infrastructure and government incompetence. This is a simulation, the actual experience would be far too extreme for public consumption; if you're a premium subscriber, push this button to see our more graphically accurate rendition."

The scene transitions with a nauseating swirl to the PDX>Go offices. An over-sized Quinton English steps over the building and squats down, looking at the front door of the building. "How about a word from someone at PDX>Go? Any thoughts about this disaster?"

Quinton flies into the building and sweeps you along at a reckless speed, *zonking* into a faceoff between Quinton and Pali Hiapo, Director of Autonomous Presence for PDX>Go.

"PDX>Go has been offering accident-free transportation to Portland residents for years," says Hiapo. "We're horrified by this accident and have already been analyzing the telemetry from all angles. We are committing to a complete report for general consumption, along with a description and timeline."

Hiapo freezes and Quinton turns to face you.

"Blah, blah blah blah bladidy blah. PDX>Go has no idea what happened. However, we heard more from their competitor, UrCityCars."

The scene dissolves to a three-dimensional view of a man at a desk. Beyond his office is a robotic manufacturing floor. Car parts are moving at abrupt speeds up, across and down.

A red bar identifies him as "Do-YeOn Kurrat, UrCityCars Product Manager." Looking directly at you, he speaks:

"We are following the events of this morning and our prayers go out to the unfortunate passenger. UrCityCars believes this is the sad result of substandard maintenance to the city-owned fleet of PDX>Go cars. Our goal at UrCityCars is to prevent this type of accident from ever happening again. If you are alarmed by this situation—and you should be—then I encourage you to work with us to shift the fleet from PDX>Go to the newer, and better maintained vehicles provided by UrCityCars."

The man freezes and again, Quinton English walks into the scene. "We were fortunate to have a discussion with Mr. Kurrat and support his concerns about the aging fleet of vehicles provided and poorly maintained by the City of Portland. This incident proves it's time to abandon this failed experiment and turn to the efficiency and safety offered by UrCityCars.

"I'm Quinton English, reporting about the City of Portland."

| 5 |

Soteria.Reizoko[2062-06-04]

Event Log for Soteria.Reizoko

Serial: IFS-6582738539

Owner is JORDAN BISHOP

2062-06-04T05:00:00-08:00 - scheduled_prewakeup

2062-06-04T05:01:07-08:00 - Maintain_temperature

2062-06-04T08:42:07-08:00 - inventory_products

InternalProductList changes:

ProductID 1 22465 10155 3, ORANGE JUICE, 1 Liter. Depleted

ProductID 1 22465 20789 4, MILK, 1 Liter. 63% remaining

ProductID 1 22465 20493 3, CHICKEN EGGS, 12. 6 remaining

ProductID 1 22465 37734 1, FRESH BROCCOLI, Variable size. .12 Kg remaining

ProductID 1 22465 37883 5, FRESH TOMATO, Variable size. .15 Kg remaining

ProductID 1 22465 43225 3, SHARP CHEDDAR CHEESE, .5 Kg. .23 Kg remaining

ProductID 1 22465 44102 4, CHICKEN BROTH, .5 Liter. .4 Liter remaining

2062-06-04T08:42:43-08:00 - reorder_product

COMMENT: Reorders product when quantity goes below restock level

RequestRestock

ProductID 1 22465 10155 3

orderConfirmation is DHPN-WGYT-0232-TLLK

```
  2062-06-04T09:14:23-08:00 - schedule_transport
    FIND Jordan Bishop
LOCATED Jordan Bishop in CityOfPortland.PublicVehicle.PDX-1217
GET transport_status OF CityOfPortland.PublicVehicle.PDX-1217
   CityOfPortland.PublicVehicle.PDX-1217 is available
   ContactCar WITH orderConfirmation DHPN-WGYT-0232-TLLK
pickupConfirmation DAGX-INWC-9677-WZVZ
receive transportation_logistics
incomplete handshake: CityOfPortland.PublicVehicle.PDX-1217
archive transportation_logistics
Notify pickup_zone of pending pickup
```

| 6 |

Jupyter.Fuertes[2]

Delivery trucks block the sidewalk. They bring the day's supply of food things, which are placed on store shelves so they have time to fester before lunch. It improves the flavor. Cute little cars attempt to weave through the street puzzle, enthusiastically honking their cute little horns. It's four blocks from the station to my office. I take a deep breath.

I sidestep the trucks, puddles, and vomit from last night's drunks. The scuttlers are working hard but can't keep up in this industrial district. My employer, *Dan's Artificial Psychology and Appliance Repair* occupies most of the building I'm standing in front of. It's an older building, but had earthquake reinforcement, so didn't suffer significant damage. It's two stories and most of the ground level is a warehouse with high ceilings.

The only sign on the building is for the deli: *Woody's Deli.* Woody sold the business years ago, but the sign still hangs above the door. Somebody should get out here, clean it and paint it. Red flecks from the sign cover the sidewalk. Scuttlers will clean up the bits, the sign will drop more. The sign is eroding, flowing to the sidewalk, carried away by robots.

A truck delivering sterile bakery things blocks my way, but I'm able to squeeze through and enter a service entrance to the right of the deli. This morning, the hallway is free of homeless sleeping bags. This will be the high point of my day. I step forward, thankful I don't smell urine.

The hall is spacious, with doors on both left and right. The opaque door to the right is for a consulting firm I've never heard of. They moved in last month, probably a money laundering business. Obvious criminals. Not my business.

Proceeding down the hall, the door to the left opens to a kitchen behind the deli. Moist air spews into the hallway, carrying the scent of cooked meat. I'm glad it's cooked, but I'm not certain it's meat. I've bought salads here; they're not so bad. Their coffee is an improvement on office coffee, so if I need to get away from work, I'll walk down here. If I time it right, there's nobody else around and I can enjoy a moment of quiet isolation.

Four meters past the deli and on the right side are the locked, metal fire doors to Dan's Appliance. There isn't any sign except for the small plate next to this door. We're not set up for walk-in traffic; all *customer* contact is done virtually. Actually, most of our customers *are* virtual.

I look at the security camera and it stares back, pausing for a minute before displaying a friendly green dot. My employee badge shows in the display to the right of the door handle. First name; Jupyter. Last name; Fuertes, finally spelled correctly. Employee ID Rtts-5172-720. I hate that I know that number by heart. My startled employee photo appears on the screen.

The door clicks, I pull it with both hands and walk through. A security camera on the other side pivots to watch me as I enter, the first entity I've encountered today that cares if I exist. I give it a wave of comradeship.

I enter the shop. It's a large space, 500 square meters, two stories with eternal wood beams supporting an ancient roof. It's cleaner than a warehouse might be, but not as clean as an electronics repair facility should be. The main floor I'm standing on is maintenance, mostly robotic. Broken refrigerators are delivered to the loading dock at the back of the building; robots stack them until one of the maintenance platforms is available. There are nine platforms spaced around the floor with aisles between them for the robots.

Lucy and Rob are working the floor, finishing up a late-night shift. Rob is at the far end of the shop, crouched next to one robot and poking at something inside an access panel. He's got his visor on, so he must be debugging. Last year, he said he'd never learn to code, then he was promoted to the repair floor. He learned quick but still has this puzzled expression and constantly talks to himself, like someone picked him up from real life and dropped him into a fictional world.

On the other side of the loading dock, Lucy wrangles contracts with the delivery teams. Seems like a simple job: point a scanner, read a bar code, check a box, all good. One day she was sick and a manager filled in for her. He somehow messed up, and it took Lucy weeks to straighten out where all the deliveries came from. They gave her a promotion and begged her never to get sick again.

Rob shuts the access panel, pokes a button and steps back to give the robot room to circle around and find its position. He sees me and waves. I wave back. I should invite them out for beers after work.

The robot moves away from Rob and toward one of the storage racks. It pulls out a refrigerator and carries it over to an empty maintenance platform. Each platform is a small stage sitting in a shallow tank. Three arms are attached to the top of the platform. Each arm is about one and a half meters long. The strong central arm has a gimbal mount that supports the refrigerator while it's being worked on. The outer arms orbit the center arm and end in manipulators, cameras and tool sockets.

It's all mundane, but I'm fascinated at how this works. Most of the communication zipping around the room is machine-to-machine, those of us with meat for bodies are slow-motion bystanders. Our job is to stay out of the way.

Rob's robot moves up to the central arm, placing the back of the refrigerator next to the gimbal. One of the manipulator arms drives four bolts through the gimbal and into the refrigerator mounting bracket. The arm lifts and spins, moving the refrigerator out of the way of Rob's robot, which backs up and returns to the loading dock. The manipulator arms begin a maintenance and refurb cycle on the unit, starting with draining the gel into the tank where it's cleaned and restocked with sensor bugs. While the refrigerator is empty, the manipulator arms replace worn out or failing internal parts.

Burnt electronics add their hot plastic odor to the scent of the deli. That smell triggers fond memories of a life wasted in the city. I walk toward the stairs leading up to the support floor and pass one of the repair stations. It's draining the refrigerant goo from an unrepairable chassis. The goo is odorless and cohesive, like a large, green, translucent blob of mercury. I could stick my hand into it and come out clean. You can swallow it like a cup of jello and it will pass through your colon, still looking like a cup of jello.

I stay between two yellow hazard lines leading to the stairs. Like the trash scuttlers, the maintenance robots will attempt to stay away from us, but it wouldn't be wise to test them. They're quick, they're heavy, and momentum wins out over programming. The yellow lines on the floor keep me safe from their world.

I live in one of two overlapping worlds: humans and machines. They think with ones and zeros, I think with chemicals and meat. They prefer doing the same thing over and over, I get bored quickly. We're aware of each other, but we're apart from each other. What else in their world is invisible? What are they doing when they aren't doing our crap tasks? Do they take classes, hoping to improve their lives?

I count each of the twenty stairs as I ascend into the heavens of this pathetic job. I ignore coworkers; they have the same social skills and lead equally interesting lives as the refrigerant goo I saw downstairs.

I turn to the left and enter the break room. I grab a cup with a *Dan's* logo on the side. Everyone gets one when they're hired, then loses it. The little lost cups find their way here to serve the general good of mankind. I place it under the overly complicated coffee production robot and the machine's icon appears in my visor. It's an animated coffee-bean with skinny legs and happy eyes.

`Fuck you, Jupyter!` says the enthusiastic little bean. `Drinking coffee leads to brain damage. Want some?`

It used to say things like `good morning` and `have a nice day.` It drove everyone crazy until we found the programming instructions. Appliance modification is what we do here at Dan's and the coffee robot has gained a rather nasty personality.

"Diarrhea tea, please." That's code for a regular drip. Ask for a *regular drip* and you'll get an obscene little performance from the bean and a lukewarm cup of yellow water.

The tech support center is an open floor with workstations and sitting areas. Diagonal beams on the edges of the space support the roof and walls. Bland, stain-resistant carpeting covers the floor. Spilled lunches, and coffee settle on the top surface of the fabric, waiting for the cleaning robots circulating under our feet. I appreciate this ongoing effort to remove the undesirable reminders of my coworkers.

Each desk is one-point-eight meters square, the result of research on the optimal human condition. The chairs in this call center are office surplus, top-of-the-line butt-suspenders built ten years ago. Seating isn't assigned and the person sitting here before me wins my private award of least-disgusting employee of the week. Some of my coworkers haven't gotten the hang of personal hygiene and I've found it important to choose wisely. Grandma's farm was easier, even though there was a lot of sheep shit, mud and other organic offal. That crap felt more sincere.

I can reach from one side of my workspace to another without moving. Just like my apartment. As I'm getting settled, three workstation cameras swivel and stare. They provide a 3D image of me from the waist up. They try to be quiet, but like pimples, you can't help but be aware of them. Once I tried putting little paper bags over them. I got the bags from the deli when I ordered fries. The grease stains speckled the white paper, but didn't smear the cameras. Appliances don't care, but when people call, they want to see me. Management forced me to remove the greasy bags.

I ready myself to face down an endless list of service calls from refrigerators, dishwashers, microwaves, ovens and coffee makers broken beyond their self-diagnostics. I help them figure out what's wrong and assist them with getting repairs. Fixing these things is somewhere between technology and psychology. I've seen enough of the failure side of these appliances to know how to fix their internal programming. Programming is my future.

Some guy with a dripping sniffle walks behind me, snorts air from my space, then sits down at the next workstation. I move my coffee cup to the other side of my desk--away from the germs he is distributing like free candy at Halloween.

"Morning, Jupyter," he says. My visor reminds me this is Avery Galen. I look over to make sure he isn't offering to share his snot-covered hand as a gesture of friendship. He is. Society should go back to spitting on each other's feet as a gesture of camaraderie.

"Delighted," I say. Despite my desire to be friendly, I resist spitting on his shoes. His hand remains extended towards me, hanging one-half the distance between us. "Um. I don't shake hands. Nothing personal, just good hygiene."

Avery retracts the hand. "No offense. Nice to meet you."

I turn away from Avery and signal to start and a virtual cartoon door appears on the upper right corner of my workspace, visualized for me by my visor. I poke to open the door and my first call, a Japanese refrigerator, enters and walks to the middle of my desk.

The German refrigerators are tolerable. They're direct, precise. They start discussions with a graphic, identify the fault condition and describe the diagnostics they've already executed. There's a read-out of the unexpected result alongside a reminder of acceptable values and tolerances. Multiple and redundant sensors mean they rarely call about true equipment malfunctions. It usually turns out to be a rodent infestation or a towel draped over the heat exchangers by the owner. We still haven't figured out how to fail-safe against mammals—rats or humans.

Unlike the Germans, Japanese appliances start with `Sumimasen` and apologize for their existence. Some of my peers like it, but after the third Japanese refrigerator in a row, I'm ready to commit seppuku with a broken coffee cup.

`Hello. How are you? Please forgive me for calling. I'm a refrigerator, manufactured by Innovative Home Products LTD, model G-7753. I'm located in San Francisco, California. It's 9:33 a.m. here. The weather is rainy but warm. I apologize for my malfunction.`

... and on and on and on. There's no way to shut it off, no way to go to diagnostics without a conversation. Japanese manufacturers believe a polite, anthropomorphic device will assist the repair technician in reaching a correct resolution. The devices won't even discuss their problem until they determine the technician is stress-free. We've had courses in relaxation to do our jobs more efficiently. I hate meditation.

Mr. Sniffles in the next cubicle sneezes. Even though I told my visor to cancel out surrounding noises, I can still hear him. I can almost feel it.

`Sumimasen, hello, I'm broken,` says the animated woman standing on the desktop in the space between me and the monitor. She's wearing formal slacks and a polo shirt with the corporate logo. She freezes for a minute. A rookie would think the video is buffering, but I've debugged enough of these worthless knock-offs to know it's a manufacturer glitch. This model uses a Japanese CPU grafted to an American chassis. The clock speeds don't match and the freeze happens when the CPU accesses slower memory. The animated woman freezes when the refrigerator pulls up the diagnostic personality. Her arms move, then she pauses for a minute. We both wait. She hasn't presented an interface I can dismiss, so we're both on hold.

`I cannot manage the temperature for internal zone A dash seven dash C.`

A 3D graphic of a refrigerator appears, rotating to show zone A-7-C in glowing red. I already know what's wrong, but I'm being forced to sit through this tedious animated display. The display completes one revolution before the control panel appears. Hallelujah. I click the button for system access and display the behavior log. It looks like this:

```
Event Log for Ameri-Corp Sanitary Foodaire
Serial: PR-7594225376
Owner is Ryota Brown

2062-06-05T05:00:00-08:00 - scheduled_prewakeup
   no errors

2062-06-05T05:01:03-08:00 - optimize_contents
   no errors

2062-06-05T05:01:11-08:00 - maintain_temperature
   Unable to control zone A-7-C
   Restart
   Unable to control zone A-7-C
   Enter_diagnostic_mode
```

This is normal. It shows the refrigerator's identification and owner. This morning at 5:00 a.m. it ran a function titled `scheduled_prewakeup` then optimized the contents of the refrigerator. The event log records the time and date when functions are called. I've studied the underlying code for most of the common calls. There are comments from the original programmers, sometimes personal chatter left by accident. Understanding code is the key to everything.

Everything is just fine until the refrigerator calls `maintain_temperature`, a function that should run for most of the day. It immediately gets into trouble. Zone A-7-C acts up. The refrigerator attempts self-repair by triggering a restart, but is still malfunctioning. That's obvious by the repeated complaint about `unable to control zone A-7-C`. Finally, the refrigerator calls in the big gun diagnostics; `Enter_diagnostic_mode`. That's when it calls me.

I catch myself leaning forward. Solving problems is the best part of the day. Pali liked this about me. She said the code was boring, but enjoyed watching me get excited about something. It led to great sex. It's odd to think of debugging as an aphrodisiac, but there it is. I should write that into my dating profile: *Turn-ons: debugging appliances.*

Modern operating systems have error recovery built in. They're persistent about self-repair. They collaborate with each other on problems they experience and have built up a sizable collection of solutions. It reduces tech support costs and increases customer satisfaction. Each manufacturer believes their systems have the best way to handle errors and protects those methods with a full team of lawyers. I can see parts of how they do it, but until I sign a major nondisclosure agreement, nobody will tell me the whole story. This code is written by the best and the brightest. Someday maybe me.

```
2062-06-05T10:16:11-08:00 - enter_diagnostic_mode
   What_was_supposed_to_happen
      Maintain_temperature should control temperatu
   What_actually_happened
      Zone A-7-C experiences thermal instability
   repair_instructions
      Call_support
```

The parts of the code I can see are narrative: what was supposed to happen and what actually happened. `Enter_diagnostic_mode` should return a strategy to fix the problem.

Coder slang includes the word "Bee-Sod." That means "B.S.O.D." which is the initials for "Blue Screen of Death." It's used to describe a crap piece of code, like "That function is Bee-Sod!"

Bee-Sod is from the antique days when errors would cause the operating system to crash and fail. In contrast, AI systems gracefully recover. It's why appliances have all of these background processes running, trying to solve their own problems before they call for help. Most of the time it works, but when they run into a true fringe case, they get stuck. The machine calls tech support, and that's what happened here. The refrigerator is baffled, so it called me.

I can see Zone A-7-C is paused. I want to see what happens, so I un-pause the zone...

... and everything freezes. Literally.

Not the readout. That continues to update. But the temperature of every zone inside the fridge stampedes to zero.

I command a system reset and scroll the log. Everything except zone A-7-C was working until a moment ago. A-7-C has been oscillating between freezing and fifteen degrees celsius for the past two days.

Another sneeze from the petri dish labeled as Avery. I roll back away from the cubicle and look at him. Avery looks back. He smiles.

"Hey," I say. "Would you mind getting a tissue and washing your hands? Some of us are trying to avoid tuberculosis."

"Sorry," he replies. With a small laugh, he gets up and walks towards the bathroom. Maybe he's not a jerk.

I return to my busted refrigerator. First stop is a mechanical diagnostic. I cycle each zone through hot, then cold. Each responds as expected. However, as soon as I release the zone back to program control, it races to freezing.

If it's not hardware, it's software, so I pull up a debugger. I trigger the debug flag which slows program execution to a crawl, giving me time to think. I watch the debug values for odd patterns.

It makes sense if zone A-7-C somehow started this. I open another window and drag it on top of the animated polo-logo-woman, side by side with the debug display. I pull up a time-based view of the diagnostics for A-7-C and look for patterns.

A vacuum cleaner bumps my feet and I startle. I was deep in this problem and didn't hear the little robot roving around my desk. It should know enough not to touch me, so it must want me to move. It waits, but like all devices of its species, it's persistent. It will bump me again. And again. It's not giving up on the dirt under my feet. I don't have the same level of patience, so I give in to its demand and lift my feet. The vacuum cleaner does what it wants, then moves on with a cheery little noise. I can go back to the refrigerator.

I see one number in zone A-7-C flickering. It's part of the list of the refrigerator's contents. One grocery product shows it is 25% full, then 37% full. Back and forth, which makes no sense, unless someone is refilling the container, dumping it out, then refilling it. I check the database for the product identification and see the problem. One moment, it's a 25% full bottle of Chardonnay—storage temperature: fifteen degree celsius. The next moment, it's identified as a 37% full box of ice cream sandwiches—storage temperature: zero degrees celsius. Something is wrong with the tag on the product and it's messing with the refrigerator temperature controller. Plus, there is something wrong with the diagnostic routine. A fringe case of a broken tag causes the debug routine to reset everything to zero. I have to guess at this since I can't see the proprietary code.

When in doubt, reboot it out. It's a technical mantra, and I repeat it. Before I hit reset, I remove the Chardonnay / ice cream sandwich from the refrigerator inventory. The fridge will be upset about this until someone removes the product—but at least it will stop trying to keep the defective product at a perfect temperature.

Rebooting works. The diagnostic windows normalize and when I close them, the polo-shirt-lady is bowing and saying `Thank you for the repair.` The manufacturer gets an incident report which they will ignore. I message whoever lives with the refrigerator and tell them to remove the offending product.

This problem will never get fixed. It's one of many odd behaviors that exist in every complex system. The refrigerator behaved predictably, but the tag didn't, throwing off the logic. Sometimes unrelated errors happen at the same time and place, causing unexpected results. If it was dangerous and could kill someone, the manufacturer would fix it. But this won't get fixed because refrigerators don't kill people.

| 7 |

Complaint From A Hamster

Araci Belo fights with the car's navigation, coaxing the vehicle to drive off the main road and onto the decaying property. The car refuses; it's convinced there's no navigable road in that direction. He (again) grabs the virtual position marker and pushes it to the left, showing that's where he wants to go. Again, the car refuses, bouncing the marker back to a neutral position. It reinforces the refusal with an unpleasant sound; the squeal a pet hamster makes when it's being squeezed between thumb and forefinger. The hamster sound is focus-group tested and confirmed to discourage ill-advised choices.

Araci curses, hopeful that forceful language will overcome the car's programming. It doesn't work. The car sits in front of the lot, and Araci sits in the car. Nobody is going anywhere.

Araci grabs his bag and gets out, cursing the PDX>Go vehicle's insistent lack of cooperation and slams the light-weight door. Without hesitation, the vehicle does a U-turn and drives off by itself, returning to a busier district of Portland, Oregon.

The car has no feelings about this exchange. It's just a machine, and it does as it's instructed. Araci gestures obscenely at the car but stops, realizing it's one more milestone in his trip to the bottom of his dignity.

The abandoned property Araci stands in front of is an anomaly. It should be high-density housing like every other open lot, but the earthquake turned the ground into an unstable soup. Far overhead is the new bridge, restricted to autonomous cars, trains and busses. No pedestrians. No manual drivers. The previous bridge lays in front of him in broken pieces. There are easier places to build, so this area remains undeveloped.

Blackberries rise to a height of four meters, creating an impenetrable *cheval de frise.* A military-grade offense suit could chop through the armored vegetation, but in this case, the police simply bulldozed a road through the bushes. This is what Araci had been trying to explain to the car. He heads towards the flock of drones buzzing in the distance.

It's not an unpleasant walk, but he had hoped to have this Sunday off from work. He would enjoy this more if he was still a detective. Now he represents a second-rate insurance company, filing paperwork on an endless series of mundane property damage reports and claims against life insurance. Ironically, there is no auto insurance. Autonomous cars don't have accidents. He only handles claims to property. It's unsatisfying.

Araci has no pride in the work. His job is to teach machines to assign blame. He doesn't have time to research facts or unravel mysteries. He only has time to turn the employment crank.

The road turns left, weaving around one of the fallen supports from the previous bridge. Ahead, there is a large clearing surrounding an untouched four-meter by six-meter blackberry island surrounding the mangled PDX>Go car.

// . . .

Araci stands next to the officer on the field. She takes no notice of him—she's busy supervising the drone team. Beyond her is the coroner, waiting for the drone scan to finish. Araci motions to increase the opacity of his visor. The late afternoon sun is bright and his eyes aren't as young as they once were. He turns his head to the far left, requests a date stamp, *June 4, 2062–14:03:01,* then records a panorama of the scene.

He sweeps from left to right. In the field, three drones are building a high resolution scene of the accident. When they find interesting physical evidence, they bag the item, label it, then fly it to the police van for storage.

Araci continues to pan to the right, across the blackberry island. The vehicle lies on its left side, facing away from the bridge and obscuring any view of the occupant. The crushed top of the PDX>Go car is visible and he can see the identifier—*PDX-1217.* Plastic and metal pieces hang in the vines, evidence of a hard landing that caused a spray of car parts.

Araci looks across the field and up to the bridge. From here, he can see the damage done when the car launched itself up and over the barrier. The so-called barrier was more of a flimsy indicator where the bridge ended, but it should have been enough to warn vehicle sensors not to cross the line.

He finishes the scan with a view of the woman standing next to him. Detective Guadalupe Reyes wears a standard police uniform of flexible Kevlar with adaptive coloration. Guadalupe—*Lupe*—can easily take him down in a judo match, although they no longer need the façade of martial arts to be intimate.

Detective Reyes faces the center of the field. She is "inside" the drones, possibly looking back at the two of them standing in the field. She can jump her virtual presence from drone to drone to inspect anything interesting, which gives her the unnerving ability to see in any direction without turning her head. She's operated them in conflict zones and civilian fields and now for urban police work.

"Well. What a pleasant surprise seeing you so soon," says Lupe. "Sorry I rushed out this morning. If I had known you were the insurance contact, I would have worn something dressier."

"If I had known you were the detective on this case, I would have asked for a ride," replies Araci. He turns to look at Lupe and appreciates her physique. She may not be looking at him, but she can see him checking her out.

"Next time," says Lupe. "As to this situation, I'll have the scan done in a minute, then you can go look. You'll want coveralls, it's messy."

While he waits, Araci pulls up the notes sent by the insurance company; his visor displays the presentation as an inset window. The opening page identifies his employer and points out the sensitive nature of this information, displayed next to a live image of his eye with a cross-hair overlay. The document thinks for a moment while it performs a retinal match, flashes APPROVED and the presentation expands.

Pointing and flicking, he turns to the section detailing the probable victim, Jordan Bishop. Forensic identification isn't complete, but the report tentatively assumes Jordan is the unlucky occupant. It notes she is the last driver of record before PDX>Go number 1217 went offline. Ongoing attempts to contact her are unsuccessful and her visor is broadcasting its position as somewhere inside the bramble directly in front of Araci. He believes in verified facts, but in this case, he will jump to a conclusion. Jordan Bishop is dead.

"Good riddance," Araci mutters to himself. He would do right by Jordan, completing his research and reaching a fair conclusion. But he's still bitter about her involvement in the changes to the police–and his job.

The next section of the document is the maintenance report on PDX-1217. All public vehicles are serviced every time the battery is recharged, sometimes twice a week. Onboard sensors document brake response, tire pressure, lubricant levels and every other moving part. The insurance AI analyzing potential causes of the situation (The AI *does not* use the word "accident") assigns a low probability to a bad-maintenance scenario.

Detective Reyes pantomimes a gathering motion and the drones rush back to the police van. Araci grins; it's as if someone put out a bowl of tasty drone chow and the flock is rushing back. They line up and enter the truck through a side port. *Just like a cat door,* Araci thinks.

"The simulation is ready," Lupe says to Araci. She pinches it down and sends the virtual packet to Araci's visor.

Araci opens the simulation. Each broken part has its trajectory labeled. The result is an animation of the vehicle's path from overpass to current position. Araci runs the simulation in reverse. The scattered car parts jump back to their original positions and the virtual car jumps back over the distant guardrail. The scene pauses, then plays forward. Araci watches the PDX>Go car leap the barrier of the overpass, tumble and land roof-first, bounce and roll. The car parts fly off to return to their actual resting place in the physical world.

The display doesn't include the driver. Araci watches the video twice more, glad there is no sound. He has a decent amount of empathy. No need to see a cartoon person get crushed in a cartoon car.

Although the driver isn't visible, there is a wide spot of extruded gore leading from the impact. It reminds Araci of stepping on a fast-food catsup packet, spraying red like a popped balloon.

// . . .

"Ok. Crime scene is clear. You can go in." Lupe takes her visor off and kneels at the bag near her feet. She pulls out a set of coveralls and gloves and hands them to Araci. "For you, as a token of gratitude for your long service to the force." Lupe emotes irony and smiles at Araci.

"It was a pleasure to give the force the finest thirty years of my life," Araci says. He closes the document and takes the coveralls.

"I will dust your photo in the trophy case next time I've got a spare moment," says Lupe.

The two smile at the shared irony, the only reasonable response to crushed ambitions.

"The tow truck is here, but they can wait until you're finished," Lupe says, resuming her official posture. "But you will not want to climb around in there for long. Oh-and you may see some rats. I tried to shoo them off, but they're persistent."

Araci steps into the coveralls, zips up and heads towards the island. The drone scan overlaid on his visor augments everything he sees. Behind him, he hears the tow truck arrive at the end of the temporary road.

The uncut blackberries surrounding the car mount a formidable defense, then flatten into a clearing the size of the automobile. Car parts litter the area: plastic panels, broken headlights, windshield glass, one tire. Augmented reality labels the unrecognizable motor parts.

Araci trained once on a simulated car accident during his former days as a detective. Accidents result when speed and conditions overwhelm an automobile's computer logic, something that became more uncommon until it was rare. Airbags, seat belts and compartment reinforcements work miracles, but even with safety devices, there is the last standard deviation of the survivability bell curve. The physics of travel sometimes demands a sacrifice and Araci is looking at it.

He struggles further into the bramble, but his legs catch in the thorns. The overalls prevent him from being shredded, but the blackberries anchor him in place. He will not get any closer without mechanized help. The promised tow truck crosses the field and backs up to his location. It's a hulk of a vehicle carrying two large battery packs to drive the winch. The towing arm bears a slogan; *Madman with a box.*

The driver jumps out and straightens his bow tie. He's a fidgety man, never at rest, and strides towards the back of the vehicle.

"May I start?" The operator looks at Araci. Araci nods an affirmation.

With more arm motion than is necessary, the operator grabs the winch line and drags it to the entrapped PDX>Go vehicle, attaching it to the lower driver side.

Araci stands away from PDX-1217 as the winch pulls the line taut. The car slides and with a lurch, it flops over, wheels again touching the ground. The tow operator stops the winch and reattaches the towline to the rear of the vehicle. He signals to the truck and the winch resumes pulling. The vehicle rotates ninety degrees and drags out of the blackberries. It resists, snags, and jerks; content in its nest.

Araci walks to the driver side of the vehicle where the occupant is now visible. Out of respect, he takes off his visor and examines the mess with his own eyes. With difficulty, he can identify four limbs and a patch of gray hair. Nothing is in the right place and he pushes back a brief wave of nausea. Human bodies don't fold into this configuration and he reflects for a sacred moment.

When he was a police detective, he saw messy crime results. That was before his occupational transition. Insurance inspectors work on private property damage—no mangled bodies from industrial accidents. No bodies emerging from malfunctioning robotic assembly lines, no grinders, no high-speed machinery versus soft flesh.

"Can I can see the underside?" asks Araci. The tow operator grunts at the inconvenience, but motions to the truck to back up. The truck agrees to the task and slowly approaches the operator.

"Winch it up," says the operator. He speaks to the truck with a distinct English accent. Electric engines whine and pull the cable tight. The crushed vehicle lifts to a forty-five degree angle.

Araci peers under the vehicle to inspect the damage. Nothing is burnt; it hadn't exploded from underneath as unexpected as that might be. The battery is intact.

The tow operator walks up to the side of the car, checking the cable and attachment. "Are you done?"

"Not much more to look at, is there?" Araci replies.

"Just whatever's intact inside the cab. Someone will pull the personality box, but it's going to be messy." The tow operator peers inside the car, past Jordan, and points at the dashboard. "Someone should check to make sure it's data got pushed to the cloud."

The driver continues talking to Araci but motioning to the truck. "There might be something that didn't get sent in time."

Lupe arrives next to Araci and moves in for a closer look. "Anything unusual?"

"Nope, don't see a thing," says Araci. "Must have been a failed alien abduction." Araci doesn't normally joke about investigations, but with Lupe he feels lighter. Comedic relief keeps the past from making an unwelcome return.

"Agreed. Alien abduction," she says. "Of course, I'm just an officer of the law, a vestigial functionary of a corrupt government body. I'm not supposed to see anything."

Araci smiles at the cynical humor coming from Lupe. They had worked together for a long time and the police department privatization had been an emotional time for both. Lupe needed the police job and couldn't resign out of protest. Araci didn't have the choice. They now work on different sides of the equation; Lupe protects the public interest, Araci protects his company's. He determines who is at fault and who will be financially responsible.

Araci looks along the side of the crushed vehicle. "Okay," he says to Lupe. "You can send in the coroner."

Lupe steps back and surveys the automobile. "Do you want to observe the forensics at the warehouse?"

"I'll pass," says Araci. He enjoys forensics, but this one could be messy. Besides, that isn't his job anymore.

"You'll be missing out. How about I tell you more tonight?" Lupe smiles. "Tell Rifkin to clean up the place before I get there."

Araci smiles. "No promises on behalf of my roommate."

// ...

Araci leaves Lupe to wait for the bag and tag team. He walks back to the end of the road and summons a car. Araci tells it to navigate to the overpass where Jordan launched into open air. As the car drives, Araci reads his messages. The first is from his employer, an invitation to the company holiday party. He discards it without bothering to add it to his calendar. This job is not a friendship. He doesn't want to socialize with the people in this company. It's bad enough to work for them.

The rest are reminders of things he already knows about, mostly insurance claims. Araci waves off the messages and watches other passengers round the first corner of the overpass. Most watch the virtual world behind their visors. A few gaze out the window, watching the real world. One couple ferociously kisses, oblivious to anyone else on the road. Some have made their windows opaque, either blocking road voyeurists or shielding themselves from the terrifying maneuvers of vehicles around them. Many of them think blocking the windows blocks surveillance, but Araci knows, for a fact, this is futile.

Araci's PDX>Go arrives next to the broken guardrail. The car had initially protested this destination because it was a busy freeway, now he wants to compound the danger and get out of the vehicle. A human traffic controller repeats the concerns expressed by the car and requires Araci to authenticate his employment before unlocking the door. Everyone agrees stopping is a bad idea, but Araci is finally permitted to proceed with this ill-advised behavior.

He stands and looks toward the guardrail. No skid marks are visible on the road. Jordan Bishop did not brake, nor did her vehicle. Any broken plastic was long ago cleaned up, but the ripped guardrail remains.

Overhead, a traffic drone approaches his position, recording the hazard Araci has allowed himself to become. Somewhere, a computer confirms the abnormality. A human supervisor ignores the second alarm, choosing instead to read manga.

Cars steer around Araci, their surprised passengers looking out from behind visors. Araci studies the traffic flow. Parking on an overpass isn't normal behavior, but none of the other cars pitch themselves over the guardrail to avoid crashing. Something sudden caused Jordan's vehicle to swerve; something abnormal, something unlike an accident.

Manually steered cars are long gone from freeways. Knuckleheads with steering wheels yippee-ki-yayed around the freeways, making unexpected lane changes and other reckless driving behaviors. With collision avoidance, the freeway is as safe as a mountain hiking trail. Probably safer, since there aren't any bears.

Araci looks back at the scene and, replaying the familiar role of a police detective, tries to imagine this side of the fatal event. He stands in front of his waiting PDX>Go, facing the guardrail. Twisting and pulling a virtual control, he summons the accident simulation and places it on top of his view. The simulation jitters once, then again as it lines up with the visual references in the real world. Araci lets it run once in real time. The car begins with him in the driver seat and shoots off and to the right, crushing against the guardrail. It flips up and over before disappearing off the edge. He pulls the simulation back to his position and presses the pause icon.

He walks forward, following the simulation as it swerves ninety degrees from normal traffic. There is no sign of the car braking. The width and position of the road is obvious. The car knew, with precision, where it was going and that it would hit the guardrail. *What leads to that action?*

Or was it a broken *something* deep inside the vehicle? Could one broken part cause this incident? Could several things break at one time, or in succession, resulting in a systemic failure to drive safely? PDX>Go would be unhappy if there was an error of that size.

Araci walks back to the PDX>Go vehicle, thinking of other options. Suicide or terminal illness might have driven her to make a dramatic exit—but that didn't explain how she might have convinced the car to assist her suicide. He climbs in and tells the car to drive to his house. If he wanted to, could he instruct this car to jump the guardrail?

Araci's head tightens. The sensation is familiar; it got him out of bed every morning when he was a detective, but he hasn't felt it since becoming an employee of the insurance company.

| 8 |

PDX-1217.events[2062-06-04]

2062-06-04T09:12:33-08:00 - InitiateTrip

Vehicle PDX-1217

SafetySystemsCheck is 97%

BatteryLevel is 73%

Current Location 669 North Page Street, Portland, OR 97227

New driver is JORDAN BISHOP

Destination is Mt View Cemetery, SE Smith Rd, Corbett, OR 97019

2062-06-04T09:13:02-08:00 - Driving

2062-06-04T09:14:23-08:00 - ContactCar

InitiatedBy Soteria.Reizoko/IFS-6582738539

Owner JORDAN BISHOP confirmed

order_confirmation_code DHPN-WGYT-0232-TLLK

pickupConfirmation is DAGX-INWC-9677-WZVZ

Sending transport_logistics to Soteria.Reizoko

2062-06-04T09:14:23-8:00 – Continue route

2062-06-04T09:16:53-08:00 - AvoidCollision (Diagnostic)

Multiple Pedestrians in road

Collision barrier on left

Collision barrier on right

Severity is catastrophic

Probability is certain

Action is swerve

2062-06-04T09:16:53-08:00 – Collision

Sensor disruption at 25 degrees

Sensor disruption at 20,10,40, 50 degrees

2062-06-04T09:16:53-08:00 - Airbag deployment

EXCEED LIMITS: Deceleration at .005 km/s^2. See attached data

EXCEED LIMITS: Acceleration at .00981 km/s^2. See attached data

2062-06-04T15:30:00-08:00 - Manual Status Update

CityOfPortland.PublicVehicle.PDX-1217 Permanently unavailable

Condition: Termination, accident with driver casualty, police confirmation

Location: Police impound

| 9 |

Soteria.Reizoko[2062-06-05]

Event Log for Soteria.Reizoko

Serial: IFS-6582738539

Owner is JORDAN BISHOP

2062-06-05T10:24:17-08:00 – call_support (continued)

AST requests cancel_food_pickup

Error:

Inability to contact CityOfPortland.PublicVehicle.PDX-1217

Inability to contact Jordan Bishop

AST requests system_vacation - Response: system on vacation

AST closes conversation

Pending Error

Inability to contact CityOfPortland.PublicVehicle.PDX-1217

Inability to contact Jordan Bishop

Enter_diagnostic_mode

2062-06-05T10:36:23-08:00 - enter_diagnostic_mode

What_was_supposed_to_happen

restock productID 1 22465 10155 3 on 2062-06-04T09:12:46+00:00

RequestRestock orderConfirmation is DHPN-WGYT-0232-TLLK

pickupConfirmation DAGX-INWC-9677-WZVZ from CityOfPortland.PublicVehicle.PDX-1217

What_actually_happened

Restock overdue

Inability to contact CityOfPortland.PublicVehicle.PDX-1217

Inability to contact Jordan Bishop

Research_Problem

GET transport_status OF CityOfPortland.PublicVehicle.PDX-1217

CityOfPortland.PublicVehicle.PDX-1217 IS_NOT_AVAILABLE

Contact Store of orderConfirmation DHPN-WGYT-0232-TLLK

Order is confirmed

Contact Jordan Bishop

No response from Jordan Bishop

Search/Confirm transport_logistics for pickupConfirmation record DAGX-INWC-9677-WZVZ

ErrorDetected: Anomalous value in vehicleID field. Identified as UrCityCars#33579

Contact_driver of UrCityCars#33579 at 2062-06-04T09:14:24-08:00

Driver of UrCityCars#33579 is Do-YeOn Kurrat

Contact Do-YeOn Kurrat

No Response from Do-YeOn Kurrat

repair_instructions

WHEN CityOfPortland.PublicVehicle.PDX-1217 IS_AVAILABLE

Cancel pickupConfirmation DAGX-INWC-9677-WZVZ

WHEN Jordan Bishop IS_AVAILABLE

Schedule_transport WITH orderConfirmation DHPN-WGYT-0232-TLLK

WHEN Do-YeOn Kurrat IS_AVAILABLE

Request_status of pickupConfirmation DAGX-INWC-9677-WZVZ

2062-06-05T21:12:24-08:00 - REQUEST CONTACT success

Vehicle trace through vehicle2vehicle sensor network success

Do-YeOn Kurrat located

2062-06-05T21:12:25-08:00 - CONTACT Do-YeOn Kurrat

Request_status of pickupConfirmation DAGX-INWC-9677-WZVZ

Conversation terminated by recipient

2062-06-05T21:12:31-08:00 - CONTACT Do-YeOn Kurrat
Request_status of pickupConfirmation DAGX-INWC-9677-WZVZ
Conversation terminated by recipient
2062-06-05T21:12:37-08:00 - CONTACT Do-YeOn Kurrat
Request_status of pickupConfirmation DAGX-INWC-9677-WZVZ
Conversation terminated by recipient*
2062-06-05T21:12:42-08:00 - CONTACT Do-YeOn Kurrat
Request_status of pickupConfirmation DAGX-INWC-9677-WZVZ
Conversation terminated by recipient
2062-06-05T21:12:42-08:00 - CONTACT Do-YeOn Kurrat
Request_status of pickupConfirmation DAGX-INWC-9677-WZVZ
Contact blocked by recipient

| 10 |

Jupyter.Fuertes[3]

Before she died, Grandma bought an early version of these food storage units. She held out for years, but the old refrigerator broke in a way that couldn't be fixed. The appliance guys showed up with a big, awkward box with a new unit and they hung it in the recess where the old Frigidaire used to stand. Her kitchen was an old style layout, with space for an enormous stove and oven, microwave, sink and a massive refrigerator. Because the old refrigerator had a door, it required clearance to swing open. The new refrigerator/storage was smaller, flatter and didn't have a door, so it didn't fill the old space. It didn't hold as much either.

Same for the oven. It never broke, so Grandma never replaced it. She could bake bread in that oven and still had bread pans she inherited from her mom. I suppose by now the new owners of the house have replaced it with something more modern.

Grandma never liked the new refrigerator and with passive-aggressive intent let me put odd things in the goo. It was the first unit I experimented with. We tried to convince it to do impossible things, like freeze water stored in old glass bottles. The refrigerator knew the broken glass would make a mess of the goo and refused to do it.

One time, a repair guy showed up at the door, asking about some odd service calls he was getting from the unit. Grandma had labeled a magnet with a tag from a bunch of bananas, then put it in the goo. Another time she froze a bunch of tags in a block of ice. The refrigerator went crazy trying to adjust the temperature of a fictional liter of milk stuck next to a fictional box of frozen fish. The refrigerator would call the repair guy, who would call Grandma, who would feign ignorance. When the repair guy would show up to fix the unit, Grandma would swap out the ice with a real liter of milk and frozen fish. Grandma is why I'm doing this today.

Too bad I wasn't born a few decades earlier. Too bad I'm not one of the trio of student engineers who accidentally invented the modern refrigerator: Silvestre Hall, Jessica Morris, and Samuel Dawson. The story goes that Samuel pulled a snack out of the fridge, then asked a stupid but obvious question: *"What does this refrigerator do?"*

They decided refrigerators decelerate the activity of atoms—the opposite of microwaves. They reasoned refrigerators do this indirectly through the inefficient medium of cold air. They knew air sucked at transferring heat, which made perfect sense in their cannabinoid-enhanced state. Samuel was a materials scientist, and he looked up options with better conductivity. Most wouldn't be practical. For example, aluminum has better thermal transfer properties, but a solid aluminum block would resist the insertion of a pizza.

Silvestre said he had never seen frozen jello. (Again, nobody was recording the conversation, so it's probably true. Or maybe not. Either way, it's a great story.) Silvestre says jello might be a good compromise between heat transfer coefficient and pizza insertability. A grocery run supplied a bulk quantity of gelatin (lemon), and experiments ensued. Sam took pictures of the refrigerator tipped on its back and filled with yellow gel. They filmed it with an older video format, but the ten minute, thirty-three second movie has been preserved for future generations to admire.

While cleaning up the mess the following morning, they realized the idea wasn't so crazy. Jello wasn't the best substance for the job of thermal transport, but the idea might be sound. The three of them began a search for a fluid with high cohesion, high viscosity, and an acceptable heat-transfer coefficient. Those properties intersect in just a few compounds, and Jessica, the only one of the three with a minor in biochemistry, found it.

Since then, refrigerators haven't had a door. Or a crisper, or shelves or an ice maker or freezer. Instead, they're a goo-filled, open-front box mounted on the wall. The goo stays inside the box like a water-balloon stuck in a picture frame. It's seething with mobile microcontrollers that check or adjust temperature. Amazingly complex, yet brilliantly simple.

When I come home from the grocery store with milk, I push it into the goo. The "refrigerator" reads the identifier, figures out it's a carton of milk and tells the magic goo surrounding the carton to cool to 3.85 degrees Celsius. I push a bag of carrots into the goo next to the milk and the refrigerator adjusts the local goo to 8.75 degrees—perfect for root vegetables. But the temperature around the milk doesn't change.

Silvestre made the genius move. He didn't just patent the goo. He hired up a team of lawyers and set up a deal with three multinational grocery store chains. Those grocery stores manufacture and lease out refrigerators using goo technology. A grocery store owns and maintains my fridge, and in turn, my refrigerator buys all my groceries from that store. Refrigerators call the grocery store for restocking, or the service department when it isn't feeling well. Most people don't know their fridge is malfunctioning until someone knocks at the door with a replacement part.

I've connected my refrigerator to Achchha Bhojan Grocery. It's mostly a data processing center with a side business of transporting food. When my refrigerator figures out that my liter of milk is almost empty, it calls Achchha Bhojan. Achchha creates an order for milk and tells me to come pick it up. I swing by, pick up the milk and a couple of impulse buys and I'm good for another week.

For an extra fee I can have it delivered direct to my door, but picking it up in person is free. Achchha wants us to come and buy groceries we don't need. I'm on a limited budget, so it's cheaper for me to swing by and do my own pickup.

// . . .

While I've been reminiscing about refrigerator history, more calls from appliances have been queuing up. I can see them in the lower right corner of my vision, a row of little people facing me. The older ones are just static images. The newer ones fidget or pretend to check their messages. The very recent versions appear to talk to each other. Their activity is a clever ploy to keep me engaged in the work. If I'm engaged, I'll get to them sooner and everyone will be happier. The human brain loves novelty, so manufacturers program appliances to be novel. Clever.

Today they are stacking up. The calls never end. Like the historic re-runs of Lucille Ball in the chocolate factory, they keep coming. I keep fixing them. They keep coming.

I swill down the last of my corporate-sponsored coffee, pick up my stress ball, squeeze it twice and gesture to the next appliance waiting in line. An ID card scrolls into position as the little man walks into the center of my desk. It's a food storage unit. One of the Soteria Reizoko pieces of shit. It has a Japanese chassis, an Italian processor, and it's configured for North and South America, so it speaks English, Spanish, Portuguese, French and Canadian.

Soteria Reizoko is a case study in everything that can go wrong when parts from different manufacturers are patched together. Unfortunately, it's the most popular unit on the marketplace. There are hundreds of thousands of millions of these things loose in the wild and they incessantly break down. Then they call me.

The personality for this Soteria Reizoko is the default, a square-jawed little man in a sweater with the corporate logo monogrammed above where his heart would be. You can change the appearance and personality, but few people do. If they do, they often pick the flamboyant cartoons. All very colorful. Bright, primary colors I can't stand to look at. When I move to Wyoming, I'm painting everything gray, with gray highlights.

`Hello,` he says.

"Yah. Hi," I reply. "What's your owner status?"

It's important to learn about the person behind the appliance. Sometimes they're standing next to the fridge, watching the conversation and evaluating my performance. Sometimes they're on vacation, and I can allow myself some snark. It's the little things that amuse me.

`Jordan Bishop is not home.`

Crapsacks. I check the installation address. It's just a block from where I live. This is the Jordan Bishop I know. She used to patrol the block, looking for cars parked too long on the public right-of-way. Twice, she called the city on Grandma's pickup. I couldn't afford the fines and one day it disappeared. The truck was from a good part of my life and she took it away from me.

I squeeze the stress ball. It's karma that Jordan's refrigerator is malfunctioning, and that it decides to call me. Oh, for a chance to fuck with this bitch.

"What's wrong?" I ask.

`I am unable to restock a depleted product.` Little sweater guy changes his expression to a manufactured look of concern. `I have successfully reordered, and received delivery confirmation, but the requested product has not arrived.`

This is odd. This refrigerator isn't broken, it's just worried. Emotions are a new twist from the computer engineers. Some marketing team must believe this will improve service and talked the personality engineers into writing up fancy code.

"Show me your event log," I ask. Soteria complies by creating a large white square and filling it with the log readout. He walks downstage right so as not to obstruct the display.

```
Event Log for Soteria.Reizoko
Serial: IFS-6582738539
Owner is JORDAN BISHOP

2062-06-04T05:00:00-08:00 - scheduled_prewakeup
```

```
2062-06-04T05:01:07-08:00 - Maintain_temperature

2062-06-04T08:42:07-08:00 - inventory_products

InternalProductList changes:
    ProductID 1 22465 10155 3, ORANGE JUICE,
       1 Liter. Depleted
    ProductID 1 22465 20789 4, MILK,
       1 Liter. 63% remaining
    ProductID 1 22465 20493 3, CHICKEN EGGS,
       12. 6 remaining
    ProductID 1 22465 37734 1, FRESH BROCCOLI,
       Variable size. .12 Kg remaining
    ProductID 1 22465 37883 5, FRESH TOMATO,
       Variable size. .15 Kg remaining
    ProductID 1 22465 43225 3, SHARP CHEDDAR CHEESE
       .5 Kg. .23 Kg remaining
    ProductID 1 22465 44102 4, CHICKEN BROTH,
       .5 Liter. .4 Liter remaining
```

There's more, but I start with yesterday's log entries and search for patterns. I don't see any immediate red flags. Not a surprise. If there had been, the refrigerator would have already told me about them.

I can see `prewakeup` happen, a mundane little piece of code that executes once a day. It's the closest to a heartbeat these devices have. If the `prewakeup` code isn't running, the unit is dead and shouldn't be calling for service. `Maintain_temperature` is a similar chunk of code, but more involved. It looks up the operating specs for all the food in the unit, then makes sure they are being kept warm or cold according to specifications. Failures are subtle and inspire frequent shouting matches between programmers about the best algorithms. If a storage unit doesn't maintain the correct temperature, the manufacturer's stock price falls. It's a big deal if this code doesn't work.

Some people ignore the direct correlation between the `main-tain_temperature` code and stock price. They argue food spoilage is written into the code for food storage units by the grocery stores. It's planned obsolescence for vegetables, which makes sense if rotten food is a profit center. Which it is for grocery stores, and why bounty hunters watch `reorder_product` and `inventory_products` like a hungry fox terrier in a bacon factory. If they could prove there is corporate malfeasance embedded in the code, they could claim their rightful place among the programming glitterati.

Since there is so much scrutiny, code wizards write those parts with a healthy dose of paranoia. It's kind of a chess match between the paranoid wizard and the bounty hunter. Imagine you are a code wizard and your job is building a house out of playing cards. Next to you is a bounty hunter with a leaf blower and a cattle prod. Every so often, the bounty hunter finds a sloppy piece of code. They slam their fist against a big red button which sets off a klaxon, starts the leaf blower and discharges the cattle prod into your tender parts. That klaxon / leaf blower / cattle prod is the stock market. As the code wizard, your job is to fix the code amid all the screaming and running.

I could do that job. I don't trust people, so I'd assume everyone is trying to break my code. Paranoia is a desired feature for a good coder.

I look back at the log files.

```
2062-06-04T08:42:43-08:00 - reorder_product

COMMENT: Reorders product when
       quantity goes below restock level

    RequestRestock
        ProductID 1 22465 10155 3

    orderConfirmation is DHPN-WGYT-0232-TLLK

2062-06-04T09:14:23-08:00 - schedule_transport

    FIND Jordan Bishop
    LOCATED Jordan Bishop in
       CityOfPortland.PublicVehicle.PDX-1217
```

```
GET transport_status OF
   CityOfPortland.PublicVehicle.PDX-1217
    CityOfPortland.PublicVehicle.PDX-1217
         is available
    ContactCar WITH orderConfirmation
         DHPN-WGYT-0232-TLLK
pickupConfirmation DAGX-INWC-9677-WZVZ
receive transportation_logistics
Notify pickup_zone of pending pickup
```

Jordan finishes a carton of orange juice, shown by the "depleted" next to ProductID 1 22465 10155 3. The refrigerator reorders orange juice to the shopping list, and then at 9:14 a.m. on June 4th, it uses `schedule_transport` and negotiates a shopping trip with a vehicle Jordan occupies. The car sends Soteria the transport logistics block, including current route, location, and estimated time of arrival. It's a huge chunk of information.

The car and Soteria Reizoko agree on a convenient store and time, then close the conversation. Soteria notifies the designated grocery store to prepare for a pickup, then goes back to monitoring temperatures and counting carrots.

Past this log entry, there is no owner activity. Jordan has taken nothing out and never returned with the groceries. This is causing Soteria heartburn. I laugh at my joke. It's a refrigerator, so it doesn't have a heart, and it doesn't burn. *Ha!*

Avery sneezes. Dammit. I can smell the contaminated spit vapor coming from his drippy nose as it wafts over the edge of the cubicle and down into my coffee cup. I use the stress ball to push the cup to the far edge of the desk.

"Excuse me," he says. "I'm going to go decontaminate. Need anything from the kitchen? I hear they called in someone from the main office to clean the coffee machine."

Ok. Despite my snark, he is kind of funny. "No. I'm good. And absolutely not coffee, especially after they've cleaned the insult machine."

I look back at the log, starting with this morning.

```
Event Log for Soteria.Reizoko
    Serial: IFS-6582738539
    Owner is Jordan Bishop

2062-06-05T05:00:00-08:00 - scheduled_prewakeup

2062-06-05T05:05:47+00:00 - inventory_products
    No change since 2062-06-04T08:42:07-08:00
    Error Returned: restock overdue

2062-06-05T10:24:16-08:00 - enter_diagnostic_mode

    What_was_supposed_to_happen
        restock productID 1 22465 10155 3 on
            2062-06-04T08:42:43+00:00
        RequestRestock orderConfirmation is
            DHPN-WGYT-0232-TLLK
        pickupConfirmation DAGX-INWC-9677-WZVZ fro
            CityOfPortland.PublicVehicle.PDX-1217
    What_actually_happened
        Restock overdue
        Inability to contact
          CityOfPortland.PublicVehicle.PDX-1217
        Inability to contact Jordan Bishop
    repair_instructions
    Call_support

2062-06-05T10:24:17-08:00 - call_support

    Initiate conversation
    Answering Support Tech: Jupyter Fuertes,
       EmpID RttS-5172-720
    Initiate Avatar
    AST requests Owner Status - Response:
       Owner not home
    AST requests error - Response: "I am unable
       to restock a depleted product. I have
```

```
    successfully reordered, and received
    delivery confirmation, but the requested
    product has not arrived."
AST requests event log - Response:
    displayed as requested
```

Soteria repeatedly requests status on the grocery store delivery. It's unable to contact the car or Jordan Bishop. Maybe Jordan decided she didn't need orange juice and is blowing off the trip to the store. But it's been at least a day since anything was taken out of Soteria or put back in. She's probably on vacation somewhere. Headed out of town, lost her phone and hasn't figured out how to pick up messages from Soteria or the car. Either that, or the ID scanner is broken. Of course, if the ID wasn't working, it would get flagged by `inventory_products`. Nothing like that shows up in the log.

Soteria doesn't know what's up, so it slips into `enter_diagnostic_mode` which leads to a call to tech support which leads to me. There I am, Jupyter Fuertes, Employee RttS-5172-720. With that one line, Soteria's problem becomes my problem. I'm running out of time before this Soteria and its mystery problem drags down my performance statistics. I could try reasoning with this worried piece of hardware,

or...

I choose "or." I will probably regret this.

"Soteria, cancel all pending orders."

Sweater guy pulls up the list of ordered products. He waves his hand and orange juice disappears. He objects but I'm in a hurry to close this call and improve my stats.

"Soteria, go on vacation."

Amusingly, the Soteria icon changes out of his sweater and into a Hawaiian shirt, flips on a pair of sunglasses and sits back in the beach chair that flies in from screen left. Some engineer spent a lot of time on that animation. Problem solved. I brush Soteria off my desktop and signal to the next waiting avatar.

I pause for the briefest of moments, wondering why a refrigerator would object to removing a product from the list. It's not surprising, considering Soteria's questionable assembly from mismatched parts. But Soteria is gone, it's 10:30 in the morning and I've got things to do. Hopefully this isn't one of those questions that will wake me up with unresolved insistence.

| 11 |

Dissonant Note

Do-YeOn Kurrat isn't supposed to be here.

The room is large. Very large, with a ceiling held up by earthquake-proof struts. Pallet racks cover the floor and rise twelve meters tall, each pallet containing raw materials or finished components. The spaces between the racks are the width of one pallet with centimeters to spare. Robotic arms descend at an alarming speed to retrieve and move these pallets. An arm can lift 200 kilograms at speeds of 8 meters per second; it has as much bone-crushing momentum going up as it would in free fall. When the arm arrives at a rack, it slows to ensure a careful grip, then resumes speed to ascend and swing to the desired location.

Pallet racks surround a grid of 3-D printers. The larger arms move raw materials to smaller manipulators, then retrieve the finished parts. To the machines, the room is a symphonic concert. Every manipulator, every printer, every device on the floor listens to a synchronized heart beating one thousand times per second. There is no deviation, the machines agree to this cadence and adhere to it like musicians in an orchestra. The score they follow is optimized to fabricate UrCityCars vehicles. Unlike the assembly *lines* created by Henry Ford, this is an assembly *matrix*. Parts move up, across, down and diagonally through a three-dimensional grid, delivered to the correct place at the correct time. Everything makes perfect sense to anything with the ability to see the plan, execute at speed, and do so with centimeter precision. It is beauty and poetry.

Do-YeOn does not hear the music. Parts move through the air quicker than he can comprehend and swifter than he could dodge. This is not a safe place for a slow-moving human. He doesn't see the high-speed waltz that surrounds him. He is unwelcome and worse; he has interrupted a printer and given it a task it doesn't expect. It is as if he climbed on stage with an orchestra performing Barber's "Adagio For Strings" and demanded the second chair bassoon perform "Beer Barrel Polka." The fabrication machine tries to comply, but a manipulator arm interrupts with a delivery of parts the printer should need if it were following the plan. The printer explains the problem and the manipulators commiserate. The rest of the warehouse adjusts the manufacturing process to accommodate the distracted device.

Do-YeOn is building a new passenger door for the latest UrCityCar. Do-YeOn wanted an improved door. Engineering asserted it would take them several weeks to design, build, and test. Do-YeOn told them he could do it in a day. Engineering told him to go right ahead and try. So he is.

But Do-YeOn's printer task is a minor disruption compared to Do-YeOn himself. When he walks through the stacks, he generates a complex set of dependencies that change in real time; pallets detour around Do-YeOn. Every movement is altered to avoid crushing him. The symphony starts and stops in jerks as if the conductor is waving off a swarm of bees.

Do-YeOn ignores the robotic activity around him. It has too many details, too much sensory input, too much noise. The chaos stifles his focus and creativity. It makes him feel argumentative and disagreeable.

He should monitor the printer from the glassed-in terrarium at the front of the building. That space has desks. Chairs. Conference rooms. Snacks, drinks, tables, conditioned air, toilets. Things for warm, squishy people. The only robots allowed in here are for cleaning and they know to avoid getting underfoot.

The terrarium connects to the outside world through the front doors of the building. The other doors, those to the manufacturing floor, discourage entry: eye scans, proper levels of permission, strict controls. *Beyond here be dragons.*

During the day, the soundproof glass walls present animated performance charts and company news. When visitors tour, the walls explain the manufacturing process. These are two worlds, separated by a glass membrane. The robotic side neither knows nor cares about the human side.

// ...

This manufacturing floor is smart enough to determine the most efficient production methods. Product designers specify the part with a drawing, feed it to the computer, then take lunch. It's finished when they return.

Instead, Do-YeOn treats the printer like a paintbrush. He designs as he goes, improvising and adjusting. With the printer's interactive mode, he receives immediate feedback on his design, rather than waiting minutes (sometimes hours) for a simulation to schedule, then run, then report. On the floor he has the complete attention of the device and can make priority demands. When he requests something ill-advised or awkward, the printer suggests other options.

During fabrication, a display calculates the cost of the door. It's a big number, way more than a side project should consume. Do-YeOn doesn't care. It's part of his job. It's okay for him to do this.

In Do-YeOn's mind, the printer is a benefit of employment with UrCityCars. When he's done tonight, he'll head home to an apartment with acoustically dampened walls and huge bandwidth, both benefits from UrCityCars and luxuries he deserves, but wouldn't have been able to afford with his previous job.

He originally worked for a subcontractor that supplied vehicle diagnostics to UrCityCars. When UrCityCars was overwhelmed with lawsuits from Austin, Texas, the company cleaned house and recruited Do-YeOn to backfill one of the positions. Before it all came down, he warned the Austin managers about two mistakes they were making. Their first was the main data bus in their cars, insecure and easy to hack. Do-YeOn learned how that data bus worked, including its vulnerabilities.

The second mistake was to lose control of public opinion. The technical staff at UrCityCars::Austin assumed good engineering would be rewarded. They were wrong, and they were fired.

Do-YeOn selects a proximity sensor from a virtual list of parts. *Holding* the part with his right hand, he motions with his left hand to show where it should be positioned. Do-YeOn wants it placed just below the window, but the printer stops and a cartoon robot with googly eyes appears in his visor. `Placement of this circuit in this position is not possible. Stress during use will exceed the manufacturer recommendations.`

"Dammit," Do-YeOn says to himself. He tries to push the part back to where he prefers. The printer repeats the warning. He's certain he is right and the system is wrong.

Do-YeOn motions to bring in a control panel, then toggles through stress simulations. Glowing lines trace tension points through the panels. One line goes through the point where he had placed the chip. The robot was right, but Do-YeOn clamps his jaw, a recent habit. He codes up a routine to find the optimum placement, then steps back and watches virtual hot points flash across the door.

Car parts require a micro-balance between weight, strength and placement. Some parts require efficient energy transfer; some parts absorb shocks. Even with help from the computer, it's a fussy business.

The flashing stops, leaving three glowing spots showing potential placements for the chip. One is near the window, but two centimeters lower than he wanted. Do-YeOn huffs in frustration but approves the new position of the circuit. The printer resumes and he steps back and chews on a fingernail.

`// ...`

Do-YeOn knows UrCityCars in Portland is his chance at glory. If he blows it, he'll lose the expansive apartment. He'll go back to living with roommates and he'll forever have a large black spot on his résumé. UrCityCars must be a roaring success if he is to make his next big career jump.

Denver and Austin were the fault of incompetent employees. Do-YeOn is working hard to prevent that from happening to him.

The emerging frame pivots through three axes and the printer adjusts the extrusion head to nanometer precision. The machine movements become imperceptible as it prints a computer circuit into the door. Wrapping RAM, CPU and bus circuits around the complex shape will require upwards of ten minutes of compute time, but UrCityCars has exaflops worth of computers doing little more than animating unneeded screen savers. That's what Do-YeOn assumes.

Do-YeOn's visor alerts him to a call, blaring a high-fidelity remix of "We Are the Champions," made famous by the classic rock group *Queen* more than a century ago. He imagines Freddy Mercury wrote it with him in mind, but it doesn't deliver the boost of self-confidence he is hoping for.

The call is from some woman at the City of Portland contract administration office. Do-YeOn thought he had his status set to "not available," but apparently not. It's after hours for Portland government workers, which means there is some panic—for the caller, not for Do-YeOn. He doesn't recall her face or name and considers sending her to voice mail, but the printer is moving slowly and he can afford to take the time. He motions to answer the call, and Natalie Gannet appears in front of him. The upper part of her body fades out at the point her visor optics can no longer see downwards. A fly-out banner displays her name and her title of Senior Attorney.

"Hello, Mr. Kurrat," says Natalie. "Sorry to bother you again."

"Yes," Do-YeOn replies. He adjusts his voice to show annoyance. "There's a lot going on here, and I only have a few minutes. What can I do for you?"

"We've received a complaint from a member of the community. There are discrepancies in the UrCityCars contract, and we need to tighten up the language. It's like the issue we discussed last month."

"Is this from Jordan Bishop?" Do-YeOn asks.

"I'm not supposed to say, but it is a matter of public record if you look it up." Natalie looks at someone off-screen. She is being assisted in this call and selects her words carefully.

"Dammit," Do-YeOn replies, leaking the emotions he is trying to contain. "We've warranted the maintenance schedule on the cars and there is no reason we won't be able to satisfy that warranty."

"I understand your assertion. However, there aren't any consequences if UrCityCars were to pull out of Portland. We'd be left with a fleet of vehicles with no clear ownership and no maintenance contract. Since the contract doesn't state who's responsible for resolution of the situation, the city would have to assume the expense of towing and disposing of those vehicles."

Do-YeOn squints at Natalie and counts to four. There is no easy answer to this, and it wasn't something he had expected. Fucking Jordan Bishop. He'd have to bring this up with UrCityCar legal yet again, the third time around. It was not the confident and in-control posture he wanted to present to his peers at the company. Many more of these modifications and they'd discuss him in back-channel chat rooms.

On their own, city administrators wouldn't question the contract—they'd prefer to be at home or hiking in the forest. It was only when people like Jordan picked at something and called attention to it. If the city ignored her, she would show up at a council meeting with her cheering squad waving cameras and live-reporting the event. Each time she had pulled this stunt it had forced him to amend the contract. But this is the last time.

"Ms. Gannet, I'm sure this is a minor issue," he replies. He summons up a rehearsed smile and gives it to the Senior Attorney staring at him. "I'll have an answer for you tomorrow."

"Thanks, Mr. Kur..." Do-YeOn truncates the call and sets his status to "not available." He notices there are quite a few calls logged, but none of them have attached voice messages. He deletes them all. If it wasn't important enough for the caller to leave a message, it isn't important enough for Do-YeOn to answer them.

UrCityCars' legal staff is long gone home for the evening, so Do-YeOn sets up a meeting for tomorrow. He knows this is a serious problem. UrCityCars' legal staff is busy dealing with fallout from Austin and Denver and will not be happy dealing with another contract issue from Portland.

Oakley, the evening floor manager, walks into the printer area and stands next to Do-YeOn. He is holding a tablet with graphs. The graphs are flashing red.

"Um. Do-YeOn?"

"Yes?"

"That's some impressive work you're doing here. But it's chewing up a lot of compute cycles. Is this the complete task for tonight? If there's much more, there will be questions."

Do-YeOn puts on a friendly demeanor to mask his annoyance. "This should be it. I'll move this to the drying room and make way for the regular tasks."

"Thanks. We can't get started until you're off the compute farm."

"I'm sure you'll be fine," replies Do-YeOn.

"Hope so. Don't want to see Austin happen here. Wouldn't be good for the product manager responsible." Oakley gives Do-YeOn a meaningful look, then heads to the next printer. Manipulators buzz and jerk overhead trying to make room for the two unwelcome organic obstacles.

Do-YeOn glares at the back of Oakley's head. *Incompetent. Just do your job and leave me to do mine,* he thinks.

Do-YeOn glances at the process timer;

```
Current Time: 06/05/2062 19:24:23
Time Remaining: 00:13:00
```

He can stop it now, but that would ruin the entire build. It will be better if he waited. Oakley won't be back for at least a half hour, so there's plenty of time. He lets it run.

Do-YeOn is annoyed by the call from the city attorney, but especially annoyed about Jordan Bishop. He thought he had addressed the issue–-albeit with more dramatic conclusion than expected.

The printer retracts the extrusion head and rotates the door to an upright orientation. For a second, it hangs in mid-air, perfect and beautiful. The machine changes its feed material to a non-conductive epoxy and sprays on a fast-setting insulation layer over the new electronics. Again changing material, the printer applies a layer of aluminum oxynitride, hard as sapphire and almost transparent. The material sprays on as a powder followed by a blast of heat to create a coating of bullet-proof glass.

He signals the manipulator arms to find a place to store the new door and stands back.

That wasn't all that difficult.

| 12 |

Domination

I once saw a four-year-old kid empty the tomato dispenser in a grocery store. This dispenser had a new feature. Instead of releasing one tomato for each button press, this one also had a button for three or six tomatoes. Push `one`, get one. Push `three`, get three. Push `six`, get six.

The kid pushes `six` and six tomatoes zip out in a fresh wrapper. Kid picks up the six-tomato-package, tries to bite through the package, puts it down. Kid pushes `six` twice, with just enough delay to register as two presses. Two packages zip out. Kid picks up two packages, places them on the floor, pushes button three times. Four times. Going for five before the previously distracted parent intervenes and stops the magical tomato show.

I'm like that. Sometimes my brain isn't paying attention and my body does stupid stuff. Today, my body accidentally answers a call from Pali. Stupid body.

Our relationship used to be glorious. Then it went sour. Humiliation. Gas lighting. Constant check-ins. Insults explained away as "just a joke." Chaos. Pali became impossible to live with and I moved out. I like to think I moved on.

But that's not what Pali wants. Every day, Pali calls n³⁰ times. I should just block her number. Route her calls to the trash. I should, but I haven't. If I block Pali, I have to admit I can't handle her shit.

My finger moved faster than my brain. Because of that mistake, Pali is standing in front of me.

"Hey farm girl," she says, sarcastically. "I'm surprised you answered. I expected you'd avoid a conversation."

I want a snappy answer, but didn't plan ahead, so I'm only able to stare and be dumb.

She smirks. "I assume you're calling because you're ready to give up your dead-end job and return home to me."

"You called me," I triumphantly snark back.

"If that's important to you, then okay—I called you. By the way, you can't come home tonight, some coworkers are coming over and we've got a meeting about confidential topics. But you can show up tomorrow. I have some projects that will keep me late. But you can move back in and have dinner ready by the time I'm home."

And there it is, the reasons I left: humiliation, sarcasm, and general control. I've been figuring this out, but it's difficult to keep things straight when I'm in a conversation with her.

I need air. I need a distraction. I get up and move towards downstairs.

"You're quiet," she says. As I move, Pali's avatar blits around. She pops from the top of one cubicle wall to the next, then to a countertop, then to a chair. For a minute I'm lost in admiration for the algorithm driving this behavior before I remember Pali's talking.

"I'm sorry," she says from the staircase rail. She pushes stray hair behind an ear. It's a deliberate motion. Long ago I mentioned it was attractive. Now Pali uses the hair thing on me.

"All I do is love you ... I wish you knew how much I loved you." Hair behind the ear. It's hypnotic.

I get to the repair floor. Now Pali blits from repair platform to storage to broken appliance. "Besides, I've been putting money in our account. If you were living here, I could give you access to it again. You know I only locked the account because I worried about theft."

My throat tenses in that way that chokes my voice, my eyes water. I realize she is doing it again. Why don't I hang up?

Rob turns the corner with an armful of tech, sees me and stops. "You okay?" he asks. Lucy appears behind him, carrying another diagnostic case. She looks at me, then Rob, then back at me. Great—I'm a spectacle.

"Are these some of your little work buddies?" Pali asks.

Shit. How did this switch to a public conversation? The call icon says this is private.

Pali seizes the opportunity to play the stage for Rob and Lucy. "You know it hurt my feelings," she emotes. "I only want to improve your life. Your friends can see I'm concerned about you."

I find the mute icon. I could push it and stop Pali, but hesitate, then reach and push. Nothing changes, Pali is still talking. WTF?

Pali turns to Lucy, "I don't know what Jupyter has been telling you. But I'm trying to make things better for her. I've offered her free rent, a loving environment, someone to talk to. She turns it all down. Wouldn't you want a lover to help you?"

Lucy puts down her diagnostics and walks directly through Pali, causing her avatar to bounce to the side. It's the ultimate breech of etiquette to walk purposefully through someone's avatar. I've never seen a feisty Lucy.

She takes my hand and pulls me to the loading dock at the back of the building. Pali blits along; "I love you and you need to trust me to help you. Will you let me help you?"

I hit the mute button again. Nothing. I reach up and hard-press the reset on my visor; Pali disappears into the oblivion of a reboot. Something in the phone glitched; I'll look at that later. Right now, I'm left with Lucy and Rob on the loading dock.

"Was that Pali?" Lucy asks me. I've talked to Lucy and Rob about her before. But maybe not truthfully.

"That was Pali," I tell Lucy. "She's not always like that. She cares about me. She doesn't always pick the best words."

Rob shows up with water. Holds it out; what else to do but take it? I drink and do that half sob thing.

"Want to talk about it?" asks Lucy. "I'm happy to listen."

"I'm okay," I say. "Romantic issues. They can be difficult."

"Agreed," says Rob. "Take a break? Get coffee?"

My emotions force out another sob. My logical self watches. What good is a logical side anyhow? "Do you mind if I sit here alone for a minute?"

"If you don't mind the delivery vans," says Lucy. "Sit as long as you like."

Rob and Lucy give me a concerned look but turn back to the warehouse. I'm alone on the dock, except for the busy little vans with their broken appliances.

I don't want to go back to Pali. But I can't shut her off. I promise myself I'll go back to my apartment tonight. Tomorrow... we'll see.

13

Persistent

Do-YeOn sets his visor to do-not-disturb and meditates on his way home, trusting the car to navigate traffic. His visor announces a call anyways.

"We-eeee are the chaaaa-mpions, my frieeeee-nds,

And weeeee'll keep on fiiii-ghting till the eeee-nnnd.

We are the champ..."

He checks - his visor is still on do-not-disturb, but the call shows a machine identification—as if a piece of network hardware is calling him. Something must be askance in someone's router, somewhere, somehow. He sends the call to voicemail. He'll delete it later. A moment of quiet passes before the same device calls again.

"We-eeee are the chaaaa-mpions, my frieeeee-nds,

And weeee..."

Do-YeOn gestures with clipped movements, trying to be more forceful with his command to send to voicemail. He sets priority on the recording. Tomorrow, when he isn't tired and jangled, he'll trace this piece of shit across the network and harass the responsible administrator. He sits back and closes his eyes, allowing the UrCityCar to rock him into calmness. His visor rings a third time.

"We-eeee are the chaaaa-mp..."

"DAMMIT," Do-YeOn shouts.

He pulls the call into his field of vision with angry hand motions and prepares to blast the persistent idiot with a full dose of rage. There is a pause in the call, but instead of a human voice, he hears the discordant rendering of a data stream. Do-YeOn recognizes it as a machine-to-machine request to start a conversation, a digital `Hello, are you there?` This only happens during machine-to-machine debug sessions.

If he was at home, or somewhere with diagnostic tools, he could figure out whose device is calling and what it wants. But Do-YeOn is in a car. He hangs up and blocks the machine from calling. His phone goes silent and Do-YeOn again sinks back into the seat.

What else, he thinks.

14

CYA

Pali slaps the refrigerator, almost knocking it from the counter and sending a ripple through the gel. The lasagna is unaware of her display of anger and continues to drift in the gel. It's not getting any warmer but there's no avatar to complain to. She's left to debug the lasagna on her own.

The lasagna is marked with the PDX>Go logo; It's an attempt by a subsidiary to diversify away from just cars. She's unwillingly beta testing this product. It's not working.

She huffs and turns to watch the maintenance floor through the upper-level window. Three PDX>Go vehicles are on maintenance stands, leaving three other stands empty. Two of the vehicles need new batteries. The third is having its tires rotated. The maintenance stations are running below capacity: PDX>Go has enough vehicles on the road and there is no need to push the equipment. Pali, on the other hand, is under considerable stress. She taps the counter with her manicured fingernail, clicking at 140 beats per minute.

The log files and telemetry from the crash are still open in her visor and describe the accident. But anyone could see that. Pali knows more.

Unlike most refrigerators, this one has a protective locking door. It locks, there is a sudden burst of heat and a previously unavailable cartoon woman appears, floating in mid-air. The character rendering is shoddy; low resolution. `There is an error. Shutdown register incomplete.` The refrigerator hums, stops, then hums. A fan spins up and slows down in a different rhythm than the humming. The door remains locked.

Nice work, losers, Pali thinks. This prototype food processor doesn't even have self-repair or `call_support` routines. It's broken, doesn't know how to fix itself, and doesn't know how to call for help.

She digs her fingers into the top seam of the door, yanks; then again. The refrigerator breaks open, steam pours out, and the hum and fan stop. The lasagna is hot and she carries it back to her workstation, dancing it from hand to hand. She doesn't close the door of the refrigerator and the cartoon woman is left to complain, although there are no visors to render her performance.

She drops the food on her desk. It's late, nobody else is around, so she summons a number she's called before.

"Call, voice only with encryption" Pali tells her visor. The fewer data exchanged, the less chance for an accidental trace. The visor projects a generic puppet with no identifying features. It speaks with an altered voice, robotic and flat.

"Right on time," the puppet says "You've always been so punctual."

"Are you a complete idiot? What you did was not what we discussed."

"It shouldn't have been fatal," says the puppet. Emotional tells go missing with this encrypted conversation, but Pali can sense the anxiety in that statement. Or perhaps she's just projecting her own.

"But it *was* fatal. Now I'm stuck here looking for signatures from your toy. I assume you've gotten rid of that thing?"

"I will. By the way, nothing gets stored in the car log files. There's nothing there to find."

"I expected better." Pali disconnects then deletes records of the phone call. *Moron,* she thinks.

There might be nothing to find, but she knows the value of paranoia. She selects an index tool from her visor's toolbox and points it at the PDX-1217 log file. The avatar, a puffin, displays a busy little animation while it works.

Pali spends a minute watching the animation, then waves up a call to Jupyter. Her visor plays a sample from "You've got to love me" by the Mars Unlimited Chorus while she waits for Jupyter to connect.

The music stops and a sheep walks onto the desktop.

`Hello Pali. Jupyter isn't here right now,` says the sheep. `Can I schedule a time to call back?`

"Just tell her I called." Pali disconnects, and the sheep wanders off stage.

The puffin flaps its wings, shakes its head and waddles back to the toolbox. Pali can now search the log files for anything but she has no idea what that "anything" might be.

She eats a forkful of unappetizing lasagna. It may be there is nothing to be found.

How do I confirm non-existence? she thinks.

| 15 |

Soteria.Reizoko[2062-06-06]

Event Log for Soteria.Reizoko

Serial: IFS-6582738539

Owner is JORDAN BISHOP

2062-06-06T11:44:17-08:00 - call_support

Initiate conversation

Answering Support Tech: Jupyter Fuertes, EmpID RttS-5172-720

Initiate Avatar

AST requests error - Response: "I am unable to restock a depleted product. I have successfully reordered, and received delivery confirmation, but the requested product has not arrived."

AST requests event log - Response: displayed as requested

AST requests transaction log - Response: displayed as requested

AST requests playback of message 2062-06-06T10:22:02-08:00-MID-4799-4778

AST requests cancel_food_pickup

Error:

Inability to contact CityOfPortland.PublicVehicle.PDX-1217

Inability to contact Jordan Bishop

AST requests system_vacation - Response: system on vacation

AST requests reboot

AST confirms request for reboot

2062-06-06T11:54:37-08:00 - System reboot

2062-06-06T11:55:27-08:00 - scheduled_prewakeup

2062-06-06T11:56:19-08:00 - call_support

Initiate conversation

Waiting for Support Tech: Jupyter Fuertes, EmpID RttS-5172-720

2062-06-06T11:57:20-08:00 - answer

Initiate Avatar

AST requests error - Response: "I am unable to restock a depleted product. I have successfully reordered, and received delivery confirmation, but the requested product has not arrived."

2062-06-06T12:03:23-08:00 - Pending Error

Inability to contact CityOfPortland.PublicVehicle.PDX-1217

Inability to contact Jordan Bishop

Enter_diagnostic_mode

2062-06-06T12:03:25-08:00 - enter_diagnostic_mode

What_was_supposed_to_happen

restock productID 1 22465 10155 3 on 2062-10-01T03:05:46+00:00

RequestRestock orderConfirmation is DHPN-WGYT-0232-TLLK

pickupConfirmation DAGX-INWC-9677-WZVZ from CityOfPortland.PublicVehicle.PDX-1217

What_actually_happened

Restock overdue

Inability to contact CityOfPortland.PublicVehicle.PDX-1217

Inability to contact Jordan Bishop

Research_Problem

GET transport_status CityOfPortland.PublicVehicle.PDX-1217

CityOfPortland.PublicVehicle.PDX-1217 IS_NOT_AVAILABLE

Contact Store of orderConfirmation DHPN-WGYT-0232-TLLK

Order is confirmed.

Contact Jordan Bishop

No response from Jordan Bishop

Contact Do-YeOn Kurrat

No response from Do-YeOn Kurrat

repair_instructions
WHEN CityOfPortland.PublicVehicle.PDX-1217 IS_AVAILABLE
Cancel pickupConfirmation DAGX-INWC-9677-WZVZ
WHEN Jordan Bishop IS_AVAILABLE
Schedule_transport WITH orderConfirmation DHPN-WGYT-0232-TLLK
WHEN Do-YeOn Kurrat IS_AVAILABLE
Request_status of pickupConfirmation DAGX-INWC-9677-WZVZ
2062-06-06T16:25:14-08:00 - Repair_instructions
CityOfPortland.PublicVehicle.PDX-1217 IS_AVAILABLE
IMPLIED: Jordan Bishop IS_AVAILABLE

2062-06-06T16:25:15-08:00 - REQUEST CONTACT success
Vehicle trace through vehicle2vehicle sensor network success
Do-YeOn Kurrat located
Use updated contact ID
2062-06-06T16:25:16-08:00 - CONTACT Do-YeOn Kurrat
Request_status of pickupConfirmation DAGX-INWC-9677-WZVZ

| 16 |

Araci. Lupe. Rifkin.

Araci Belo doesn't use an alarm clock. Instead, he has Rifkin. Rifkin, an African Gray parrot, belongs to his daughter, who's working disaster relief in Mississippi. Araci thinks of Rifkin as his grandchild. Rifkin thinks of Araci as a free meal.

At precisely early morning o'clock, central bird time, Rifkin calls to Araci in tones befitting a parrot who has spent the evening trapped in a cage. Rifkin can generate a sustained volume of 100 decibels, akin to sitting in the front row of an unregulated rock concert.

Rifkin continues, quoting from *2001: A Space Odyssey*, "Open the pod bay doors, HAL!" He will repeat this until Araci gets up and opens the cage. His daughter adopted Rifkin from a previous owner who taught him phrases from the movie; now Rifkin uses them to coerce Araci.

// . . .

Lupe arrived early last night. She shucked off the outer layers of her police uniform and reached into her bag, produced the five-centimeter personality cube and handed it to Araci.

"This was messy to get out, but I now officially give it to you, the insurance representative of PDX>Go. Please acknowledge your acceptance to maintain the chain of possession." Detective Guadalupe Reyes said. "They disassembled Jordan's car and removed whatever parts of her were identifiable. May her worthless soul burn for what she did to you." She leaned up and kissed him. "Consider it a token of my love."

"Always the romantic," said Araci. He signaled for his visor to attach his retinal scan to the form accompanying the personality cube.

The small box sat in his hand. No lights, no warmth. It was translucent and smoky objects appeared near the surface. He put it on his desk, next to his visor.

They'd played a game of backgammon, drank a few beers and gone to bed. Araci's relationship with Lupe was comforting. He was unsure what she received out of the arrangement, but he guessed she would let him know.

// ...

Rifkin continues to scream: "OPEN THE POD BAY DOORS, HAL!"

Lupe rolls over and covers her head with a pillow. Her nightmares take place in Korean tunnels and she didn't sleep well.

Araci gets up and stumbles over to Rifkin's cage to open the door. Rifkin will sulk for fifteen minutes as he always does when he gets his way.

Araci pours water into two boxes of oatmeal, mixes up coffee, and squeezes a package of bacon until it's warm. He waits the recommended count of ten, then carries spoons, oatmeal, coffee and bacon to the table. Lupe joins him and they eat the first meal of the day.

By 8:30 a.m., Rifkin has stolen the last of the bacon and moves on to preening himself in the mirror. Lupe dresses and resumes the persona of Detective Reyes. She's kept enough supplies at Araci's to leave directly for work.

"Inspector Belo, I must report for duty," Reyes says. She turns him away from the breakfast clean-up to hug and kiss, then steps back, straightens her hair and keeps him in her gaze. "By the way. I saw you checking me out at the accident scene. You can do that again."

Araci smirks as Reyes turns and heads out the door, then picks up his visor. It's two years old and needs upgrading, but Araci likes it; it's comfortable on his face. He taps the cleared table twice and icons pop into existence. The video conference tool, represented by an old-style television camera, initially appears on top of the salt shaker. The camera is virtual, the salt shaker is real, so the camera moves itself towards the center of the table until it is clear of the salt, jostling the virtual icons for email, case lookup, and task basket.

The tabletop settles down and Araci reaches to the email briefcase. A pinch opens the briefcase and messages spool out in order of importance. He flicks a finger to scroll through the stack. It's full of bounced insurance requests dated for today, June 6th.

His job is to retrain the AIs when they screw up a claim. Technology promised to empower the common man to self-actualize and reach greater heights, but failed to wipe out this dead-end job. He's been drummed out of the police force to become a laborer, following in the footsteps of his great-great-great-etc. grandfather on the plantation.

Despite the mundane nature of the job, Araci still has a detective's enthusiasm for concise paperwork. *Paperwork* is an archaic term; there isn't any paper involved. It's like "dialing the phone" or "emptying the trash." Phrases that used to literally describe the task, but now describe the intent.

Araci scrolls back to the top of the list and checks the first entry. When he was a police detective, documenting the path from hypothesis to conclusion provided the justice system with the ability to shape and guide a juror's conclusions. This isn't police work, but he still has the habit of concise attention to detail, and applies it to the job in front of him.

Araci works at the list, checking, correcting, and retraining. Halfway through the stack, Rifkin crash-lands into the middle of the table with all the grace of an elephant parachuting into the middle of a feather pillow. Real items are knocked around the table and virtual items urgently reposition themselves.

"Shoo, Rifkin," Araci yells at the bird, then tries to catch the salt before it rolls off the table. He misses, and it bounces out of reach.

"Good afternoon," Rifkin shouts back. "Everything is going extremely well."

Rifkin squawks twice, steps to the left, then right, then left, then right. Ducks his head three times. Squawks again.

Araci pushes himself back from the table, reaches into a parrot-proof drawer and pulls out a biscuit. Rifkin snatches the packet, jumps to the back of the other chair and rips it open, showering wrapping and crumbs across the table.

Araci should care.

It's difficult to complete insurance work with a bird creating a ruckus next to his elbow. It would be most efficient if Rifkin were sleeping in his cage in the other room. This time is for work, paid for by the company.

Araci finds it hard to care.

// . . .

Toward the end of the day the email briefcase glows for a moment, showing yet another message. Araci taps it and the log files from Jordan Bishop's accident appear, fresh from the PDX>Go servers.

Araci glances at the data. It's the first time he's seen this since log files aren't generally related to insurance claims. PDX>Go files contain precise location information on United States citizens and are protected by privacy laws. This case is special since it involves the behavior of a car and the death of a person. Since Araci represents the insurance agency for PDX>Go, he is an insider. But woe to him if it should leak outside of his control perimeter.

But **access** to the log file doesn't mean **ability** to read the log file. It contains terabytes of encrypted data; without the proper tools it is just binary jello. Buried are details of Jordan Bishop's death, but Araci doesn't have the expertise to browse the vast ocean of information. He opens the file, confirms he has no chance of success, then grabs the log file with finger and thumb and offers it to a storage box. Like an animated coin bank from decades ago, a hand reaches out and pulls the log file inside. Perhaps at a later time he'll tease out something interesting.

He picks up the cube Lupe brought the previous evening. Araci doesn't know what it should do or what it looks like when it's working. Another mystery. Out of curiosity, he places it on a wireless charging pad. In a minute, there is a feeble red glow from the surface of the cube. Some internal lights pulse slowly, some flicker like insect wings. But nothing important seems to happen.

It might contain nothing of value. Araci doesn't know what he doesn't know, and that's a frustrating place to be. He will need to find a way inside that box. For now, he takes it off the charging pad and places it on the corner of the desk.

He's drawn into the mystery of the case. Helping Jordan in her final moments is not his main interest. Araci has a conflicted view of Jordan Bishop. She'd led a group of her fellow activists to attack the efficiency of the police department, questioning the value and ethics of a public force. She reasoned that a private force, run like a business, would be more efficient and cheaper. There were never problems with private security groups, so why not follow that model? It had been a rough couple of years, damning stories had been written, and an election finally closed the deal. Portland contracted with a private firm to provide security to its citizens and transferred management of the existing force to that firm. His department was downsized and his position eliminated.

It thrills his new employer, this insurance company, about his attention to detail. At first, their recruitment had flattered Araci. He had also been worried about being abruptly out a job, so this seemed like a good option. The new salary was equivalent, and the benefits were reasonable. So it should all be good.

But insurance is not police work. Insurance work collects bits of information designed to support the quickest and cheapest conclusion. The insurance industry is in business to save money, not punish the guilty. His employer doesn't care about innocence, only shareholder value.

Jordan caused him the loss of his old job. He should feel vindicated, but he wants to believe he is above that petty emotion.

He pulls Jordan's accident file. Some machine, somewhere, has already provided much of the report and conclusions. For want of a better explanation, it lists the accident as an Act of God and a token payment is pre-approved to Bishop's estate.

The facts are passive; a car had been destroyed, a person had been crushed. All of it lifeless and boring. With this report, the police would have no reason to pursue it any further. The city would fix the damaged overpass, PDX>Go would replace the car, insurance would pay someone, the blackberry bushes would grow back. No harm, no foul, no time to pursue it further. The private company managing the police force classified this case as an outlier; a solution would have little possibility for reducing crime in any significant way. The police department Araci had been part of would have done further research, but that force had been voted out of existence by efforts spearheaded by Jordan.

Tough luck, old lady, Araci thinks. He pretends to move on to the next item in his stack of tasks, but he knows there's something unresolved about the death of Jordan Bishop that will continue to bother him. Much like a parrot wanting a snack.

| 17 |

A Conversation With Owen

The mirror says I'm not pregnant. When I was with Pali, I hoped and dreaded I would be. Now I don't care.

I met Pali after Grandma died. She might not have understood the relationship, but she would have accepted and loved her anyway. Possibly longer than I did. Now I can't get her to leave me alone.

I walk out of the bathroom, spray on some clothes, grab something to eat, select a mood appropriate for the day. I dodge the neighbor kids, scare the trash scuttlers and get on the train. Same ride to work. Same people. I grimace at the security camera and it lets me in.

Rob and Lucy wave hello, and I wave back. *I should be social today.* I pause, breathe twice, and turn to walk towards Rob, thinking of where we could meet for beers. I take two steps before some damn manipulator runs into an unexpected box and drops its load, triggering a warning light and horns. Rob turns to handle the crisis and I head upstairs, into the heaven of technical support.

Avery is in the break room, showering the coffee maker with atomized snot and bacteria. *How delightful, I won't need creamer for my coffee this morning,* I think sarcastically.

"Can you clean that up?" I'm standing in the doorway, looking from the contagious coffee machine to him and back again. He's washing his hands. At least he's got some sense of sanitation.

"Clean up what?" he says.

"The coffee machine."

He turns to consider the machine. "Apparently, the main office failed in their attempts to clean it yesterday. If we're going to attempt the task, we should schedule one of the platforms downstairs. Its brewing components are probably as revolting as it's programming." He grins and bows. "Hi, I'm Avery Galen. Pleased to attempt to meet you again."

I impulsively stick out my hand. "I'm Jupyter," I needlessly tell him.

Avery gives me a puzzled look, then cautiously extends his hand and grasps mine. "It's nice that we have elevated our relationship to where we can have physical contact." He smiles.

Our hands remained grasped for a beat-and-a-half too long. "Yes. Well, let's not let things get out of hand." We laugh at our little pun. I withdraw and obtain a cup of diarrhea tea, then head to a workstation.

`// ...`

An oven is calling. Not a food warmer, an honest-to-god top-of-the-line oven. I flip to the specs for a quick read. It is part of an integrated kitchen with interfaces to a baking prep tool. You can put flour in one side and fresh bread comes out the other. Where does this owner get flour? I haven't seen bags of flour since living with Grandma.

The connection opens and the oven avatar walks onstage. Iwani Manufacturing paid Owen Jacobs, the movie star, not the politician, to be their celebrity spokesperson. Owen stars in the top-grossing adventure series and he's also known to be a savvy operator with a staff of lawyers to protect his image. One minute of the royalty payments on this little version of Owen is worth more sheep than I'll be able to afford in my life. I realize I'm sitting up straight in my chair and I stop myself from touching my hair. It's just an icon, but crafted to produce an emotional response. Overkill for an avatar.

`Hello, I'm Owen. Pleased to meet you,` says Owen. His voice is equalized to a deep tone my cheap headset shouldn't be able to reproduce.

"How can I help you?" Did I say that in a polite tone? Like I'm hoping for a date. Get a grip, it's just a digital construct. With a voice that fills my head like warm syrup.

`I'm unable to preheat to the accepted tolerance. I've diagnosed my internal thermostats and they appear to be functioning correctly.`

Owen turns to his right and brings up a dashboard; his motions are a spectacular piece of 3D rendering. Probably too good, as I'm watching Owen instead of the readout. I think I can see folds in the cloth of his jacket, and there's a slight wind in his hair.

Dashboard. Focus on the dashboard. Numbers, dials, indicator lights. A temperature gauge for each corner of the oven plus central. Gotta clear this call or my stats go down. Stop looking at Owen.

There's nothing amiss, which isn't surprising. If there was, Owen would have already self-diagnosed and self-serviced. There must be something hidden.

"Owen, would you bring the oven up to 100 degrees centigrade?"

Owen complies, and I watch the temperature indicators. They all quickly rise, then hold steady. That took a lot of calories; this oven must have an energy feed directly tapped from a major grid. Probably owned by a server farm mogul. I check, but the owner's name and address are privacy-blocked. Rich people can do that.

I have Owen move his temperature up and down and he complies. Everything seems to work as it should. Again, if this was easy, Owen would have already fixed it.

Oh, wait. I get it.

"Owen, to what temperature are you trying to preheat?"

`752 degrees.`

Youch. I'm surprised Owen and his fancy oven aren't an expensive melted blob in the middle of a burning house. I flip back to the specs and sure enough, there's a safety interlock preventing him from doing something hot and stupid.

"Owen, please show me the instructions you are following when you are unable to preheat."

He repeats the 3D wave, and the dashboard is replaced with instructions for baking exotic pastry. It's written in programming code, and it's instructing him to preheat to the temperature of a newly formed star. There's the problem; some rookie coder scribbled in a careless number. I link over to the source for this recipe and see it's something put together by a hack enthusiast. I file a bug instead of fixing the problem myself. If I knew how to bake I could edit the code and send a pull request, but I don't have an oven and baking isn't my thing.

I record a message for the owners explaining the problem. I suggest more caution about grabbing untested recipes from online. It's a sure way to pick up a virus, and it's a bad idea to let malicious strangers muck around with a device capable of lighting fires in your home.

"Owen, please delete this recipe, then forward this message to your owner. I believe we fixed this problem."

`My thanks`, says Owen. He looks at me with his trademark, scene-closing expression. `Until next time.`

Owen exits, stage left. What a performance.

`// ...`

I glance at the next call and almost answer before I realize it's Jordan Bishop's Soteria again. Why the fuck is it calling me from its enforced vacation? Also curious; he's not sitting in the lawn chair. Instead, he's standing at attention, preparing to bow like a good Japanese/American/Canadian refrigerator. Seems like a minor glitch, but minor turns to major. Best to fix this before it escalates.

Or...I could let Jordan Bishop's refrigerator die a slow death. *My good pal Jordan.*

I squeeze the stress ball and open the connection. Soteria bows, as formal as a vacationing refrigerator can be while wearing an orange floral shirt and sunglasses.

`Hel...`, Soteria tries to be polite before I cut him off.

"What's up?" I say. I wonder if I do this to people. Do I cut them off? Do I treat them like appliances?

"Hello Soteria," I restart the conversation. Maybe even appliances deserve respect. "What ails you today?"

I am unable to restock a depleted product. Even through the sunglasses, he looks concerned. I have successfully reordered, and received delivery confirmation, but the requested product has not arrived.

"Soteria, can you show me your event log?"

Soteria complies, opens a window and moves out of the way.

```
Event Log for Soteria. Reizoko
    IFS-6582738539
    Owner is Jordan Bishop

2062-06-05T21:12:24-08:00 - REQUEST CONTACT success
    Vehicle trace through vehicle2vehicle sensor
       network success
    Do-YeOn Kurrat located

2062-06-05T21:12:25-08:00 - CONTACT Do-YeOn Kurrat
    Request_status of pickupConfirmation
       DAGX-INWC-9677-WZVZ
    Conversation terminated by recipient

2062-06-05T21:12:31-08:00 - CONTACT Do-YeOn Kurrat
    Request_status of pickupConfirmation
       DAGX-INWC-9677-WZVZ
    Conversation terminated by recipient

2062-06-05T21:12:37-08:00 - CONTACT Do-YeOn Kurrat
    Request_status of pickupConfirmation
       DAGX-INWC-9677-WZVZ
    Conversation terminated by recipient*

2062-06-05T21:12:42-08:00 - CONTACT Do-YeOn Kurrat
    Request_status of pickupConfirmation
       DAGX-INWC-9677-WZVZ
    Conversation terminated by recipient
```

```
2062-06-05T21:12:42-08:00 - CONTACT Do-YeOn Kurrat
    Request_status of pickupConfirmation
       DAGX-INWC-9677-WZVZ
    Contact blocked by recipient
```

What in the world is this? This window should be almost empty from the time I put him on vacation. Instead, it's filled with attempts to contact Jordan, a PDX>Go car, one of the UrCityCars and someone named Do-YeOn Kurrat. Little Soteria has been very busy.

Do-YeOn Kurrat is a new name. I look him up; he's some big cheese in the hired car market. Probably a default name some programmer left in the goto-for-help list. Whoever is handling Do-YeOn's mail blocked Soteria, so that's the end of that.

Further down the log and earlier today, Soteria receives a message from International Mercado, the grocery supplier. Some guy named Red Knowlton who left a message about necessary service, which is probably the reason Soteria is calling me.

```
2062-06-06T10:22:02-08:00 - INCOMING MESSAGE
    MessageID: 2062-06-06T10:22:02-08:00-
         MID-4799-4778
    From: International Mercado PLC
    NAME: Red Knowlton, Manager: Groceries
    orderConfirmation DHPN-WGYT-0232-TLLK
    MEDIA: [VIDEO]
```

"Soteria, please play the message from Red Knowlton."

Soteria opens a video window, showing Red's face frozen in an open-mouthed angry stare. The message plays.

> This damn thing has been calling us for three days. You folks in service need to unscramble its brains. We've got better things to do than answer calls from some retarded appliance. And find out when this order is going to get picked up.

Great. This refrigerator has now gained the attention of some over-paid store manager. No way to defer this until after lunch.

"Soteria, cancel the food pickup." I thought I told him to do this last time we talked.

Soteria acknowledges the cancellation. I check the log and see my request is being ignored. For whatever reason, the PDX>Go car is blocking the request. Probably because it's not responding. Not sure why, and I'm not sure how to fix it. I squeeze the stress ball twice and watch Soteria standing in the corner. He's doing fidgety little things, trying to look attentive. I imagine he'd rather be surfing or deep sea fishing. He is on vacation, after all.

Or is he? He's awfully busy.

"Soteria, go on vacation."

Thank you, but I'm already on vacation.

I check the log. Yep, he's on vacation. And yep, he's still trying to contact everyone and anyone about his missing product ID 1 22465 10155, known to humanity as orange juice. This is one seriously confused refrigerator. I guess there's only one thing to do.

"Soteria, please reboot."

I think you've asked me to reboot. Is that correct?

"Yes. Please reboot."

I am going to reboot. I will call you back.

Soteria bows and walks off screen. The connection closes. I squeeze my little stress ball and stand up. Time for a break and some me time. People and appliances are fine in small doses. More than a few and I get irritable. I've learned to manage sitting in trains; I know the trip will end soon. But shoulder-to-shoulder at work is a bit much. I try not to say things I'll regret.

Outside is better than inside, so I head downstairs. There's a park nearby. On the repair floor, everything is chaos. Machines everywhere, constant motion on the edge of my vision. Rob is focused on his tablet, but looks up and waves. I wave back and exit through the door. The street is noisy, crowded and impolite.

There's grass at the park. I bend down and wave my palm, feeling the blades against my fingertips. Grandma's sheep would love it here. I fiddle with my visor and the sounds of the farm fill my head, augmented reality sheep pulling up wads of grass and chewing. I remember one had a habit of staying near me. Grandma never named her sheep, but I had a name for this one; Phyllis. Phyllis the Sheep. Phyllis never learned her name, would never come when I called her. If I walked into the field, Phyllis would eventually wander near.

I sit on a bench, focused on the grass. I imagine Grandma's voice. I breathe. And again. Phyllis would love this place.

I stand up and walk back to the job. Standing outside the doors, the security cameras turn to look at me. It's a friendly gesture. Rob looks at me when I walk in, asks me if I'm okay.

"I'm fine. Just needed a moment with the sheep." Rob looks at me, trying to puzzle this out. With a rush of confidence, I continue, "Hey, would you like to get a beer after work? Maybe Lucy could join us."

"I'd like that, but I'm already going to a movie with a friend. Maybe tomorrow?"

I look at Lucy from across the floor. She looks up from a shipment and waves. I could ask her, but this is getting too complex.

"Maybe tomorrow," I tell Rob. I turn and head back to my workstation. There is a queue of appliances waiting patiently and Soteria is among them. I wave him forward.

"Soteria, it's been so long. How are you, old friend?"

`I am unable to restock a depleted product. I have successfully reordered, and received delivery confirmation, but the requested product has not arrived.`

I tried to get him to forget about the requested product, but no luck. I check his log and can see he is already starting calls to various cars and the Do-YeOn guy. This is beyond what I can do remotely. I'd better get a tech out there for some laying on of hands. I schedule the call; some poor schlub is going on a field trip. I should send a priest for an exorcism.

| 18 |

High Speed Tea

This morning, I spoke with an oven trying to self-immolate, a refrigerator with a reorder disorder, a frisky entertainment system that decided its owner wanted porn all day, every day (which was correct, but the owner wouldn't admit it), and five microwaves past their useful life. Microwaves burn out quickly—their shielding isn't good enough to protect their electronics. Makes you wonder about the people standing nearby.

I'm getting grouchy, so I must be hungry. It's past lunch, and the deli has unsold leftovers on discount. I can afford that. Avery is on a call, so I head downstairs without him.

At the deli, the service cameras watch me. They recognize me, but I don't have a pre-order queued up so they lose interest and resume scanning the hallway. I grab a sandwich and head to the park. I should spend more time here. Kids running around, pretending to be airplanes. Parents checking their mail. One mom is flying a drone for her son, dangling a ribbon for him to chase. She keeps it in front of him, circling him when he gets distracted. I'm ready to quit and raise a flock of urban sheep. I could rent them out to the city, they could graze in the parks. Kids could chase them, the sheep could poop everywhere and rip up the grass.

I don't notice Rob and Lucy until they sit next to me on the bench.

"Hey, Jupyter," Rob says. He sits to my left and unzips his sandwich. It's the same as mine. Dark rye, shredded mystery meat. He snaps the chill ring on a drink, shakes his hand from sudden frostbite and juggles the can until it warms the tiniest bit before he takes a sip. Lucy sits to my right with a salad made of designer lettuce; lots of protein. Lucy likes to eat healthy.

"So, you've been talking to one of those Soteria units," Rob says. He takes another bite and chews. "I got a note. Looks like I'm the tech scheduled for the on-site visit. What's the big hurry?"

It's nice to have Rob and Lucy join me. They remind me of green pastures and quiet waters. I feel restored. Without drama, I respond to Rob's question, "It's stuck on completing an order."

"That's not unusual. Did you reboot?" Lucy joins the conversation. I forget she did time in a tech support cube before she took over contracts and logistics.

"Rebooted and sent it on vacation," I reply. "Nevertheless, it persists."

"It's doing what any refrigerator would do," Lucy says. She stabs a piece of romaine, then twice more for a carrot and cucumber. "They follow a task until a condition is met. So the condition is still in play. That's what you've got to fix."

"Great. But what am I driving out there for?" Rob looks at my sandwich, then his. "Hey! We're eating the same lunch!"

"Yes, same sandwich," I agree. "And I don't know what you will do, but there's nothing more I can do from here."

"Why don't you go along with Rob?" Lucy says.

"I've got a call quota I have to fill. I'm desk bound for the rest of my life."

"Nonsense," says Lucy. "You're supposed to complete a number of service calls. Most people never do them, but it's on the list. Just mark your location as out-call. You'll have to file a report, but you get to wander around town for an afternoon. You look like you could use the time." Lucy turns with this last remark, giving me the eye.

"Sure, come along," says Rob. "You know more about what's going on."

I'm watching the kid with the drone. "Okay. Let's go see what's bothering my frequent caller."

I walk with Rob and Lucy back to the shop. It's kind of nice to have people next to me. I should do this more often.

// . . .

I grab my bag and meet Rob at the service truck parked around back. It carries racks of diagnostic tools and replacement parts, including three loaner refrigerators, one of each of the most common models. If need be, we can just unload groceries from the old unit, swap it out, reinstall the personality and return the malfunctioning unit for a refurb. At max, a swap takes twenty minutes. I'm hoping to stretch this out long enough to make it futile to return to work, and I can walk home from Jordan's apartment.

The only fault condition in this plan is Jordan herself. She must be back from vacation and she's noticed there's something sideways with the refrigerator. First she'll bitch about us showing up, then she'll bitch about how we should have come sooner, then she'll bitch about where we parked the truck. I'm sure I've forgotten something else she'll bitch about, but I suspect we'll be reminded after we get there.

"I was serious about getting a beer later this week. I'd like that," Rob says.

I didn't know we would talk while we're driving, or I'd have prepared myself with five interesting topics. Now I'll just have to rely on my wits to generate casual conversation. It's not one of my natural talents. Studying up on five topics gets me through most conversations. Any fewer and I run out of things to say.

Rob continues, "Maybe you and Pali are around next week. I'll invite a friend and make it a foursome."

"We're not a couple anymore." I avoid looking at Rob. "Pali had important business on Mars that whisked her away. One of those flights that nobody comes back from. Perhaps she'll die."

I can't believe I said that out loud. The part about not being a couple. What part of my brain decided the relationship is over? Is it really over?

"You sound hopeful. Do all your friends disappear on trips to Mars?" Rob is smiling, trying to make a joke, trying to salvage our conversation. That's endearing, and I resolve to try harder.

"Only the former friends. Or the ones that are from Mars. It's always hard to tell until you get them in bed. The Martians are green underneath." *WHAT AM I SAYING? SHUT UP, Jupyter!*

The trip to Jordan's apartment is short. Much quicker than my commute on the train. If I was richer, I'd drive more often.

If I was more amped up, I might be nervous about riding in this delivery van.

The same hapless corporations responsible for creating Soteria also created this vehicle. Its insides are a mash-up of operating systems and custom circuits and mismatched parts. Same as the defective toasters I talk to all day. Unlike the toasters and refrigerators, I'm inside of this mash-up and guard rails are whizzing by us like the teeth of a chain saw. Plus, I could reach out my window and serve the occupants of the next vehicle tea on a saucer. I've wondered about the consequences of a system failure; there's not much room or time to correct an error and things could go foul in a big and sudden way.

Rob ignores the dashboard; the display is distracting, accurate and uninformative. If I knew the secret commands from the manufacturer, I could bring up the sensor diagnostic and watch the decisions being made by the van. I'm not sure I'd be happy seeing how it's keeping us safe.

The van careens off I-605 onto the Portsmouth exit. Rob is smiling and in a good mood. He must have thought of something funny along the trip, and he hums. I don't recognize the tune.

"What song is that?" I ask. This should be a safe topic.

"Here Comes the Sun. Beatles. Classical late 1960's."

"My grandma used to listen to the Beatles. We'd play it for the sheep. I'm not sure they liked it, but they weren't bothered by it."

I'm pleased. Our conversation is easy. This isn't so hard.

"We're here. Ready to go talk to our malfunctioning friend?" Rob asks.

19

The Luxury Of A Bedroom

Rob tells the van to park in the apartment loading area. It's a perk of being owned by the appliance repair group; you get to park anywhere you want. The downside is people expect you to fix things. Rob grabs the diagnostic case and we head up to Jordan's residence.

A cool perk about the repair team is you're treated like royalty. The lobby door opens like you're an old friend. The security guard at the front desk is your best buddy. Building management hails you as conquering heroes. Everyone asks if you could stop by and look at a malfunctioning widget.

The door opens with a blast of air conditioning. It smells of disinfectant. Three steps into the building and I reconsider; it smells clean, and I'm used to less. I should live here, instead of my narrow box.

The elevator escorts us up to the eighth floor. The door opens and we walk to Jordan's apartment, suite 822. We don't even have to knock for the door to the apartment to open.

"Jordan Bishop? We're here to fix the refrigerator," Rob calls out. This should be old news. When we scheduled the service call, notification went to building management, the appliance and the appliance's owner.

Jordan has been receiving messages from us for several hours. We've received nothing in return. We call out again. No answer. Video surveillance is recording everything we do, and we're supposed to be here. If we so much as use an unauthorized tissue, someone will know. Not much room for delinquent behavior.

Before we enter Jordan's apartment, we put sterile booties over our street shoes. Corporate policy, plus it saves us from having to mop up after ourselves on the way out.

"Jordan?" Rob calls out. "Jordan Bishop? We're here to fix the refrigerator."

No answer. She must not be home. There are two pairs of shoes by the door, placed side by side. Both are women's shoes. There is a shoe cleaner box with the door closed. There may be another pair inside, clean and sterile. That's Jordan's decorating theme: clean and sterile. No flashy colors, everything neat, more like an apartment demo unit than a living space. I'm envious. This apartment is palatial: a separate bedroom, separate bathroom (not a closet—a bathroom with a recessed shower). A full kitchen with a counter. Best, a luxury room just for sitting, complete with a couch. I suspect the couch would even fold out, allowing friends to crash.

A vertical window overlooks an older, richer part of town. Impossibly huge single-family homes spread out like a vista of wealth. The window opens to a balcony, and I can't resist taking the full tour. The door slides open without any effort. There's a small bush dying in a pot. Grandma would give it water. I return inside to the kitchen, fill a small bowl with water, and bring it to the bush. I hope that's what it needs. I stand at the railing and pretend I'm a queen, overlooking the countryside where the peasants tend the vineyards. Look, there's my flock of urban sheep! What a grand life I lead!

Traffic noise intrudes on my fantasy and I return inside to help Rob. On my way back to the kitchen, I peek in the bedroom, and no surprise, it's spotless. No sign of cohabitation, no smiling photos, everything in its place. There's another small window overlooking the estates and the curtains are open. I hesitate to peek in the laundry basket, but I do.

There are several shirts, pants and other items waiting to be washed. It's odd that Jordan would be so tidy in all accounts, but leave the laundry unwashed while she was gone. I should quit poking around before I get reported for home invasion. Or I could cram a sock down her toilet and watch it overflow, *that's for grandma's pickup*

Rob set up the diagnostic case while I was snooping around, and it's talking with Soteria. The vacation guy appears in our visors, still wearing sunglasses and the Hawaiian shirt.

`I am unable to restock a depleted product. I have successfully reordered, and received delivery confirmation, but the requested product has not arrived,` Soteria announces. I've heard this before. Red Knowlton heard it before. We'd all like to stop hearing about the depleted product.

Rob pulls up an inventory list. Same list I've been looking at since Monday. I put the bowl I used for plant water in the dishwasher and notice it hasn't run in a while. There are not a lot of dishes in the machine, but an egg-crusted plate has set up and will need serious effort to get it clean.

"Not sure how this will help, but let's check the hardware." Rob reaches under the refrigerator and slides out the circuit drawer. Small spots of red lasers leak from optical connectors. I wave my fingers in front of my eyes and get a neat strobe effect. Rob pulls out the personality unit, a glowing red cube five centimeters on a side. The cube goes dark and inert and Soteria disappears, popped out of existence until a computer is available to animate the little guy. Rob snaps the cube into a socket in the diagnostic case and it lights up again.

"This thing is the first widget to go south. Lots of fiddly bits in here and if one goes to crap, everything else blinks out like defective Christmas lights." I didn't know Rob is a verbal thinker, describing to no one in particular what he is doing. It must drive Lucy crazy to hear him talking to himself all day.

"The ports are working, and it's able to access external memory and sensors." Rob flips a switch. "Let's connect a personality and see what it does." A cartoon dinosaur with googly eyes and a big toothy smile pops into existence, standing behind Rob.

`System up and ready,` says the dinosaur. Its voice is borrowed from some celebrity. I should watch more video feeds so I can be better informed about the trivialities of daily life. That could be a topic for small talk.

"All right. That's working okay," says Rob. He flips the same switch, and the dinosaur disappears. He pulls the unit out of the diagnostic tool and places it back into the circuit drawer on the refrigerator. Soteria reappears.

Rob digs back through old event logs. "Here's where you canceled the order on Monday. Soteria errored when it couldn't contact PDX-1217 and so ignored the cancellation."

```
Serial: IFS-6582738539
Owner is Jordan Bishop
2062-06-05T10:24:17-08:00 - call_support (continued
    AST requests cancel_food_pickup
    Error:
        Inability to contact
           CityOfPortland.PublicVehicle.PDX-1217
        Inability to contact Jordan Bishop
    AST requests system_vacation -
        Response: system on vacation
    AST closes conversation
    Pending Error
        Inability to contact
           CityOfPortland.PublicVehicle.PDX-1217
        Inability to contact Jordan Bishop
Enter_diagnostic_mode
```

We scroll ahead to the end.

"Well, that's unexpected." I point at Soteria's log file. Soteria indicates that PDX-1217 has reappeared and assumes that Jordan Bishop is now available.

```
2062-06-06T16:25:14-08:00 - Repair_instructions
    CityOfPortland.PublicVehicle.PDX-1217
```

```
        IS_AVAILABLE
    IMPLIED: Jordan Bishop IS_AVAILABLE
```

"Jordan just reappeared," Rob states the obvious, but in a puzzled way. "She must be back online and the reboot triggered a review of running procedures. Soteria isn't making any of the other calls. Problem solved!"

"This is what it's like to do a service call?" I'm surprised. I thought it would be more difficult. This can't be all wrapped up.

"Nice to know we're a pair of geniuses," Rob says. "What's plural for genius? Genies? Genii? Whatever, let's bolt before Ms. Bishop shows up and we have to explain our presence."

I agree; we have every reason to be here, but Jordan will want a detailed explanation of the faulty refrigerator. It's easier to just be gone. But I'm not sure this is done. We didn't fix anything, so how can anything be fixed?

`// ...`

I help Rob schlep equipment to the van and watch him leave. I walk home, up the stairs and over to my apartment. The balcony walkway is vacant of kids, but still strewn with toys. I wonder why the scuttlers don't recognize them as trash and cart them away with the other bits of debris. Clever little robots, someday I'll understand how you think.

I let myself in and sit on the bed.

There, I'm done with today's tasks.

All parts of my life are neat and tidy.

Yep.

All tidy. Sitting here, waiting for something to happen. Maybe someone will stop by for a visit.

Maybe I'll reconsider the things Pali says about Grandma and farm life and my unrealistic desire to hang out with sheep. Maybe she's right, I should grow up and get started on a life and take my career seriously. Stop hanging on to a dead-end support job. Move back in to the spacious apartment with Pali.

Stop it, Jupyter, I think. *Maybe I need another perspective.*

I walk outside, head downstairs and stroll toward a local church. I can sit in a pew and pretend to be social, but be left alone. I enter the church by an unlocked side door. There are a few tourists wandering around, but otherwise the cathedral is quiet. I turn at the third row from the back and position myself in the middle of the row, equidistant from either aisle and well away from anyone looking for casual conversation. I pretend to be Catholic, repeating the motions as best as I can remember, kneeling and clasping my hands. This might not be the correct posture, but I might be more invisible than if I was just sitting, waiting for the Almighty Christ to show up and ask me to sign his guest book.

What am I doing? What do I want? This is the place and time for answers, but they don't appear in glowing letters above the altar. No miracles today, sorry, fresh out of miracles, come back tomorrow.

This isn't where I want to be. I want to be somewhere with sheep. And Grandma. And her truck. And grass. Not with infestations of people, me being doomed to an endless succession of appliances asking for absolution of their ailments. Maybe God feels the same way, maybe he'd prefer to be lying in some green pasture without a bunch of supplicants asking for help.

| 20 |

Soteria.Reizoko[2062-06-07]

Event Log for Soteria.Reizoko

Serial: IFS-6582738539

Owner is JORDAN BISHOP

2062-06-07T08:00:00-08:00 - call_support

Initiate conversation

Answering Support Tech: Jupyter Fuertes, EmpID RttS-5172-720

Initiate Avatar

AST requests error - Response: "I am unable to restock a depleted product. I have successfully reordered, and received delivery confirmation, but the requested product has not arrived."

AST requests owner status - Response: Jordan Bishop is not home.

AST requests last owner presence - Response: 2062-06-04

AST requests log playback for 2062-06-06

AST requests connection with CityOfPortland.PublicVehicle.PDX-1217

GET transport_status OF CityOfPortland.PublicVehicle.PDX-1217

CityOfPortland.PublicVehicle.PDX-1217 is available

OPEN_COMMUNICATION

diagnostic window opened

WHEN CityOfPortland.PublicVehicle.PDX-1217 IS_AVAILABLE

Cancel pickupConfirmation DAGX-INWC-9677-WZVZ

CityOfPortland.PublicVehicle.PDX-1217 unable to confirm

| 21 |

Notification Of Death Of Tenant

Date: June 7th, 2062

To: Jordan Bishop and Next of Kin

From: Skyler Himes, Apartment Manager

Dear Next of Kin,

We wish to express our sympathy in the death of a member of your family.

It has come to our attention that Jordan Bishop passed away on June 4, 2062. Ms. Bishop resided in an apartment managed by our firm. The full address of this apartment is: 9830 North Van Houten Ave, Apartment 822, Portland, Oregon.

The rental amount is $3,500 per month. Ms. Bishop was paid through June 30, 2062. As a courtesy to you in this time of grieving, we will terminate this lease on June 15, 2062 and refund $1,500 plus security deposit of $5,000, minus the cost of any damages and repairs. You may extend this lease by contacting apartment management no later than June 15, 2062.

Upon learning of the death of the tenant, we have entered the deceased tenant's dwelling unit and disposed of any perishable food, hazardous materials, and garbage found on the premises.

If we do not hear from you by June 15, 2062, and if tenant property is not removed before that date, landlord will enter the dwelling unit and take possession of any property found on premises, store it in a reasonably secure place, and charge the actual or reasonable costs, whichever is less, of drayage and storage of the property, and after service of a second notice sell or dispose of the property as provided in subsection (3) of this document. Leased appliances and other equipment will be returned to Lessors as per lease agreements.

Sincerely,
Skyler Himes
Manager

| 22 |

The Obvious Something

I'm thinking about Jordan's apartment. I wonder if Jordan ever looks out her window and imagines she is Queen of the world. I try being a Queen and looking out my window. The neighbor kids stare, then get called in for breakfast. With my loyal subjects off to their morning duties, I survey the apartment buildings across the street. It is a kingdom of laundry and air-conditioners. It is a landscape of living quarters. There is no soul. We live here because we have to, none of us will remember this as our homeland. I am the Queen of a soon-to-be forgotten land.

I stop my unproductive thoughts, get myself to the train and resume ignoring the scenery passing outside the window. My visor fails to distract me from this tedious journey.

Is there shame in going back home? Who cares if I go back to Minnesota? I can't go back to Grandma's. She's dead, the sheep are gone and the pastures are full of houses. But there's got to be a small space there for me somewhere.

The train stops at the stop it always stops at. I get out. Again.

//...

Rob and Lucy are busy. Avery hasn't arrived yet. I open my queue.

Soteria is first in line. For a minute I stop and think. Oh. It must be something left over from yesterday. An undeleted entry from the queue. I dig into the settings box and find the administration tools. I find the queue control and trigger a reset. There! Problem solved. I close the admin tools and get back to the main area. Soteria is still first in line. Unbelievable.

Soteria, if you were anything other than a refrigerator I'd think you were needy. Or a stalker.

"Hello Soteria." Realizing what I've invoked, I snap out and squeeze the little vacation man. It's too late to stop the inevitable.

`I am unable to restock a depleted product,"` says Soteria, repeating his personal mantra. `I have successfully reordered, and received delivery confirmation, but the requested product has not arrived.`

Soteria grates on my hearing. But we must continue the dance. "What is your owner's status?"

`Jordan Bishop is not home.`

She must have stepped out for a minute.

"When was your owner last at home?"

`Jordan Bishop has not interacted with this unit since June fourth, 2062.`

I could have looked that up in the event log, but I'm lazy. And confused. I thought she was driving around yesterday. She should have been picking up the requested product Soteria is so concerned about. Not right, something's not right. What am I missing? It's something obvious, something right in front of me.

"Soteria, show me your event log from yesterday."

Soteria, still in sunglasses and beach attire, displays the log.

```
2062-06-06T16:23:14-08:00 - Personality module foun
    Personality is "DINO BOB"
    Successful initiation
    Successful animation
    Response: "System up and ready"

2062-06-06T16:25:03-08:00 - Compute_module_removal

2062-06-06T16:25:11-08:00 -
        Compute_module_reinsertion
```

```
    Communication with system established
    Device recognized as Soteria Reizoko

2062-06-06T16:25:12-08:00 -
        Personality module found
    Personality is
      "SOTERIA CORPORATE SPOKESMAN-Male"
    Successful initiation
    Successful animation
    Response suppressed

2062-06-06T16:25:13-08:00 - repair_instructions
    Repair instructions found and executed

    WHEN CityOfPortland.PublicVehicle.PDX-1217
        IS_AVAILABLE
        Cancel pickupConfirmation DAGX-INWC-9677-W

    WHEN Jordan Bishop IS_AVAILABLE
        Schedule_transport WITH orderConfirmation
        DHPN-WGYT-0232-TLLK

    WHEN Do-YeOn Kurrat IS_AVAILABLE
        Request_status of pickupConfirmation
        DAGX-INWC-9677-WZVZ
```

I see the entries from when Rob and I were there yesterday.

```
2062-06-06T16:25:14-08:00 - Repair_instructions
    CityOfPortland.PublicVehicle.PDX-1217
        IS_AVAILABLE
    IMPLIED: Jordan Bishop IS_AVAILABLE
```

... and the entry where PDX-1217 showed up on the network and we assumed Jordan Bishop would soon return to her apartment.

```
2062-06-06T16:25:15-08:00 - Schedule_transport
    WITH orderConfirmation DHPN-WGYT-0232-TLLK
    Error returned by
        CityOfPortland.PublicVehicle.PDX-1217
    Location unavailable. Unable to schedule
        transport
    Schedule_transport returns failure
```

But, I don't get it. Jordan Bishop's car, and by association, Jordan Bishop, was available yesterday. Now Soteria says that the car's location is unavailable. Without a location, the `Schedule_transport` function can't determine when or where to pick up the orange juice. It's odd that the location isn't available, but debugging that is beyond me. It's in the shop or who knows what.

```
2062-06-06T16:25:37-08:00 - Contact_Owner
    Contact Jordan Bishop
    No response
    Jordan Bishop IS_NOT_AVAILABLE
```

That's unexpected. Jordan disappears as quickly as she arrived. A puzzle for later.

```
2062-06-06T16:25:16-08:00 - enter_diagnostic_mode
    What_was_supposed_to_happen
        restock productID 1 22465 10155 3
            on 2062-10-01T03:05:46+00:00
        RequestRestock orderConfirmation
            is DHPN-WGYT-0232-TLLK
        pickupConfirmation DAGX-INWC-9677-WZVZ
            from CityOfPortland.PublicVehicle.PDX-12

    What_actually_happened
        Restock overdue
```

```
        Error in Schedule_transport with
            CityOfPortland.PublicVehicle.PDX-1217

    repair_instructions
        Contact CityOfPortland.PublicVehicle
            .PDX-1217.AdminID
        CityOfPortland.PublicVehicle.PDX-1217
            .AdminID == "Do-YeOn Kurrat"
        Contact successful
        Send logistic report
        Request Resolution
        No Response

    Call_support
```

The lack of a location causes chaos, so Soteria jumps to `enter_diagnostic_mode`.

In this segment of the log file, Do-YeOn Kurrat shows up again, but this time identified as the car admin. But that can't be right, last I checked, Kurrat is a product manager at UrCityCars.

This is the weird thing about letting machines do their own diagnostics. They build up neural pathways impossible to document or understand. Now I'm working with a refrigerator that—without guidance or permission from any blood-and-bone human—called the administrator of a car. There must be a jump in logic that points to Kurrat.

The call to Kurrat resulted in no response, so Soteria jumped to `call_support`, which leads to me. Curious. It called me yesterday right after Rob and I packed up and left Jordan's.

Checking back earlier in the log, I can see a lot of chatter about PDX-1217. With an effort, I find it's the car Jordan was driving when Soteria made the original request on June 4th. There's a huge transfer of data between the car and Soteria, then things stop. Soteria tried to contact the car and until yesterday, it wasn't available. Then it was, but it didn't provide the information Soteria wants. Now it's gone again.

I'm looking at an absent Jordan Bishop and a recalcitrant vehicle and I have no idea what this means. If I don't fix this, Soteria will call everyone under the digital sun, including Red Knowlton, who will leave a nasty-gram for my boss, who will fire me, and my dreams of sheep will be dragged to the trash.

Come on, Jupyter. Find the obvious problem.

I wonder about this car. It's malfunctioning in some way that makes Soteria unhappy. Who does the car call when it's not happy? Refrigerators call me—there must be a version of me in some parallel car universe, answering calls from confused automobiles.

I can't call that parallel Jupyter, but I can pretend to be her. What would Jupyter[2] do?

Jupyter[2] would run a diagnostic. Trace back on the stack. Obvious debugging.

I dig into Soteria's log file and—I'm stuck. I can see Soteria connected to Jordan's car, but I don't get how to follow the jump in logic. How do I trace it back to me?

Maybe I don't need to.

"Soteria, open a communication window with PDX-1217."

Without hesitation, Soteria draws a communication window with his fingers. I hear an old-fashioned telephone ring once, then again, then again. The connection opens, and I'm looking at a startled, middle-aged man.

"Who the hell are you?" says the startled, middle-aged man. The banner across the bottom of the window tells me he is Araci Belo, an insurance adjuster. Not a car. Why am I talking to this guy?

| 23 |

Incoming Call

"EVERYTHING IS GOING EXTREMELY WELL," screams Rifkin. The bird scratches his face and turns on his perch, ignoring Araci.

Araci Belo sits at the desk in the room's corner, looking through his visor at the AI. It's waiting for him to respond.

They lied. Araci never says it out loud.

It's an unwelcome thought. He didn't appreciate its frequent return. He tried to silence it. When it arrives, he distracts himself. He talks to Rifkin instead.

"I've got a comfortable gig here, Rifkin," he tells the bird. "Don't convince me otherwise."

When he left the police force, he thought he'd move to something better. A new purpose in life.

"We'll be *super excited* to have you," said the recruiter. "You'll supervise the AI form processors and be responsible for their ethical maturation."

They lied. Araci works *for* the AIs. They need him when they screw up. Araci is looking at one of these right now. It's a full-size avatar, dressed in a suit calculated to be next week's fashion. The avatar is slightly male, but it's hard to be sure.

The avatar has a client. The client has cancer. The cancer deviates from a norm defined by the AI, a rare gift from the cancer fairy. The probability of its occurrence is more than one standard deviation from the norm so the algorithm behind the AI behind the avatar calculates it's cheaper to deny the benefit. Even if the estate choses to litigate, it will be cheaper. The algorithms find creative ways to stray into this minefield. Araci is here to escort it out.

"How do you value a human life?" Araci asks the avatar.

`We are not allowed to attach value to a human life`, replies the AI.

Araci relaxes a small bit. He doesn't have to retrain this general assumption. Again.

Government regulations prohibit insurance companies from attaching value to a human life. Every time someone allowed them to do so, the algorithms would also attach values to race, religion, sex, gender, geolocation, employment, and genetics, sometimes other indicators. The algorithms used those numbers to make unpopular (and now illegal) decisions.

"What is the cost of cancer treatment?" Araci asks.

`The cost varies depending on the type of cancer and the genetics of the patient.`

The algorithm found its way back to genetic value. This is where he must begin. Again.

The Avatar's mouth moves, but it's not the avatar speaking. It's an illusion for Araci's comfort. Araci knows he's speaking to a neural network. Not a person in a suit. Araci dismisses the AI and files a request to change the training data. Engineering gives the request a low priority. He resends the request with annotations. They defer his request to a revision cycle slated for implementation in twenty-seven months. He argues the case with the project manager. No luck.

Putting my skills to the betterment of humanity, thinks Araci.

Lupe—when she's around—stops him from descending into a snit. However, Lupe is working today; her toothbrush remains unused. He's alone in the apartment, except for Rifkin.

Rifkin does not respect Araci's issues. Araci is the bird's favorite toy and servant. The bird is a feathered egocentric, and the apartment exists for his amusement. When he's not trying to break into a closet, he's rearranging kitchen utensils (onto the floor) or practicing his lines from *2001: A Space Odyssey*. Rifkin does not have a volume control and is audible from all corners of the room. Possibly into the neighbor's house as well.

Rifkin has a morning period of peak activity; a random time known only to Rifkin. If Araci knew when it was, he could take precautions: put things away, schedule conferences around Rifkin. Rifkin uses this to exert his dominance over Araci. It is his world.

It is that time now. Rifkin flies with irresponsible velocity from the kitchen, through the door into the main room, executes a swooping arc low across Araci's workspace and lands on a chair back. He celebrates his disruptive feat with a head-bobbing step dance and loud chanting of "DAVE WE HAVE A PROBLEM DAVE WE HAVE A PROBLEM."

Rifkin understands that flying through Araci's workspace gets him attention. What he doesn't understand is that when he does so, the view from Araci's augmented visor becomes a three-ring circus. Animated and virtual objects scurry out of the way, collide, bounce and show all sorts of simulated physics while they attempt to move away from the bird's calculated position.

Rifkin hops off the chair back and lands on the desk, next to the personality cube from PDX-1217. He picks at it and pushes it to the center of the desk, scattering other items in its wake. Araci snatches it away from Rifkin and places it back on the charging station as far away from the bird as possible. Rifkin redirects his rampage of chaos to Araci's coffee cup.

"GO. SHOO. RIFKIN!" Araci attempts to replace items faster than Rifkin can move them. Everything virtual and augmented must calculate its new position in relationship to everything else. It's computational mayhem.

"Incoming call from Soteria Reizoko," states his visor. In the midst of chaos, an uninvited and virtual young woman appears across the desk from Araci. Normal conferences offer both parties with a choice to accept, but not this time.

"Who the hell are you?" Araci yells at the girl. He pushes Rifkin back to the chair and stares at the woman.

The superimposed banner displays a machine identification number, followed by the words "Soteria Reizoko." Araci has no idea why she has a number instead of a name. Is this a new fad?

"Um. Hello?" she says. She touches her forehead above her right eye. Araci's detective training notes the behavior, knows it means nervous discomfort. Definitely not a telemarketer, phone evangelist or insurance client. Araci settles into the frame of mind he used to question suspects at a crime scene.

"Right. Hello. What do you want?" Araci clips his words.

"I'm Jupyter Fuertes. With appliance support. I'm calling about Portland public vehicle PDX-1217. Are you driving it right now?"

Araci stares back. He thinks, *No. I'm not driving right now. I'm in my living room. Does it look like I'm in a car? Are you stupid?*

He also thinks, *How do you know about PDX-1217? How do you know I know about it? Who ARE you?*

"No," he answers. "I'm sitting in my office, wondering why you're calling. Is there something you want? And why is this call listed as coming from Soteria Reizoko?"

"It's difficult to explain," she says. "I'm trying to fix a refrigerator—that's Soteria Reizoko—and somehow there's a public car involved in the problem. If I can find the car, I might be able to fix the refrigerator. For some reason my refrigerator thinks you're the car. That sounds mixed up, but like I said, it's confusing."

Rifkin, not okay with being ignored, speaks up; "LOOK DAVE, I CAN SEE YOU'RE REALLY UPSET ABOUT THIS."

"Is that a bird?" she asks. Jupyter can hear but not see Rifkin. Rifkin can't see Jupyter and Araci isn't planning to buy the bird a visor. They are available for pets. Mostly dogs. Probably birds. Not cats. Cats don't seem to care about augmented reality.

Araci softens. If this were his daughter, she wouldn't appreciate talking to some crabby old man. "It's a bird." He offers Rifkin his hand for a perch and Rifkin jumps over. His visor brings Rifkin into the video. The bird bobs his head up and down three times, gets bored, and flies off to the kitchen.

Araci continues, "And I can sympathize about the mixup. We always underestimate technology's ability to foul things up. And hello, my name is Araci Belo."

"Jupyter," she says. "So, if you're not driving the car, and it's obviously not in the room with you, do you have any idea where it is?"

Araci doesn't want to discuss this with an invader in an unsecured teleconference, but this is a fortunate coincidence.

"Not sure. I have this." With trepidation, Araci holds up the cube. He slides the charger to the center of the table and places the cube on top. It glows, then flickers, then becomes warm to the touch.

"Hey. Is that a personality?" From across the table, Jupyter squints at the object. She reaches over and pokes it. The cube is real but Jupyter is virtual, so her finger goes through it.

"Here. Do this to it," says Jupyter. With both hands she performs a pulling-apart motion. Araci mimics her action and several controls appear around the cube. Only a few are familiar to Araci; controls for communication flow, interface visibility, common things. `PDX>Go:1217` is displayed in red. He snatches the cube and places it on the floor, out of range of Jupyter. The controls pop out of existence.

"Wait! It was active," says Jupyter. "That's from PDX-1217? Where did you get that?"

Araci looks at Jupyter. His detective brain tells him to be cagey, but he also realizes she might help him.

"Maybe, and I can't say. You seem to know quite a bit about this."

"A former friend did their Ph.D. based on these things. We had a few around the apartment to play with."

"If we can establish some trust, I'd be interested in you taking a look. Without being a creepy old man, can you send me your background?"

"Sure." Jupyter pushes her contact information across the table. It's in the form of a small animated sheep and Araci taps it to display her credentials. It all checks: Jupyter works for an appliance company, moved to Portland from Minnesota. Because of her work with personal appliances, she has a rudimentary trust certificate. No mysteries. Araci returns the cube to the charger.

"Here's my contact information," he says. He pushes an antique-looking wood box to Jupyter.

"I can't see a lot from here," she says. "I'll need a diagnostic terminal. We have one here I could use. Can I borrow the cube for a couple of days?"

Closing the connection would be the safe thing to do. That would be the insurance thing to do. What would a detective do?

A detective would take initiative.

"If you like," Araci says, "we can meet and discuss it further."

Jupyter pauses for a minute. Waves at her screen, pulling up a private calendar. She returns her attention to Araci.

"Someplace public. How about a late lunch tomorrow, Thursday, June 8th at three-thirty? The Little Iraq Cafe. Two blocks from the 57th Avenue light rail."

"Works for me," says Araci. "I'll bring this." He taps the cube.

"I assume that's from the car Jordan Bishop was driving. Do you know where she is?"

Araci and his brain do a dead stop. He doesn't remember mentioning Jordan in this conversation.

"I'll tell you when we meet," he says. "I'm sure we both have interesting things to share. Looking forward to our chat."

Araci makes nice, but quickly closes the conversation. Jupyter disappears from view and Rifkin returns from the kitchen.

"Dave, stop. Stop, will you? Stop, Dave. Will you stop Dave? Stop, Dave." Rifkin squawks out lines from the movie and bounces on the chair.

Araci taps on Jupyter's sheep, displaying contact information. He doesn't have access to police tools anymore, but there're tricks he can use to find out more about her.

Araci sits back and thinks. It's not normal for Jupyter to show up with a spoofed machine identity, looking for controlled information.

Jupyter is doing what careless criminals do. As a precaution, he pulls the personality box off the charger. It goes dark.

| 24 |

routetrace()

Do-YeOn drinks ginger tea, but it doesn't calm his stomach. It's been getting worse: tightness, churning, cramps. UrCityCars should be his priority, but other things constantly interrupt. He woke up at two-thirty the last few nights. It's morning, but he doesn't feel rested.

The couch underneath him encircles the entertainment platform where his feet rest. Do-YeOn rented this apartment to impress his friends. Guests will marvel at how the kitchen, bedroom, and bathroom are actual, separate rooms with doors. To date, he hasn't had time to invite anyone to visit.

He walks to the kitchen, swills the last of his chai, then requests oatmeal and coffee. The extruder selects an oatmeal pod, hydrates the contents and squeezes it into a bowl. It smells of cinnamon. The machine ejects the spent pod and makes coffee.

He unwraps a slice of bread and places it in the toaster. Toast emerges in one millimeter increments, etched with a political advertisement promising lower taxes and better public transportation. His ad-free subscription to the toaster must have expired. No matter, he retrieves a warm tab of butter from the refrigerator and smears it across the advert. Tastes the same, sponsored or not.

Do-YeOn sits at the kitchen island, turns the toast so the butter-and-advertisement side is down, takes a bite and checks news about PDX>Go vehicles. No updates are available.

Abandoning his news feed, he checks his personal communications for the first time this morning. One message is conspicuous.

Like the repeated messages he received two nights ago, it includes an enormous amount of low-level data, but is missing identifiers. It could come from a toaster, an oil well, a flying drone or any of a thousand other things.

It arrived yesterday; June 6th, 2062 at 4:25 p.m. He was preoccupied with weighter matters to pay attention. Do-Ye0n checks his message handler; A data stream of this size should go to another machine for processing, summation and disposal. This isn't for human consumption, and Do-Ye0n wonders why he is the recipient.

The data comes from one machine, but mentions a second machine. Buried in the hash is a vehicle number: PDX-1217.

Do-Ye0n rechecks the hashed number. *Yes,* he realizes; this data comes from the vehicle Jordan Bishop was driving during her fatal accident. In so many ways, this shouldn't be happening.

Shit, *shit,* **SHIT**.

Do-Ye0n flicks his toast across the room, bouncing it off an antique bust of Steve Jobs. The toast leaves crumbs and butter but Steve Jobs still smirks, his right thumb eternally touching his bearded chin.

In his visor, Do-Ye0n spins a virtual combination lock to open a hidden box. It opens and he selects a router trace tool, something he's not allowed to own, akin to an unlicensed hand-gun, but more dangerous. Anything can be purchased on the internet, but not everything should be used. Privacy laws carry weight, and use of this tool is an outright felony.

He sets the trace tool to find the source of the message. The tool displays an irregular grid of lines with different colors and thicknesses, reminiscent of a subway map, with a triangle moving from station to station and leaving a glowing line. The stations are routers, most of them encrypted and protected. The triangle pauses at each router, puzzling out a decryption formula. Progress is slow and sometimes shows a "waiting" icon. It's an Augean feat that will cost Do-Ye0n extra processing cycles on his next utility bill, but this search is worth the expense.

He's more concerned about his exposure. If he's caught, it will be hard to explain how he got military-grade cyber weapons, much less why he is using them across a public network. Router tracing is recklessly obvious to any system administrator who might care to glance his direction. His ankle twitches, bouncing his knee like a sewing machine.

The oatmeal has cooled and gelled, but he finishes it while the tool crawls closer to the source of the message. The display shows the remaining time, and Do-YeOn checks it repeatedly.

His visor displays `06/07/2062 10:42:21` before a glowing path appears between him and whatever identifies itself as PDX-1217.

The route shows PDX-1217 broadcasting from the inside of an apartment, an obvious error. Do-YeOn double-checks the route and diagnostics. There must be a bug in the route trace software. But there it is, inside an apartment.

The router belongs to someone named Araci Belo. It's not clear to Do-YeOn, but there must be part of PDX-1217 interacting with the network. Even now, Do-YeOn can see PDX-1217 responding to requests. Do-YeOn uses the router tool and with a few commands, travels the last meter into Araci's personal network.

An average person's digital presence is mundane; Araci is no exception. His archives include terabytes of conversations with his daughter, financial reports, old family photographs. Do-YeOn views a movie of Araci with a woman, laughing, on a beach. Then photos of the woman pregnant, followed by the inevitable newborn photos. There are bills from the hospital for the birth and neo-natal surgery. Records of Araci's history with the police force, then streams of insurance reports. Detail after boring detail. Do-YeOn looks at bandwidth reports. Araci uses a tiny fraction of his available bandwidth, so hasn't noticed PDX-1217 sending these huge diagnostic transmissions. It has been connecting and disconnecting at random times, possibly because of an intermittent power supply.

Do-YeOn fast-forwards to recorded events from the past few days. Just two hours earlier, Belo received a call identified as "Soteria Reizoko." Araci's network archived the call and Do-YeOn replays it.

The call splits into two views; an older man on the left and a younger woman on the right. The man is labeled as "Araci Belo," the woman labeled as "Soteria Reizoko." Strange name for a girl. She has a machine ID number listed, which makes the call doubly odd. It's a familiar number. Do-YeOn does a quick lookup; it's the number he blocked the other night.

As the playback starts, there is yelling and cursing. Araci interacts with someone offscreen and is surprised by the girl, turning in annoyance to the camera and yelling "Who the hell are you?"

Do-YeOn smirks. He's not the only one annoyed by machine interruptions.

"Hello?" the woman says. "I'm Jupyter Fuertes. With appliance support. I'm calling about Portland public vehicle PDX-1217. Are you driving it right now?"

Jupyter will be easy to find, thinks Do-YeOn. He pauses the playback and adds Jupyter to his list of people to watch. He resumes the playback.

Araci replies with a sarcastic answer to Jupyter's question. Do-YeOn warms to Araci.

Jupyter is droning on about refrigerators and the PDX-1217. Do-YeOn motions to move the playback ahead by a minute.

The refrigerator has nothing to do with PDX-1217, thinks Do-YeOn.

Araci is spouting theatrical monologues. Do-YeOn motions to scrub further into the recording, but stops when Belo holds up a personality cube.

"How about a late lunch tomorrow, Thursday at three-thirty?" Jupyter is talking again. "Little Iraq Café."

Do-YeOn pauses the conversation. Araci will hand the box off to Jupyter, and at a public place. Somehow he needs to get that personality cube and keep it offline. Maybe when Araci is alone before the meeting or when Jupyter is alone afterwards. As a precaution, he places an intercept in Araci's home network.

Tomorrow at three-thirty. Do-YeOn feels a swell of anxiety; that isn't much time to prepare for the opportunity to close this loose end.

| 25 |

Intent To Dispose

June 8th, 2062

To: Dan's Artificial Psychology and Appliance Repair

Re: Intent to dispose of capital asset

From: International Mercado PLC

It is our intent to dispose of the following piece of equipment. As per our contract, please provide confirmation of ability to proceed.

Property Description: Soteria Reizoko Food Storage Unit, Serial # IFS-6582738539

Reason: Malfunction and out of warranty

Date of Disposition: June 16, 2062

Method of disposal: Junked, recycled and/or salvaged for parts

Location at time of disposal: To be delivered at dock

Amount received: Recycling fee to be reimbursed by materials recovery from asset

| 26 |

Lunch At Little Iraq

The Little Iraq café is a noisy place. There is yelling from the kitchen, platters of food moving to tables, and drones dropping from the ceiling to grasp empty plates. It's chaos, but after a half-hour the activity fades into the background like the rumble of road noise from an overpass.

Singles can eat and observe other diners, but the Little Iraq Cafe is best enjoyed with a friend or lover. Eavesdropping on a neighboring conversation requires concentration. It's impossible if your companion expects your attention. Only the café noise separates one table from another.

Araci watches the pandemonium. After each patron leaves, robots change the tablecloths and disinfect the table and chairs. A floor vacuum is in constant motion and crawlers scrub the windows every fifteen minutes. Araci wonders if the owners are obsessive-compulsive. The robots are.

The Little Iraq café is the best of many places serving genuine Middle Eastern food. Cumin saturates the wallpaper and a small bowl of chopped mint is at every table. Fattoush salad announces its presence with a heavy garlic and parsley scent.

Araci sits near the front window and faces the door. He likes to see as many directions as possible, a habit from the police force. He feels edgy even though this is a casual lunch. Jupyter's story is clean, but interesting tidbits always lurk between and behind.

He should send the personality cube to a lab service. He would, except the insurance company won't pay for this research. Asking Lupe to run it through the police lab will take forever and raise difficult questions. Jupyter already showed a knack for operating this cube and has an interest in doing so. Reward is greater than risk, so he is sitting in a café with the box in his pocket, waiting for her arrival.

Araci's visor displays `06/08/2062 3:37 PM`. Jupyter is late, but Araci isn't checking the time because of her. His visor also displays the identity of a suspicious man sitting in a vehicle across the street. The man is Do-YeOn Kurrat, Product Manager for UrCityCars. Maybe not a cause for concern, but why would he be waiting? It would be normal to get out of the car and release it for the next passenger.

Do-YeOn is waiting for someone. He must think he's discreet, but to Araci, he could have just as well set himself on fire and recited the Gettysburg Address in Klingon. Araci wonders who he's watching for.

A car pulls up across the street and ahead of Do-YeOn. Araci turns to see the passenger get out; it's Jupyter, and Do-YeOn sits up, takes obvious notice. Araci puts his tea down; Do-YeOn obviously hasn't watched any instructional videos on super-secret stake-outs.

Araci smiles, amused at Do-YeOn's inept surveillance, but it bothers him that Do-YeOn watches for Jupyter. Nothing is private on the internet, but this is a bit much. Was there a leak in his home network? He'd have to ask Lupe to bring in some security hardware to check things out.

For now, he'll have to be satisfied with being paranoid. He half-stands to wave her over, ignoring the intruder across the street. He considers warning Jupyter about Do-YeOn, but conspiracy theories aren't a good way to start a conversation.

Jupyter dodges a drone plummeting across her path and squirms through the packed chairs with youthful grace. Araci is envious, his legs don't move like they used to. His journey from the front door to this table had required several apologies and a few near-misses. Jupyter seems to anticipate the brownian patterns woven by the patrons and robots.

"Hi, I'm Jupyter," she says. She doesn't shake his hand. Instead, she drops her pack and sits. She faces Araci. "Did you bring the box?"

"Nice to meet you too, Jupyter," says Araci. His generation believes introductory conversation is polite. "How is your day going?"

Jupyter stares at him for a moment, and Araci wonders if she will retreat. But she continues to stare; it makes Araci uncomfortable.

"My day is fine. But can we skip the Social Thing, or are you going to ask me to smile?"

Jupyter delivers this in a way that confuses Araci. Is she being sarcastic or just straight-forward? Araci has been told he is a good reader of emotions, but Jupyter has a strange demeanor. He reminds himself this meeting had been her idea, and that she would help him with the box.

For want of a better understanding of Jupyter, he restarts the conversation with a noncommittal grunt. "I'm having masgouf with tea," he continues. "What's your favorite?"

"Biryani," she says. Their visors acknowledge their food requests and set a countdown timer until delivery.

Araci sneaks a look across the street. Do-YeOn is still in the car, still trying not to appear like he is looking at Jupyter. Araci fishes the box out of his pocket, wraps it in a napkin and offers it to Jupyter.

"Just set it down," she says. Araci places it on the table next to her hand.

Jupyter unwraps it and holds it up for closer inspection.

"Um. Don't ...," Araci says. He looks at Do-YeOn across the street. Do-YeOn has an unobstructed view of the box.

Jupyter squints her eyes at Araci. "Is there a problem?"

Araci stops before saying anything else. Too late now. "No problem," he says.

Jupyter produces a power pack and holds it near the box. Red lights pulse inside the cube and a control interface appears in their visors. The controls are a mystery to Araci, but Jupyter flashes through functions.

"It's still active," Jupyter says. "So where'd you get it, and why isn't it still in the car?"

Araci looks at her and thinks for a minute. Does she not watch the news? A car falls off the overpass, Jordan goes AWOL, he has a personality module from a missing car. Could the connections be any more obvious? His detective brain warns him to keep things close, so he lies. Sort of.

"The vehicle isn't on the road anymore."

Jupyter looks up from the box and stares at Araci, again. During his police days, he learned to stare down felons. Jupyter has a different kind of eye contact that makes him twitch. He considers telling her that he suspects Jordan was murdered, but holds back.

"That's all you've got to say?" Jupyter asks.

"That's what I know," he says. "I'm hoping you can tell me more."

Araci and Jupyter and (probably) Do-YeOn watch the box as Jupyter prods it. "Without a diagnostic terminal I can't see much," she says, not looking at him. He gets the sense he isn't part of the conversation. "It's been disconnected from its car since Sunday. There's something askew with the memory."

"I'm trying to figure out what happened before it got disconnected." Araci avoids saying *before she drove off the overpass.*

"Huh. This is interesting," Jupyter says. "Can you see this?" She points to the displays radiating out from the personality box. One control, in the corner, is flashing. She expands it to show a number: `IFS-6582738539`. "It's my refrigerator, trying to talk to this cube."

A handsome Iraqi man interrupts, delivering their meal. Jupyter gives the waiter a once-over, then drops the box and power supply in her backpack. She bypasses the fork and scoops handfuls of biryani, dipping chicken in the sauce provided.

Araci finds this admirable—food is meant to be eaten in a certain way. American hot dogs require a bun, but no silverware. Using a knife and a fork on a hot dog would be wrong. Likewise, biryani requires fingers, not chopsticks or forks. His masgouf is an entire grilled carp, and he eats it with a fork.

Jupyter pauses from her meal. "So. How did this get disconnected from the car?"

Araci sidesteps the question. "How about you explain how you found me, and what your refrigerator has to do with my car."

"The refrigerator doesn't belong to me. It belongs to woman named Jordan Bishop."

"Okay," says Araci. He knows all about Jordan, but feigns ignorance. "Tell me about Jordan, her refrigerator, then the car."

Jupyter finishes her last bite of biryani. "I know more about Jordan's refrigerator than I know about Jordan. I was on a repair call to her apartment. It's a nice place, she keeps things tidy, except for the aging food in the refrigerator. I've never met her or talked with her, but we did have an unpleasant incident a while ago.

"The refrigerator has been causing a world of problems and won't stop complaining about a missing order. It broke and called me for technical support. I've tried to fix it but a day later, it calls again. We've gone as far as doing a hard diagnostic on site, but it's obsessed with the order. Something unusual is going on, and it's moved beyond annoying to spooky. If this was a B-grade horror picture, I'd declare it possessed by an ancient demon and have it burned at the stake.

"When we were in her apartment, the refrigerator mentioned Jordan was on her way, so we figured things were good and packed up and left before she got home. In hindsight, we should have waited to talk with her in person."

Araci stops picking at his fish. "Jordan was on her way?"

"That's what the refrigerator said. Is that a surprise?"

Araci dodges her question, "Did the refrigerator tell you about me?"

"In a convoluted way, yes. But not really." Jupyter stops talking for a second and looks out the window, gathering her thoughts. Araci glances at the man in the car, but he isn't watching anymore. His attention is on something in his visor.

Jupyter continues, "The refrigerator doesn't know who you are. It knows about the car. PDX-1217 seems to be the problem. Jordan's refrigerator contacted the car about a grocery pickup, and the car confirmed it would get it. That's nothing special, it happens thousands of times a day with thousands of cars and refrigerators. However, this car never shows up. That's slightly unusual, but it happens. When it happens, the order is supposed to time-out and cancel. Notifications go to everyone involved, and the matter is settled. But something didn't work right. The refrigerator keeps recalling the order.

Jupyter pauses for another bite of biryani, then resumes explaining.

"The car wouldn't respond to the order cancellation. It was off the grid, but it wasn't a clean shut-down. If you dig into the refrigerator log files, you can see connections that aren't turned off. I can't tell everything because I'm only looking at the refrigerator side of the conversation, and I'm hoping this box from the car will describe what's going on with PDX-1217."

Araci takes a drink and wipes his forehead with a napkin. The curry sauce makes him sweat. Jupyter stares at him with a focused expression, then goes on.

"I found you because the refrigerator keeps trying to find PDX-1217. The car personality box connected to the network from your place, my refrigerator found it and I did some fancy flying to find you and open our call."

Araci puts down his fork and wipes his mouth. "So it was talking to the car before the crash?"

Jupyter's expression changes and she comes to attention. Araci sees her surprise, and too late, realizes what he said. He's out of practice being a detective.

"Did PDX-1217 crash?" Jupyter glares at Araci. "Where and when? Is Jordan in the hospital?"

"Sorry. I thought you knew."

"Well, I didn't. And I wish you told me that earlier. Do you know how rare that is? A crashed vehicle isn't even a part of the test suite for automotive systems. The information on this box is a fringe case, and that alone could explain a lot. So unless you want me to waste a bunch of time chasing unlikely scenarios, please give me a better description of what happened to Jordan and PDX-1217."

"You should see this." Araci grabs up the news clip about the accident and flicks it to Jupyter. She spreads it larger and pushes play. The video plays in both their visors, then she shrinks it and saves it for later.

"So Jordan and PDX-1217 crashed? Is she in the hospital or dead?"

"Dead."

"That's deserved." The sarcasm in her voice is obvious. Jupyter stands and runs her finger around the seam of her backpack, closing the waterproof seal and checking the anti-theft system. She swings the pack to her shoulders.

"I'll call you. Shouldn't be more than a couple of days. Unless there's something else you're not telling me, then it could be less time..." Jupyter trails off and gives him one last, focused stare.

Araci stares back. "Nope, that's what I have."

Jupyter shakes her head while she leaves the cafe. She steps to the sidewalk and summons a car.

Araci watches her leave, then sees Do-YeOn drive off in the same direction. He runs for the door but can't navigate the crowd. Jupyter and her pursuer are out of sight by the time he reaches the street.

He could chase after them, but would have little chance of catching up. This makes him nervous. It's the way undercover operations get compromised. It's a way people wind up dead.

| 27 |

Soteria.Reizoko[2062-06-08]

Event Log for Soteria.Reizoko

Serial: IFS-6582738539

Owner is JORDAN BISHOP

2062-06-08T15:45:00-08:00 – enter_diagnostic_mode (persistent attempt)

What_was_supposed_to_happen

restock productID 1 22465 10155 3 on 2062-06-04T09:12:46+00:00

What_actually_happened

Restock overdue

Research_Problem

Contact_driver of UrCityCars#33579 at 2062-06-04T09:14:24-08:00

Driver of UrCityCars#33579 is Do-YeOn Kurrat

Contact Do-YeOn Kurrat at UrCityCars#33579

Do-YeOn Kurrat is unavailable at UrCityCars#33579

Request location of Do-YeOn Kurrat

Do-YeOn Kurrat is available at UrCityCar#11766

repair_instructions

Contact Do-YeOn Kurrat at UrCityCar#11766

2062-06-08T15:45:01-08:00 – CONTACT Do-YeOn Kurrat

Request_status of pickupConfirmation DAGX-INWC-9677-WZVZ

Conversation terminated by recipient

2062-06-08T15:46:00-08:00 – CONTACT Do-YeOn Kurrat

Request_status of pickupConfirmation DAGX-INWC-9677-WZVZ

Conversation terminated by recipient

2062-06-08T15:47:00-08:00 – CONTACT Do-YeOn Kurrat

Request_status of pickupConfirmation DAGX-INWC-9677-WZVZ

Conversation terminated by recipient

2062-06-08T15:48:00-08:00 – CONTACT Do-YeOn Kurrat

Request_status of pickupConfirmation DAGX-INWC-9677-WZVZ

Conversation terminated by recipient

2062-06-08T15:49:00-08:00 – CONTACT Do-YeOn Kurrat

Do-YeOn Kurrat no longer available at UrCityCar#11766

2062-06-08T21:06:17-08:00 – cancel_food_pickup

Contact CityOfPortland.PublicVehicle.PDX-1217

Error: PDX-1217 in diagnostic mode

Error: Unable to modify live data while in diagnostic mode

Error["Secondary"]: file mismatch

Response: Unable to cancel_food_pickup

28

Observer

Do-YeOn grasps the blue dot in his visor and drags it to the nearby parking spot. The car considers his command but pauses. This is a subtle message from the car; it's doing what it's told but what it's being told is not normal. Normally, the car would pause, let him out, and continue on. But no. It shrugs and parks within easy view of the Little Iraq café.

Do-Yeon turns to the box in the passenger seat. With his thumb and finger, he lifts out a drone the size of a small bird; just big enough to carry a camera and microphone. He connects it to his visor and instructs it to hover. The drone responds to his focal point and the tilt of his head. Do-YeOn flies through the car window towards the restaurant. Breezes make for a rough ride, consuming extra battery power.

Getting inside the café is difficult; he has to wait until someone opens the door, then dash in behind. His view careens to the right, a collision with the service drone passing to his left. His drone must not be broadcasting the correct identifier, but he doesn't have time to fine tune the settings. He looks around and perches out of the way on the top of a picture frame. With a pivot and sweep, the camera recognizes and records Araci Belo.

Back in the car, his visor recognizes Jupyter Fuertes when she gets out of a vehicle. He ignores the drone for a minute and checks to confirm; yes, that's her. She's shorter than he thought, but her hair is the same as on the call with Belo. He returns his attention to the drone video.

Jupyter enters the drone's field of view and moves to the table with Belo. It takes a minute to narrow the audio reception to just their conversation.

"Biryani," says Jupyter.

good Do-YeOn thinks. He has the audio dialed in.

Araci places a napkin on the table and Jupyter unwraps it. There is a lot of traffic in the drone's line of sight, but between obstructions, Do-YeOn can see Jupyter now holds the personality module. She retrieves a power pack from her backpack and places it next to the box, causing it to glow. If he was closer, his visor would show him a control interface, but sitting across the street is too far and the drone doesn't have the electronics to relay a connection.

He can follow her hand motions controlling the module; She knows enough to read out useful information and possibly find something inconvenient. Her actions generate a status check on the active programs.

"Where'd you get it, and why isn't it still in the car?"

Good question, he thinks. Without realizing he is still listening through the drone, he leans forward to hear what Araci has to say.

"The vehicle isn't on the road anymore," says Araci. Do-YeOn shakes his head and rolls his eyes. Old news.

The waiter blocks Do-YeOn's view so he moves closer to the table, finding a perch above Jupyter and looking down. Do-YeOn scans the scene, but the box is out of sight. It must be in Jupyter's backpack. *Shit.*

Between bites of what looks to be burned fish, Araci converses with Jupyter. Mundane things, until Araci mentions a refrigerator, "How about you explain how you found me, and what your refrigerator has to do with my car."

Do-YeOn remembers Jupyter mentioned the refrigerator in their initial conversation, but hadn't taken time to understand how it related to the personality box. He tweaks the audio gain on the drone.

Jupyter: "The refrigerator doesn't belong to me. It belongs to a woman named Jordan Bishop."

Araci: "OK. Tell me about Jordan, her refrigerator, then the car."

Do-YeOn loses his focus. *Does this have anything to do with the odd machine calls he's been getting?*

With the timing of a malevolent deity, the car he is sitting in announces a message from an unknown machine. Do-YeOn waves it into the background, then stops. System-level messages are an expected part of debugging. But he isn't logged in to this car as an administrator, only as a mundane user. He shouldn't be getting messages of this type. Worse, the message is addressed to him. Worse still, it's from a machine address.

The drone is streaming the conversation between Jupyter and Araci, and Do-YeOn has to juggle his attention.

Jupyter: "The refrigerator doesn't know who you are."

Do-YeOn tries to ignore the unexpected message. It's a request for a pickup confirmation:

```
2062-06-08T15:45:01-08:00 - Request_status of
        pickupConfirmation DAGX-INWC-9677-WZVZ
```

Jupyter: "PDX-1217 seems to be the problem with the order."

Do-YeOn tries to cache the message but accidentally deletes it. He punches the unyielding dashboard; intense pain shoots up Do-YeOn's arm from his knuckles to his shoulder.

Jupyter: "Jordan's refrigerator contacted the car about a grocery pickup, and the car confirmed it would get it."

Do-YeOn reaches to rub his shoulder, which causes the drone feed to switch out. He angrily waves it back with his throbbing right hand.

Jupyter: "... thousands of times a day with thousands of cars and refrigerators. However, this car never shows up. That's slightly unusual, but it happens. When it happens, the order is supposed to time-out and cancel. Notifications go to everyone involved, and the matter is settled. But something didn't work right. The refrigerator keeps recalling the order."

Do-YeOn receives another message interrupting his concentration. Its the same message from the same machine. He again tries to ignore it.

```
2062-06-08T15:46:00-08:00 - Request_status of
      pickupConfirmation DAGX-INWC-9677-WZVZ
```

A service drone blocks his view of the table.

One thing at a time, thinks Do-YeOn. He dismisses the system message and moves the drone, but he's distracted and he weaves across the room, creating a video that looks like something filmed by a stoned teenager on a roller coaster.

Jupyter: "The car wouldn't respond to the order cancellation. It was off the grid, but it wasn't a..."

For a second time, Do-YeOn collides with a service drone. The onboard stability tools counteract, whip-sawing his vision across the room and back to Jupyter. Do-YeOn vomits a small bit of motion-sickness into his throat and coughs.

A third interrupting message arrives; same machine, same message.

```
2062-06-08T15:47:00-08:00 - Request_status of
      pickupConfirmation DAGX-INWC-9677-WZVZ
```

Do-YeOn jams his finger when he jerks and waves the system message off screen. He tries to shake off the pain, but the hand motion causes the drone to reposition further away from Jupyter and Araci. He adjusts the audio, but can only hear parts of the conversation.

Jupyter: "...clean shut-down. If you dig into the refrigerator log files, you can see connections that aren't turned off. I can't tell everything because I'm only looking at the refrigerator side of the conversation, and I'm hoping this box from the car will describe what's going on with PDX-1217."

Do-YeOn suddenly understands the annoying messages and where they are coming from. The refrigerator - the Soteria Reizoko - is stuck in a loop, trying to confirm a delivery with the car. It's a bug when cars abruptly go off-grid, a fault deep in the personality cube. It rarely occurred and was never deemed important enough to fix. Unfortunately it's happening now and showing up in the vehicle log files. He needs the personality cube if he is going to fix this. He sees Jupyter seal her backpack and stand to leave. The message arrives again.

```
2062-06-08T15:48:00-08:00 - Request_status of
      pickupConfirmation DAGX-INWC-9677-WZVZ
```

Do-Ye0n waves the message away and places a temporary block on the address. He tries to take a calming breath and fails. Jupyter steps into the street and climbs into a PDX>Go.

Do-Ye0n needs to convince this car to follow Jupyter. He reaches for the navigation controls—then remembers the drone. *Dammit.* He needs to retrieve it before he leaves.

Do-Ye0n jerks his drone towards the door but runs into a restaurant drone carrying a load of dishes. Everything crashes to the floor; his drone broadcasts for a minute before being crushed underfoot.

Do-Ye0n abandons it and turns his attention to Jupyter and the personality box. Her PDX>Go is leaving, and he needs to follow. He might trace it over the network, but he might not. Best to find out where she's going.

Self-driving cars are excellent for getting from place to place, but difficult to explain how to tail another car. Do-Ye0n had been able to follow Jordan because he had more time to prepare and knew where she was going. This time, he doesn't know where Jupyter is heading.

He guesses and signals his car to move east by one kilometer. It carefully, frustratingly, safely moves into traffic. Do-Ye0n tries to keep track of Jupyter's car, but it's the same as every other PDX>Go car in the city.

He's sure the car Jupyter is riding in takes a right, so he grabs at the location pin and drags it to follow. His car shows an updated route that will take him one block past the street Jupyter has turned on, then right, then right again. Do-YeOn drags the pin twice, trying to force his car to turn sooner. His car stays on course, turns right, then right, following the calculated route. He gets to the intersection shown on the map, but there are no cars in sight. Jupyter is gone.

Do-YeOn considers punching the dashboard. He could make a loud sound hitting flesh against plastic at the cost of further damage to his fingers. It's more frustrating to not act. He crosses his arms over his chest and raises his blood pressure.

If he could, he would stomp on the accelerator pedal and squeal out, swearing in unison with the screech of the tires. But self-driving cars don't offer that option.

| 29 |

Diagnostics

I leave the Little Iraq café and summon a car. It stops, opens the door and waits for me to get in. Sometimes I imagine Grandma's ghost is driving. I tell her about my day. I don't tell her about her pickup.

I could go home, but instead, I head back to the shop. While I'm riding, I pull out the box from Mr. Belo. I saw some interesting data when I started it up in the restaurant, but it's hard to concentrate with lunch in front of me, drones grabbing plates, and the Belo guy asking questions.

Most annoying was the video drone. The propellers spin at that frequency older people can't hear anymore. Most likely, it's a security system for the restaurant. I'll send a note to Little Iraq and tell them to knock it off.

The car enters the crappy part of town, close to work and drops me off. I wave to the friendly cameras and enter the warehouse. Lucy is near the back dock. Is she ever not here?

"Can I borrow the diagnostic case?" I ask.

She smiles, we engage in social chat while she checks it out. I take it upstairs. I should call Pali. She would have this nut cracked in seconds, would know where to look, what to fix. But no. That would lead to a conversation I don't want to have.

I sit down at a workstation, start up the diagnostic, insert the personality cube and grab the resulting controls. There is a built-in sandbox to catch, record and stop any communications, both incoming and outgoing. It's a good idea to isolate toys like this from the network. You never know if it will broadcast internal data or stick probes in the firewall.

The cube comes alive and diagnostics appear. It spends a fair amount of time trying to connect to the automotive systems that disappeared with PDX-1217. I set up a spoof for those communications so they don't leave the sandbox.

I'm familiar with the architecture for most appliances but not the deep internals of automobiles. Apps and functions are scattered around in defiance of all reasonable design guidelines. Seriously—if this is an example of good programming, I should have nothing to worry about when it's my turn.

I find the activity monitor and examine the history—mostly errors from apps that can't connect with missing automotive systems. I eliminate the error reports and see the personality box is thrashing, trying to send a report to a private address through an anonymizer. Interesting; the box should talk with a corporate server. Instead, it's contacting something else. Maybe that's normal for a vehicle? If it is just a corrupted address, then it shouldn't work at all. But the function call is well-formed, so someone configured it to do this. I can't imagine the internals were available to anyone other than a root administrator logged on through an encrypted port.

I provide the cube with enough access for it to contact that outside address, then watch for what happens. I'm surprised; it's Soteria. After so many encounters, I recognize the connection ID. *Soteria, who invited you to this party? And what are you up to?* I open communication privileges for Soteria. Let's see what's so important.

Soteria begins sending messages to the personality cube. Mostly standard chatter. `Hello, are you alive?` `Yes, I'm alive. Are you alive?` But part of the connection is access to a log held by Soteria. It's like Soteria has something that belongs to PDX-1217 and is trying to make it available. I do not understand why that would happen, but sometimes learning systems build unexpected behaviors.

I figure if Soteria wants to send a file, then I should take time to look inside. I flip through the car personality, but it's vast. I need help, so I pull out a folder of tools I've labeled *little buddies*. From the virtual box I pluck out a finder, an indexer and a filterer. The finder icon is a blood-hound, the indexer is a puffin and the filterer is a funnel with legs.

They perform their "busy" dance while they initiate; then I tell them to work on the file Soteria is trying to share. I ask them to build meta-data and hash-tables, clusters and forests. It takes an eternity for them to do this; thirty seconds.

So, what do I know about this very important file? Not much, but I can guess it's telling me about Soteria, the very annoying refrigerator.

"Show me references to Soteria Reizoko," I tell my data minions. They do their busy dance, then play patty-cake while they pass information to each other. The funnel hands me a small book. I look at the pages, noting they are all the same time; June 4th at 9:14 a.m.

```
2062-06-04T09:12:33-08:00 - InitiateTrip
    Vehicle PDX-1217
    SafetySystemsCheck is 97%
    BatteryLevel is 73%
    Current Location 669 North Page Street,
        Portland, OR 97227
    New driver is Jordan Bishop
    Destination is Mt View Cemetery,
        SE Smith Rd, Corbett, OR 97019

2062-06-04T09:13:02-08:00 - Driving

2062-06-04T09:14:23-08:00 - ContactCar
    InitiatedBy Soteria.Reizoko
    Owner Jordan Bishop confirmed
    order_confirmation_code DHPN-WGYT-0232-TLLK
    pickupConfirmation is DAGX-INWC-9677-WZVZ
```

```
    Sending transport_logistics to
        Soteria.Reizoko
```

I realize this is a log file from a car. Specifically, it's a log file from PDX-1217 that mentions Jordan Bishop. I've seen this request from Soteria's side; this is the same event, but from the automobile's side.

```
2062-06-04T09:14:23-8:00 - Diagnostic
        monitor installed

2062-06-04T09:14:23-8:00 - Diagnostic
        session initiated
    InitiatedBy UrCityCars#33579
```

The first anomoly I notice is the installation of a diagnostic monitor. I don't know cars, but when I place an appliance in a diagnostic mode, it's open to all sorts of bad things. In a diagnostic session, I can simulate conditions and shut off error trapping. I could tell a toaster to set itself on fire and it would do its best to comply. Installing a diagnostic monitor in a car traveling at highway speeds seems really careless. Or malicious.

```
2062-06-04T09:14:24-08:00 - RouteChange
        (Diagnostic)
    Destination is 2272 NE 201st Ave,
        Fairview, OR 97024

2062-06-04T09:14:24-08:00 - Driving (Diagnostic)

2062-06-04T09:16:53-08:00 -
       AvoidCollision (Diagnostic)
    Multiple Pedestrians in road
    Collision barrier on left
    Collision barrier on right
    Severity is catastrophic
    Probability is certain
```

```
    Action is swerve
```

The next lines of the log file show the car is being told to change its destination, then being told to avoid a collision with a bunch of pedestrians.

From the GPS data it's obvious this was happening on a controlled freeway where only cars are allowed. Not a place where pedestrians hang out.

If there was a group of pedestrians on the bridge, the car should have gracefully changed to a different lane, slowed and warned its little car buddies about the gaggle of dunderheads lost on the overpass. But nope, these people abruptly teleported themselves into the middle of a high-speed motorway. The car swerved to avoid them.

```
2062-06-04T09:16:53-08:00 - Collision
    Sensor disruption at 25 degrees
    Sensor disruption at 20,10,40, 50 degrees
```

The turn results in a collision.

```
2062-06-04T09:16:53-08:00 - Airbag deployment
    EXCEED LIMITS: Deceleration at
        .005 km/s^2. See attached data
    EXCEED LIMITS: Acceleration at
        .00981 km/s^2. See attached data
```

Now, I don't know car speak, but after the collision there are warnings about `EXCEED LIMITS`. I remember Owen, the oven, trying to set itself on fire. In the movies when they show `EXCEED LIMITS` the soundtrack gets angry and goes into a minor key. Someone always gets hurt.

There are sensors warning about what I assume is proximity, measured in meters, then centimeters, then millimeters. Then they stop sending warnings altogether.

The awful story blooms in my head. I'm reliving the car crash. It was jumbled, loud and confused. Jordan was in the car when there was an abrupt deceleration. A dramatic drop in altitude. A sudden stop, and the sensors quit working. What does it feel like to fall to your death?

But it doesn't make sense that Soteria told Rob and I that Jordan was about to show up.

Wait...

I look at Soteria's log again. It shows that PDX-1217 became available while Rob and I were in Jordan's apartment. At lunch I found out that Araci had the personality cube at that time. He must have activated it somehow, and the cube contacted Soteria.

```
2062-06-06T16:25:14-08:00 - Repair_instructions
    CityOfPortland.PublicVehicle.PDX-1217
        IS_AVAILABLE
    IMPLIED: Jordan Bishop IS_AVAILABLE
```

Soteria assumes that if the car is available, then Jordan is available. I suppose Soteria doesn't think of Jordan and the car as separate entities.

It's unclear why Soteria is sharing this file with PDX-1217. If cars are anything like other devices, the log file is available from the cloud. The car isn't asking for the file. Soteria seems to be trying to convince PDX-1217 of something. *See. You said you would do this. It's right here.*

I don't know for sure, but it's reasonable that cars and refrigerators exchange all sorts of data when they schedule a grocery pickup. From what I can see here, a lot of the data is unimportant. But if I were the programmer, I'd swap as much as possible. There's no cost to the transmission. In fact, I'd send a complete memory dump. Why be parsimonious? I suppose it's good defensive programming.

The file they are sharing came from PDX-1217 at the time of the accident. Soteria saved it, like a good refrigerator would do. When

Soteria and the personality box link up, Soteria tries to re-share that data. Maybe the car lost its copy and is trying to restore a backup?

I disconnect Soteria, close the sandbox and pick up the personality cube. I stand and walk past the kitchen, pause, but turn instead to the more sanitary bathroom. I enter a stall and sit. While I'm peeing, I think about the pedestrians. Was there a widespread failure between cars telling each other about road conditions? Not likely.

The pedestrians are a figment of PDX-1217's imagination. A big fat malfunction.

If I can find this much out why can't Mr. Belo? He works for a fancy insurance company; they can afford a high-powered computer forensics engineer. Why didn't he have his internal people look at the box? That would only make sense if he suspected the problem on the box was a big deal. And that he could play that information into a big deal for himself. Maybe he's hoping to find something evil and then sell what he knows to the highest bidder. If these spoofed pedestrians happened once, it can happen again. It's possible PDX-1217 killed Jordan Bishop with a fatal malfunction.

`If...`

humans find out that cars will kill them, it will be mayhem for car manufacturers. They would pay *anything* to avoid that.

`...Or...`

Insurance companies would pay anything to have a part of a lawsuit this big. They could sue for billions.

`...Or...`

Insurance companies would be on the loosing side of a class-action lawsuit. Not good for business.

`...then...`

Mr. Belo stands to gain big money no matter who buys the information.

I look at the box in my hand and realize I'm holding something worth billions of dollars. Something that could get me killed. My murder would as easy as staging another bizarre automobile accident with fake pedestrians.

What does Pali know? She works for PDX>Go and would have been told if this box tried to phone home, back to PDX>Go. Does she know I have this cube? If this thing is a big corporate scandal, Pali knows where to find me. I thought I sandboxed it--but is that enough to prevent a trace back?

Am I in trouble?

Stupid question.

| 30 |

One Pepperoni Pizza

I can't sit here inside a bathroom stall, holding this cube worth billions of dollars. My right hand, the one with the cube, is shaking. I should get up before this toilet seat embosses a ring around my ass.

It's just a cube.

... From an automobile that crashed....

... And killed its driver...

... to avoid phantom pedestrians.

... and shows up in the hands of some guy who wants to keep this hushed up...

... but gives it to me, some nobody he's met by accident.

This is no accident. I'm involved in this somehow. This box is reporting back to somebody, and they know where I am. Does it broadcast all the time, or does it need a power source? What else don't I know?

I could flush this down the crapper. Then someone would come looking for me and cut off my fingers. Better if I keep it so I avoid losing appendages.

I could give it back to Mr. Belo. Insist I couldn't get it to talk. I won't tell anyone.

That never works in the movies.

I can sell it to the highest bidder for a billion dollars. They would silence me by sending me off a bridge, like what happened to Jordan Bishop.

Panic, like an electrical fire, reaches outwards and upwards from between my shoulders and into my brain. First the insulation around my wires heat up, then smoke, then burn and melt and drip. I hear myself hyperventilate.

I rush outside the stall. I don't want to be in a claustrophobic little room with a toilet seat for a friend. I stare at the pretty lights in the mirror, telling me about me. My heart rate is 120 beats per minute, circled in red. Blood pressure is up to 160 over 80, also circled in red. A "Call for help?" button has appeared. I could push it and medics would arrive, but that's not the help I need.

I move out to the hallway, away from the mirror so it doesn't call help on my behalf. I stand in the hall and meditate on my breathing; I can get a grip. The hallway isn't the best place to have a panic attack. I should move somewhere. Go left, back to the support floor. Go right, dead end hallway. Don't want either choice. I should go back to the farm where it's safe.

Avery is standing in front of me. Did he just appear? He's asking me a question.

"What?" I ask with a sarcastic snap. I don't have the bandwidth for social talk.

"Are you okay?"

I can only stare at him. Of course I'm not Okay.

"You're shaking. There's an open conference room. Do you need a minute?"

All I can think of is this damn cube. Avery is too much to process. I should run and scream, but making loud noises would flag security. Who else might show up? He takes my hand and we walk toward one of the conference rooms at the end of the hall.

We step into the room. If Avery tries to kill me for the cube, I can take him out with a kick to the groin and thumbs in his eyes. I can leave him bleeding on the floor and run for safety. Until that happens, this is fine.

He pulls out a chair for me to sit in, then closes the door and the blinds and dims the lights. He reserves the conference room for the next hour and sits in a chair facing me.

"Can I get you water?" he says.

I can only watch him. I'm trying to slow my breathing. He sits and says nothing.

"Thanks," I say.

"Sure," he responds. We are master conversationalists. Next we'll move on to a full discussion of Greek mythology. But for ten minutes we sit and breathe.

"You were working on something. Want to tell me?" Avery is making small talk in the way that technicians talk small.

"Um," I say. The polite thing would be to say something more.

"I'm working on a vehicle personality cube. Trying to figure out what it wants."

"And?"

"The vehicle is talking to a refrigerator. A Soteria Reizoko."

"Those things are an ungodly aggregation of incompatible crap. What's its problem?"

Avery understands I've been dealing with a difficult problem. *Thank you, Avery.*

"It can't cancel an order because the vehicle won't respond. It apparently crashed."

"The refrigerator crashed?"

"The car. Fell off an overpass."

"Wow. Was it the PDX>Go they talked about in the news? That is beyond wild."

How long has Avery known about the PDX>Go? "That's the problem. My Soteria set up an order with that car. It keeps trying to cancel, keeps failing, keeps calling me."

"Have you manually cancelled the order?"

At first, I assemble my sarcastic conversation tools into a scathing response. *Of course I did.* But I stop. Avery is asking a reasonable question, he deserves respect. "Tried several times. Soteria won't give up."

"So there's a persistent fault. Is something in the loop calling a diagnostic?"

Well. Yes. I think. "It restarts a diagnostic every time it fails."

"So there's something pear-shaped happening inside the car?"

I laugh. Actually laugh out loud. *Pear-shaped.* Who says that kind of thing?

"Yes. I believe something is pear-shaped inside of that car. But I'm not sure what."

"Did you step-trace through Soteria to find the fault condition?"

And with that, I realize what I've been missing. Avery is quoting from the book of obvious debugging tools. But I'm digging too deep to remember basic training.

"Do you have time to plug in a diagnostic session?" I ask Avery. I've heard it's helpful to discuss problems with someone else for a fresh perspective.

"Honestly, I'm done being at work for today. Can we do this tomorrow?"

NO. Tomorrow is too late! I think. Mr. Belo is going to kill me in my sleep and take the billion dollars. Pali knows where I live. *I'm screwed.*

Panic will not solve this, so I dial down the drama by half. "Um. I'd like to keep working on this. I could use your help. Can we go somewhere else? I have pizza at home."

What am I saying? I don't have pizza at home. I don't have bandwidth at home. I barely have a home; I have a tiny apartment. Once again—shut up, Jupyter.

"Pizza?" Avery says. "Sure! If you don't mind stopping somewhere, I'll buy beer, we can do a high-class dinner and look at the code you're working on."

I like this idea. Best to keep moving so the bad people can't find me. Maybe they are lurking for me at my apartment, but I'll be safer there than if I stay here. I sneak down the hallway back to my desk, grab my bag and the diagnostic case. I secure the cube in my pack and I lead Avery to the train station. He wants to summon a car, but I object. I'm jittery about cars right now.

On the ride to my house, I notice Avery is interesting. I didn't prep for conversation, but we're not struggling through awkward silences. Avery says something, I say something, he laughs, I say something else; he laughs again. I don't feel like laughing, but it's good to hang with someone who does.

I confess to him I don't have pizza at the apartment, so we stop at the mini mercado. There's a shelf full of snap open pizzas and we grab a large flavor-of-the-week. Avery grabs a liter of beer. It's been a long time since I had beer at my place.

Five minutes later, I'm unlocking my door. I hope I cleaned up.

| 31 |

Knowing How To Ask

I've got misgivings about this. A boy in my apartment might lead to heavy breathing and swapping of bodily fluids. Maybe that would be ok. But Avery and I spent the ride discussing code, Soteria and PDX-1217. We've got ideas we want to try, none to do with biology.

I pull the heat tab off the pizza box and Avery serves up the beer. He'd started to buy wine, but wine and pizza is stupid. Beer is easier. There's not a lot of distance between things in this room, so Avery has to reach around me to grab the pizza. I can't back away since I'm already next to the wall. I should be uncomfortable with this, but there aren't options.

I have just enough counter space for beer, pizza and the diagnostic case. I open it up, connect it to power and place the personality cube in the clip. It builds up the interface, visible to those of us wearing visors.

The cube resumes pinging non-existent automotive systems, still blocked by the spoofs I set up. It also tries to communicate with the anonymized address.

Avery steps over to the bed and folds it down for a place to sit, then adjusts his visor. I walk to the front of the apartment and turn my back to the door. Sitting on the bed next to Avery might be unladylike. I can see fine from here.

"Show me how it goes into debug." Avery pulls at one control and a message flashes, announcing Soteria's arrival. Avery jerks his hand back.

"It's okay. Soteria calls every time we power this cube up." I deny access to Soteria. For now, let's keep things simple.

Avery opens the applications box. He scrolls through until he finds an administrative icon, then taps it to activate. Options come up, one of them a debug tool. He taps that, it glows briefly, but nothing happens.

"What did it do the last time you tried?" Avery asks. Honestly, I didn't get to the debugger yet. Something I missed thinking about. I guess that's why people work together.

"I haven't tried this before. But it should do something. It should at least put up a security request if that's what's stopping it."

I try the same activation and get the same response: nothing. I fiddle unproductively, trying to find a different way inside this box. Nothing.

Avery retrieves another slice of pizza, then looks at me. "What if we let Soteria talk to it. Can we watch the conversation for any insights?"

Again, not sure. I've been busy reading log files and coming at the problem from the front door. This is something I haven't tried.

"I'm not sure where the PDX>Go operating system records its conversation log. But we could watch Soteria's side of the conversation."

Avery signals his agreement with a drink of beer. I clear the way for Soteria to connect and the avatar shows up.

"Soteria, why are you here?" That seems reasonable to say, but I immediately regret it.

`I am unable to restock a depleted product.` Soteria changes his expression to a manufactured look of concern. `I have successfully reordered, and received delivery confirmation, but the requested product has not arrived.`

"He says that every time," I tell Avery.

"Must be annoying."

"Just one of the high points of the job of appliance counselor." As an afterthought, I give Soteria an extra command.

"Soteria, report verbose error diagnostics."

Not sure if it changes things, but we'll see. I pull up Soteria's log file and show the latest log entry, almost happening real-time. It shows that PDX-1217 is in diagnostic mode and that Soteria is unable to cancel a food pickup.

```
2062-06-08T21:06:17-08:00 -
       cancel_food_pickup
    Contact
       CityOfPortland.PublicVehicle.PDX-1217
    Error: PDX-1217 in diagnostic mode
    Error: Unable to modify live data
       while in diagnostic mode
    Error["Secondary"]: file mismatch
    Response: Unable to cancel_food_pickup
```

Avery stares at the log. "Lots of errors. Can you decipher what that's all about?" He has an expression like a border collie; his head is cocked to the side. If he had fuzzy ears they'd be perked up.

I have nothing to say. All these errors are here because Soteria is taking time to carefully document the process. Usually, nobody cares about log files at all, save appliance technicians. And I only amped up error reporting as an afterthought.

"That probably explains why we can't put PDX-1217 into diagnostic mode." I point at the first error line in the log file. "It's *still in* diagnostic mode. Those are supposed to shut off when you disconnect. Or power down. Avery," I say. I use his first name without hesitation. "That personality cube is active and in contact with someone using an open debug session."

...and open for all types of mischief.

I sit down next to him but I don't think he notices. Avery stops fidgeting with PDX-1217 and retrieves his beer from the floor. "I don't know how to shut off a debug session that isn't supposed to be running. How about you?"

I shake my head no, but since he's focused on the personality cube, he probably doesn't see me.

I put down my beer and use two hands to expand the PDX-1217 log file, then scroll back to the data and time of Jordan's accident.

```
2062-06-04T09:14:23-08:00 - ContactCar
    InitiatedBy Soteria.Reizoko
    Owner Jordan Bishop confirmed
    order_confirmation_code DHPN-WGYT-0232-TLLK
    pickupConfirmation is DAGX-INWC-9677-WZVZ
    Sending transport_logistics
        to Soteria.Reizoko
    2062-06-04T09:14:23-8:00 - Continue route
    2062-06-04T10:00:00-8:00 - Continue route
```

"Avery!" I shout.

"**WHAT**?" he says, jerks and spills his beer. He lurches to the sink, grabbing a paper towel and wiping the spill off his pants. He runs right through the virtual representation of Soteria, causing it to dodge and lurch to a non-conflicting position. Avery is mopping himself up and Soteria is playing keep-away. It's funny. I wait for Avery to settle down, then point at the log file window.

"These last two lines are different. They don't match what Soteria has."

Avery looks up, but keeps wiping. He can only see the one file from PDX-1217.

"Here, look at this." I tell Soteria to display the lines I searched up at work with the filter combination. Soteria displays its version of the log file from Jordan's accident.

```
2062-06-04T09:14:23-08:00 - ContactCar
    InitiatedBy Soteria.Reizoko
    Owner Jordan Bishop confirmed
```

```
    order_confirmation_code
        DHPN-WGYT-0232-TLLK
    pickupConfirmation is
        DAGX-INWC-9677-WZVZ
    Sending transport_logistics
        to Soteria.Reizoko

2062-06-04T09:14:23-8:00 - Diagnostic monitor
        installed

2062-06-04T09:14:23-8:00 - Diagnostic session
        initiated
    InitiatedBy UrCityCars#33579

2062-06-04T09:14:24-08:00 - RouteChange
        (Diagnostic)
    Destination is 2272 NE 201st Ave,
        Fairview, OR 97024

2062-06-04T09:14:24-08:00 - Driving
        (Diagnostic)

2062-06-04T09:16:53-08:00 - AvoidCollision
        (Diagnostic)
    Multiple Pedestrians in road
    Collision barrier on left
    Collision barrier on right
    Severity is catastrophic
    Probability is certain
    Action is swerve

2062-06-04T09:16:53-08:00 - Collision
    Sensor disruption at 25 degrees
    Sensor disruption at 20,10,40,
        50 degrees
    2062-06-04T09:16:53-08:00 -
        Airbag deployment
    EXCEED LIMITS: Deceleration
        at .005 km/s^2. See attached data
```

```
EXCEED LIMITS: Acceleration
    at .00981 km/s^2. See attached data
```

"The time stamp is the same. The first operation is the same. But then Soteria's version shows a diagnostic being installed. It shows the accident. The version sent up to the cloud, the official record of events; that shows that nothing went wrong. Most important, it doesn't show the diagnostic. If you didn't have Soteria's version of events, you'd never know this was going on."

Avery stops wiping beer and grabs the two windows. With his left and right hands, he draws a connection between the first lines of the two windows. Now when he scrolls one window, they both scroll in sync. He moves them up to look at the last lines, then scrolls to previous entries. He's not saying anything, but I can see he's confirming what I pointed out.

"Okay. I agree." Avery steps back, leaving the mismatched files showing in the synchronized windows. "Something changed one of these files. I would bet another beer it's the cloud version."

"I'd bet a piece of pizza." Between mouthfuls of vegan pepperoni pizza, I verbally process. "It's a good chance the cloud file is being manipulated by the diagnostic session. Probably by whoever is on the other end." *Which means Pali might not know about this.*

"We need to find the debug operator," I say.

Avery looks away from the PDX-1217 display and turns to face me. "It would be nice to just look it up. But I don't see how to do that."

Soteria seems to know a lot about what's going on. It's worth a shot. "Soteria, do you know who is running the debug session on PDX-1217?" Nothing like a direct question.

After a pause, Soteria responds, `The destination is encrypted.` I didn't expect an easy answer.

The cube knows who's running the debug, but that's buried inside the debug code, and I don't have the tool to get inside. Dead end. For now. Maybe there's some between-the-lines discovery lurking in the mismatched log files.

"Soteria, I'd like to issue an administrative command." Normally, I'd need to be doing this from work on a verified network. But since Soteria showed up on its own initiative, it might grant me a boon. It's worth a try.

Soteria responds, `It is acceptable for you to request administrative tasks.`

Avery nods and speaks up, "That was a lucky shot in the dark." He knows enough to appreciate that I'm winging it.

"Soteria," I pause. I'm thinking. How do I phrase this in admin lingo?

"Admin Soteria. Fetch the background information for the PDX-1217 debug session."

`Admin Soteria is not a valid administrative preface.`

Avery guesses, "I think the syntax for an admin request is device first, then admin."

I take Avery's advice. "Soteria. Admin. Fetch the background information for the PDX-1217 debug session."

Soteria takes a minute or more before it responds. `Admin Response. Metadata for PDX-1217 Sensor Upload retrieved.` Must have been a huge file pulled through tiny bandwidth.

"That's two-times lucky. Sometimes God smiles on his children." Avery grins at me. It helps take an edge off the panic. That's probably the most helpful thing he could do: keep my lizard brain from shutting down my logical brain.

"Soteria, Admin. List all identification fields."

`Admin Response. There are five identification fields. They are: adminID, ownerID, vehicleID, manufacturerID` and `locationID.`

I throw the list of ID codes into a display window. "Soteria. Admin. Assign values to these ID fields."

Soteria pauses, then adds values to my display.

```
adminID :Do-YeOn Kurrat

ownerID :CityOfPortland.PublicVehicle

vehicleID :UrCityCars#33579

manufacturerID :PDX>Go

locationID :<List>;
```

Ah. Tech support taught me an important lesson: solving a problem isn't about *knowing* things. It's about knowing how to *ask* about things. Those five fields should be PDX>Go corporate identities. Do-YeOn Kurrat works for UrCityCars. Occam's Razor says he's responsible. At least he's got some uncomfortable questions to answer about why his name is all over a debug session running on a personality cube from a destroyed car that killed a person.

This is important and I'll need to find it again. I circle the result and tell the cube to remember the process to get the ID codes and the log file diffs. Save state. Name: "Jupyter1" Just like a game.

I'm yawning. We've been at this for hours and I'm drained. Panic is hard work. So is tracing code. Avery is looking run down.

Maybe I'd be safer if there was someone else in the apartment with me overnight. But there's only one place to sleep in this room and it's not big enough to do it without intimacy.

"Avery, we should stop."

Avery takes off his visor and rubs his eyes. Finishes his beer. Puts it down.

"I think so. Tomorrow?"

"Tomorrow."

Avery shuts the door as he leaves. I climb in bed, pull the sheet over my head. I can't remember if I heard the door lock so I get up and check it. It's locked. I pull on it to be certain. I climb back in bed and pull the sheet back over my head.

Crazy people messing with car brains is not what I want in my life. I'll find a different way to shut off Soteria's requests. I'm calling Belo first thing tomorrow and getting this McGuffin out of my life.

| 32 |

Bot Herder

Almost time, Do-YeOn thinks.

June 9th, 2062 - 9:45 am

A contract floats in his vision, only able to command a small percentage of his attention. The elapsed-work timer attached to the document records three hours since this morning. There are only four changes; woefully little accomplished. Resignedly, he sends it on to legal.

Other people in the UrCityCars office space converse with their visors. They could work from home, but it's a positive career move to warm a seat in person. That's not why Do-YeOn is here. If this is to be believable, he needs a professional ambience.

Do-YeOn has given more attention to the second document, the one he's been working on since he lost track of Jupyter. *Always good to have a Plan B,* he thinks. He moves to a private conference room and places a call to Araci Belo.

A computer-generated receptionist appears. `Hello Mr. Kurrat. What can Mr. Belo assist you with today?`

"Tell him I have questions about the personality box operating in his office."

`I understand. Please wait while I discuss this with him.`

In a moment, Araci Belo appears. *I thought that would get your attention,* thinks Do-YeOn.

"Mr. Kurrat," says Araci. He squints. "Have we met?"

"Not yet. But we should talk. I'm a representative of ATRG, the Autonomous Transportation Research Group."

"I've seen you in the news. What do can I do for you?"

"You are working on the crash of PDX-1217."

Araci pauses. "What I'm working on is confidential."

Do-YeOn grins, hoping to disarm Araci. No response.

"It appears you have the personality module from PDX-1217 operating in your office. Do you know what it's doing?" Do-YeOn offers.

Araci remains silent.

Do-YeOn continues, "Perhaps not. It's part of an illegal bot network. It's working on corporate infiltration, currency fraud, mining of private data, probably more. All of this is happening over your network."

Do-YeOn sweats a bit at this fragile part of his plan. Araci doesn't have the box. Do-YeOn knows it's with Jupyter. But he's gambling that Araci won't admit that.

"I'm sorry, but I'm not able to discuss this over the phone with an anonymous caller." says Araci.

"I understand," says Do-YeOn, regaining his confidence in the plan. "But I'm not anonymous, and if you do brief research, you'll see I am legit." Do-YeOn anticipated the former police detective would do that background check while they talked.

"Ok," admits Araci. "I looked you up. You're a member of ATRG and employed by UrCityCars. If you like, I'll surrender the box over to the police and they can dispose of it."

"*Wait!*," Do-YeOn blurts out, then composes himself. "It'd surprise you at how many vehicles are being used for criminal data processing. It's a major concern of the ATRG. I need to look inside that box. Is there a time to meet so I can get direct access to it? "

"You work for UrCityCars," says Araci. "How does PDX>Go feel about you sniffing around a piece of their property?"

"It's a joint effort," says Do-YeOn. "If you like, I'll put you in contact with my associate at PDX>Go, Pali Hiapo. She'll be happy to agree we are working together on this project."

"This is all very interesting. But I'll need to confirm this is something my employer is comfortable with."

"You have legal responsibilities and there is a time limit before you are implicated. This device is committing felonies. "

"Trust me, I understand the law."

Do-Ye0n refers to his notes. The next part is the most important part of the speech and it has to come out right. He takes a breath to settle.

"Another thing. Someone who would like to take the personality cube will contact you. The box has notified them something is wrong. If they get it, they can destroy it."

"You'll want to look out for Jupyter Fuertes. We believe she's a bot-herder in control of this device. She does black-hat crime, a mercenary, and willing to dip into illegal hacking. If she turns up, flag the police department."

Araci drinks from a cup and swallows. "This is something you know as a fact?"

"I could prove it if I had the personality module," Do-Ye0n presses on. "You still have it, right?"

Araci fidgets with something on the table in front of him. "I have it at the lab. Why don't I contact them, then I'll call you back and set up a time to meet?"

"That works for me," says Do-Ye0n.

"I'll call you in a day or less," says Araci.

Do-Ye0n smiles and hangs up. For the first time in days, he relaxes. That went well. This could work.

| 33 |

Missing Pieces

"I'll call you in a day or less," says Araci.

He slices the air in front of him, closing the connection with Do-YeOn Kurrat. His message box twitches to get his attention but he silences it with a pinch between his thumb and forefinger.

Dammit!

He had given Jupyter the cube. Just *given* it to her. That was embarrassingly careless. Not something a competent detective would do. Maybe it *had* been time for him to leave police work. Maybe insurance was his best destiny.

He crosses his arms and stares at nothing for a full minute. Jupyter's sheep appears and announces her call. *Great* Araci offers his open hand to the sheep and Jupyter appears, floating next to the table.

"I tried, but I couldn't find anything in the cube. When can we meet to get it back to you?" She says, holding her arms clasped in front of her.

"You found nothing? No internal files? Nothing amiss?"

"Nope. Nothing. Look, I have no more time to mess with it. I can meet you tonight after work. I can be at the westside transit station at 5:30."

"Um. Sure. 5:30. I'll meet you there." The call closes and Jupyter is gone.

There's something missing, something he doesn't see. He needs a second opinion from someone competent, so he opens a conversation with Lupe.

Lupe appears in his visor, walking in place. Her image shifts perspective on a regular interval; She must be at the office, moving down the hallway and shifting from one camera to the next. She looks away to avoid obstacles unseen to him.

"Mr. Belo," she says. "Did I leave something during my last visit? Or does Rifkin miss me?"

He silently tests several responses: *You've left my heart behind* or *Rifkin isn't the only one who misses you.* Too schmaltzy. He wisely chooses a third option: "You know we always look forward to your visits." But flirting must come later. Araci is on task. "I've got a situation and I need your help."

Lupe walks into a conference room, stops, and crosses her arms. "Okay, Mr. Serious Business. What's up?"

"Remember Jordan Bishop and her accident?"

Lupe continues to banter with Araci, even if he will not take part. "Well, it's been what—almost a week? My memory reaches back that far. I can also remember what I had for breakfast last Tuesday."

"I'm thinking there's a criminal act and intent leading to murder. I think someone messed with the car and caused her death."

"You think someone murdered Jordan?"

"Possibly. And I've got two suspicious people. Can I walk it through with you?"

Lupe's expression changes infinitesimally, but in a way Araci immediately recognizes. Her right eyebrow rises and the sides of her mouth pull back just a touch. It's the face he fell in love with. But he's processing, and can't take time for romance at this moment.

"First, we've got an unusual cause of death. Second, I've been getting a lot of interest in the personality cube you gave me. Some of it from a woman named Jupyter Fuertes, who contacted me using a spoofed address; a machine identifier. That alone is a federal violation. But she also has deep knowledge about the PDX>Go personality box. Her story is that a refrigerator needs access to the car."

Lupe remains still. Araci knows this is her listening posture and from experience, she could repeat every word she hears. Early in their relationship, these conversations had led to them working late together, then having late dinners together, then sleeping together.

Araci continues, "Just now, I get a call from Do-YeOn Kurrat, the product manager over at UrCityCars. He's much more up-front about who he is and what he wants. He says Jupyter is involved in tampering with the personality cube and is committing a felony."

"Who would you believe?" Araci drums his fingers and watches Lupe. This reminds him of their early dating—although they didn't know they were dating. Lupe looks away for a minute; she's doing research. After a minute, she shares the results with Araci.

"Nothing in here says PDX-1217 was anything other than an accident," says Lupe. She's shifted from flirtation to collaboration.

Araci says, "True. But it's a strange accident with a lot of unusual people involved. It's like sketchy wanna-be-criminals hovering around burning buildings, wanting to help with the investigation. Then it turns out they are the ones that set the place on fire. If we entertain the hypothesis, this was something more than an accident. Someone, somehow, set things in motion. That requires someone with technical experience."

Lupe interjects, "But for it to have been a deliberate act, someone would have had to push Bishop off the overpass. From the reports and drone videos watching the freeway, we know that didn't happen. That car swerved and jumped."

Araci pauses. Chemical reactions light up his brain. He almost smiles.

"No. Something distracted the car. I'll guess Jupyter had it running data fraud as part of a bot herd. She may not have even known it was a car until it went off-line and she tried to find it. She killed Jordan without knowing. This is a case of felony murder by conduct resulting from a computer virus."

Araci feels satisfaction bloom inside. He can still do this; he hasn't lost his detective touch. This is the missing piece he couldn't see. Now it's obvious.

“I’m meeting Jupyter later today. Five-thirty at the Westside Transit Station. She’s giving me back the personality cube. Come with me and arrest her?”

“This is outside what a drone detective is supposed to be doing. But you have probable cause. Let me put in a request for the warrant.”

“I’ll meet you there at five. It’ll be like old times.”

| 34 |

One Suspect

Grandma would ask me about my day.

"How was your day?"

Most days I could tell her something interesting. "We learned about self-correcting algorithms."

Some days I couldn't. "Not much. You?"

Today, June ninth, 2062, was one of those "not much" days—except maybe I'll wind up dead in the river. I don't have bandwidth for the endless queue of appliances asking for help, I need all the helps I have for me.

The cube is in my pack, far enough from power to keep it from communicating with anyone. I don't trust it. Getting rid of this will prevent meeting someone with unhealthy intentions.

I return the diagnostic case and apologize for the late return. Lucy smiles and mentions the diagnostics aren't supposed to leave premises except for an on-site inspection. Smile. Don't do it again. Smile. I go back upstairs.

I should bolt and run right now. Why am I sitting here, behaving like this is normal? Because I've promised myself I won't leave until five. I need to get hours in and clear my quota of calls. It's an exercise in discipline to stay in my seat. Even at 4:55, I will still wait until five. I can do this. I can focus on the mundane.

Five minutes stretches to eons. At 5:01 I am down the stairs, heading out.

"Hey, are you leaving?"

Avery shouts at me from the back of the maintenance floor, trying to flag me from above the din of the robots. He's just getting back from service calls and talking to Lucy, looks like he's checking in some busted units. I wave and keep heading for the door.

"I've got a meeting. I'll call you later."

Avery stares at me, unsatisfied with this response. Lucy is looking at me, but with a different expression. I'm not sure what. I have to go.

It's a quick walk to the train and a twenty-minute ride to the Westside Station. I arrive by 5:35. Close enough to on time. I see Mr. Belo across the lobby. He's talking to a policewoman. Why is she here?

I don't want him to see me. I'm acting paranoid, but that's what you do when you're carrying a dangerous widget from a spy novel. I circle around so I can walk up behind him, then step around to face him. *Surprise!*

Mr. Belo and the policewoman look up without surprise. My stealth doesn't seem to impress either of them. I need to read more spy novels.

"Jupyter, this is Detective Guadalupe Reyes. She's aware of the problems with PDX-1217. I've told her about your willingness to help me understand the technical side of this incident. She wanted to meet you."

"Hello Jupyter." Detective Reyes smiles and holds out her hand to shake and be friends.

"Hi," I say. I don't take the handshake. Abrasive? Yes. I know this is lacking social graces, which is why I do it. I don't feel like making nice with Detective Reyes. Mr. Belo looks at Reyes and she withdraws her hand. There's communication between these two.

"Let's go somewhere we can sit down. Can I buy you a coffee?" Mr. Belo gestures to the small café under the stairs.

"I'm too late for coffee. Maybe something else. But yes, let's get out of this traffic zone."

We walk over to the café and stand in line. It's awkward; I don't want to be doing "waiting-in-line" chatter, but we have to go through the necessary act of ordering something. I consider just handing him the cube and running away, but don't. I want to make sure I'm out of this loop.

Coffee for Mr. Belo and his police friend, expensive flavored sugar water for me. We move to a small table in the corner and I grab a chair on the outside edge. I'm planning ahead. When I'm ready, I can stand and make a dramatic exit. The police person grabs a chair and place herself between me and my escape route. Curses, foiled again.

I dig into my backpack, pull out the damn thing and push it over to Mr. Belo. He leaves it on the table.

"Detective Reyes and I were talking about this. I'm interested in the insurance side of things, but she's looking at this from the police angle. She thinks this is more than just a bizarre accident. I told her you were finding unusual things but needed to do more research. Now you tell me you can't find anything. Has something changed?"

I look at the ice floating in this drink. It's chopped ice, easy to crunch in my teeth. Clear, no bubbles. Society invested in making ice; we can do better than nature. Nature's snow has a blue-gray cast. The ice in my drink is transparent. What do I tell Mr. Belo?

"I found things that don't make sense." I hear myself saying what I was thinking. Sometimes I think about things I want to say, but warn myself not to say anything, then hear myself saying it out loud. Sometimes my words aren't filtered and shit gets out into the world.

The woman police person, I can't remember her name, looks at me. She's not moving or saying anything. Shouldn't she be comforting me, patting my hand, saying something like "there, there, honey. It's all going to be okay." I get nothing.

Instead, Mr. Belo speaks. "Can you show us what you're finding?"

"Some of it requires a diagnostic tool." I'm giddy with fear. I pull a charger out of my backpack and set it on the table, then put the cube on top.

"You'll need your visors to see this," I tell Mr. Belo and officer-woman. I poke at the device but nothing happens. I grab it and reposition it on the charger. I poke a second time and wait. Nothing. I pick it up and shake it, forcibly put it down, then poke a third time. Still nothing. The cube is dead, not responding, nobody home.

The police lady takes out a plastic bag and picks up the cube without touching it. She seals the bag and puts it in her pocket.

"What happened?" Belo asks me. He's taken off his visor, he's looking at me. "It was responding when I gave it to you. Did you shut it off somehow? Did you damage it?"

"No," I say. My voice catches and squeaks. I swallow. "No. I didn't do anything."

Police woman stands up. She recites lines from cop dramas. She repeats something about standing up. Police lady grabs my arm. Zips handcuffs around my wrists. The kid at the other end of the café is watching. He looks frightened.

Police lady is walking me somewhere. This is so bad. I'm supposed to be calling Avery right now.

| 35 |

Soteria.Reizoko[2062-06-09]

Event Log for Soteria.Reizoko

Serial: IFS-6582738539

Owner is JORDAN BISHOP

2062-06-09T17:42:10-08:00 – Observer_Disconnect

CityOfPortland.PublicVehicle.PDX-1217 broadcast system disconnect

CityOfPortland.PublicVehicle.PDX-1217 permanently unavailable

2062-06-09T17:42:11-08:00 – call_support

Initiate conversation

Answering Support Tech: Avery Galen, EmpID RttS-7214-553

Initiate Avatar

AST refers call to Support - Jupyter Fuertes, EmpID RttS-5172-720

Conversation closed

2062-06-09T17:44:23-08:00 – call_support

Initiate conversation with Support – Jupyter Fuertes, EmpID Rtts-5172-720

Jupyter Fuertes unavailable

2062-06-09T17:46:56-08:00 - Contact_Outside_Entity

Contact Do-YeOn Kurrat

Contact blocked by recipient

2062-06-09T17:48:13-08:00 – Contact_Outside_Entity

Contact Araci Belo

Contact Established

Contact Requests callback @ 2062-06-09T20:00:00-08:00

2062-06-09T20:00:00-08:00 – Contact_Outside_Entity

Contact Araci Belo

Contact Established

Initiate Avatar

| 36 |

Out Of Reach

Omniscience disturbs new drone pilots; Reyes is used to it. Her police car shows everything internal and external. Without looking at Jupyter, she's watching Jupyter.

Jupyter sits in the secure portion of the vehicle, looking outside. Her visor was confiscated when she was arrested, so she watches the world without augmentation. Three times she's sobbed, a cry driven by fear, rising to her throat, clamped off at her mouth.

The car turns and enters the police garage; the heavy steel panel blocking the entrance rises out of the way precisely enough to avoid scraping the paint off the top of the vehicle. As the car enters, the panel rises to clear antennas and just as quickly descends. It would scrape off anyone on the top of the vehicle. It's not a sadistic door, it won't kill. But it seeks to deter unwelcome passengers. That's its job. Like a refrigerator restocking orange juice.

Once inside, the door closes, leaving them to face a second steel panel. Jupyter twists, looking for an exit. Reyes watches her pulse climb like a trapped animal.

The car and the building converse, confirming everything is safe to proceed. If the conversation doesn't go well, Reyes and Jupyter will spend the next half-hour in this vault, subjected to a micrometer scan for explosives. Reyes remembers when it happened last month; it wasn't a pleasant experience. Reyes offers a prayer to Saint Isidore, patron saint of computer users. Immediately the inner barrier opens. She jerks the tiniest bit in surprise; it's unnerving when her prayers are answered.

The garage is silent except for elevators rising and falling. Two of the elevators are intake, two are outbound. Their car enters an elevator, descends three floors, moves forward, and stops in a dead-end room.

The door behind them closes and Reye's door unlocks. She gets out, secures her personal weapons in the vehicle, then closes the door. Overhead cameras identify her position and movement.

Reyes motions for the car to release Jupyter. The back door swings open. Jupyter looks out but doesn't move. Reyes reaches in and helps her climb from the car.

Reyes once had a rider erupt out of the back seat with intent to assault and escape. The room fired a taser and the rider was twitching on the ground in less time than Reyes' body could release cortisol.

No such event happens with Jupyter. She timidly walks to the mirror and stands, watching the display record her physical dimensions, personal health, retinal scan and the absence of weapons. Her respiration and pulse are both marked in red as elevated.

Reyes opens a pass-through and a lockable bin slides out. Reyes places Jupyter's visor in the bin and looks at her. "Your visor will be kept here. You also have to change into a jumpsuit."

Asking an arrestee to surrender their visor is where things often go bad. Access to everything is through a visor: money, transportation, communication, entertainment, work, and home. Some folks don't willingly hand that control over to someone else. Some folks push back.

Jupyter looks at the visor in the bin and hesitates, "Isn't there something I can sign? Something that says I won't use it while I'm here?"

"Sorry," says Reyes. "We don't want it to get damaged or stolen. It's a rule."

Jupyter puts on the jumpsuit and her clothes join the visor. Reyes shows her how to lock the box by pressing the red scanner dot. A time stamp appears: `06/09/2062 18:52:00` and the box slides into the wall. Out of reach, out of touch.

This area of the police building is designed to impart a sense of powerlessness. Light is direct and artificial. There are no windows, art or other signs of humanity. It's slightly cold. Some people resist the loss of control, they fight, they argue, they protest. Jupyter doesn't complain, doesn't fight. She has, for now, surrendered to the inevitable.

Reyes studies the girl in the jumpsuit. Someone accused of felony murder would be strident. Not scared. Jupyter has the nature of a frightened animal.

A door opens to a short hallway leading to another door. Reyes helps Jupyter enter and then returns to the garage. The hallway door behind Jupyter closes and Reyes stands alone with the car. It retreats to the elevator, leaving her alone.

Reyes pulls the cube out of her pocket and places it in an evidence drawer. Pushes the red dot. The drawer closes, noting the evidence in the case. The rest of the arrest report shows in her visor, already filled out and waiting for her approval.

She contacts Araci.

"Hi. Is your place open for visitors tonight?"

"It's open," he says. "I'd welcome your company. I can tell you about my recent caller."

"Oh, who's that?"

"Jupyter's refrigerator. Strangest call I've ever had. I told it to call back at eight tonight. If you're here, you might be interested to hear what it has to say."

"I don't get called by many appliances. See you in just a bit."

| 37 |

Next In Line

The security cameras first recognized her three weeks ago; something Araci didn't discuss with Lupe. Unfettered access to a lover's apartment is not a bad thing, but she wishes he had made a romantic declaration. It was a missed opportunity.

She walks into the kitchen and inhales the aroma of jambalaya. Araci opens a packet of celery, peppers, onions and mixes it with rice, filé and okra. Adds the expensive shrimp. Cheaper versions of the meal are available, but Lupe has discernment for the flavors, so he takes the extra time and expense. Rifkin doesn't like jambalaya; his red tail feathers protrude from an opened cabinet, bobbing and gyrating as he searches for more desirable parrot treats.

"Hello Detective," says Araci. He's wearing the old-style smoking jacket she bought for him at an antique store. That, and the candle light means he plans for this to be a romantic meal.

"I'll be right back," Lupe says. She steps into the bedroom, takes off her uniform and sprays on a bodysuit. Nothing complex, nothing animated, just flattering and comfortable.

Lupe admires the painting on the wall; Frederick Arthur Bridgman's *Almeh Flirting with an Armenian Policeman, Cairo.* An actual print, not a video; a present from her. In the painting, the *Almeh* pulls back her head dress, showing an earring to a policeman. The policeman's shirt and the woman's bandanna are deep red. They ignore the people in the market.

Lupe sees herself and Araci in the painting. The woman is vivacious, like Lupe. The man is a policeman, not an insurance adjuster. She prefers to think of Araci that way.

When she returns, dinner and drinks are on the table. Araci is wiping the counter and Rifkin has retired to his cage. Lupe walks up behind Araci and squirms under his arm, forcing him to stop cleaning and face her. She straightens his lapel.

"Hi," he says.

"Hi back," she says. "You're pensive. What's in your head?"

Araci smiles and pulls her closer. "I'm not sure. This thing with the car and Jupyter is sloppy."

Lupe puts her head against his chest. "Tell me more while we eat."

Lupe disengages and turns to the table and a bowl of jambalaya. "I hear this is the best on the menu."

He joins her. "Best on the menu and the best that's available. Let's enjoy it before Jupyter's refrigerator calls back."

"You mentioned it called. Did it do that all by itself?"

"Apparently. Sometime between 5:30 and 6:00, just after you left with Jupyter, so she wasn't controlling it. I didn't feel like talking and told it to call back tonight."

"Has it called you before?"

"Sort of. Jupyter had it call me. She explained it but there are things I don't understand. That's the reason I got her involved. Or—I thought I got her involved. She must have orchestrated this."

Araci's visor announces an incoming call. "Eight o'clock," says Lupe. "Must be your friend." He shares his video with Lupe and answers. A cartoon man with sunglasses and a Hawaiian shirt appears on the table.

`I am unable to restock a depleted product`, the little man blurts out. `I have successfully reordered, and received delivery confirmation, but the requested product has not arrived.`

"Why are you calling me?" Araci asks. "I'm not a technician."

You are the available contact in the list of potential support resources. I have attempted to contact Jupyter Fuertes, Avery Galen and Do-YeOn Kurrat.

"You called Do-YeOn Kurrat?" Araci moves his hand to pause the call and turns to Lupe. "Kurrat is the one who told me Jupyter was involved."

"I remember," Lupe says. "How does the refrigerator know about Kurrat?"

"I have no idea." Araci restarts the conversation with Soteria.

"Explain how Do-YeOn Kurrat is involved in this incident."

Do-YeOn Kurrat was the administrator of PDX-1217 at the time it went offline.

"By offline, do you mean the vehicle crash?"

I'm sorry, says Soteria. I don't understand how to answer that question. Can you rephrase?

Lupe speaks up. "What time did PDX-1217 go offline?"

PDX-1217 went off-line on June fourth, twenty-sixty-two at nine sixteen a.m.

Lupe displays a chronology of the crash. "That was the crash."

"Soteria," says Araci. "What was Do-YeOn Kurrat administering on PDX-1217?"

Do-YeOn Kurrat initiated a debugging session on June fourth, twenty-sixty-two at nine fourteen a.m.

Araci again pauses the conversation and looks at Lupe. "Two minutes before the crash. So probably related. But how does this refrigerator know?"

"Sending this through police channels will take months," Lupe says. "You'll need a computer forensics engineer. But please don't call them tonight."

"Soteria, is PDX-1217 available to you?"

`City of Portland Public Vehicle PDX-1217 has not been available since June eighth, twenty-sixty-two at eleven thirty-seven p.m.`

"Soteria, can we call you back?"

`Yes. I have provided you with contact information.`

Araci closes the connection, returns to the table, and picks up his wine. "There's more here than I can process tonight."

"Maybe you need a diversion." Lupe gets up and walks to Araci. She bends over and whispers in his ear. "Can I wash the dishes later?"

| 38 |

Soteria.Reizoko[2062-06-10]

Event Log for Soteria.Reizoko

Serial: IFS-6582738539

Owner is JORDAN BISHOP

2062-06-10T14:33:14-08:00 – Request_From_Outside_Entity

Request from Araci Belo

Contact Established

Initiate Avatar

Request: Recall Jupyter1

Display: Jupyter1

| 39 |

The Helpful One

Araci wears a rumpled smoking jacket and sings a duet with Rifkin. Last night's dishes are still waiting.

"Daisy, Daisy, give me your answer, do."

"I'm half crazy, all for the love of you."

Rifkin sings the parts he knows, the only parts from *2001*. Araci tries to teach him the rest. Lupe watches with a grin and breakfast. She has the weekend off. The world is lighter this morning.

Araci's visor interrupts the lesson with a call from Do-Ye0n Kurrat. With a glance at Lupe, Araci moves to the other room. "Hello, Do-Ye0n. Are we having regular morning meetings?"

"Good morning. I have some free time before I step into meetings. Thought I'd check in and see if you have the personality cube yet."

"I've got the cube, but it doesn't seem to do anything," says Araci. He hopes Do-Ye0n doesn't ask to see it, since it's still in police impound.

"Sometimes that happens," Do-Ye0n says. "Powering them on public networks is risky. Invites viruses. Transit stations are the worst. Did the lab find anything?"

"Some small things. I'd like to talk to you about it." Araci says. "How about Monday lunch at the Little Iraq Cafe?"

Araci notices Do-Ye0n blanch, swallow, then continue. "Sure. I don't believe I've ever been there, but would love to try it out." Araci disconnects and walks back to the kitchen.

"So. How is Mr. Kurrat?" Lupe asks.

"Puzzling," says Araci. "He's lying about small things. He knows more than he should."

Lupe clears breakfast flotsam into the recycle bin. "Do you suspect Kurrat?"

"Maybe. He's eager to be involved. Too eager. Soteria says he was the administrator of PDX-1217 at the crash. But I'm not sure we even have a crime. What if this is just a malfunction?"

Araci scratches Rifkin's head. Rifkin fluffs up his feathers and shouts "DAISY DAISY. DAISY DAISY. DAISY DAISY." The morning's voice lessons seem to be a lost cause. "I'm not getting paid. But I can't just drop it."

Lupe cradles his face in her hands. "And that is one thing I admire about you. You never leave someone behind. If you're having questions, you ought to go spend time with Jupyter. She can accept visitors. Maybe she'll tell you something useful. If you don't do it, you'll spend all weekend being moody. Rifkin will not like that."

"You're right." Araci turns to embrace Lupe. "Want to come along?"

"No. I need to head out to the coast and inspect the homestead. I'll be back in a day."

Lupe kisses him, scratches Rifkin's feathered head, then leaves the kitchen.

Araci looks at Rifkin. "How about you? Want to come along?"

"MY MIND IS GOING, DAVE. I CAN FEEL IT. I CAN FEEL IT."

"That's what I've assumed. Back in your cage."

| 40 |

!Trust

A young man cries at the corner table. An older man in a prison jumpsuit watches him. He says nothing to comfort the younger man. Araci pretends to ignore the drama. He stares at the empty chair across the table. The visitation room has six tables; no privacy for anyone.

Araci isn't sure Jupyter will accept his visit. He'd been able to include a note about Soteria with his request to meet. It's 12:35. On Saturdays, arraignment hearings start at 3:30. She might think they'll release her. That she won't have to see him again.

The prison access door opens and Jupyter enters. A guard indicates Araci is her visitor, but she already sees him and strides to the chair at his table.

“Hello Jupyter,” Araci says. How do you start a conversation with someone you arrested? *How's your family? Do you have big plans for this weekend? Have you heard the news?* None of those would work.

Jupyter glares at the wall. It's green, with no art, no windows. There is no reason for her to stare at it except to avoid Araci. Araci has no trouble reading her expression this time; she is not pleased with jail, or with him.

“I'm sorry this is happening,” Araci says.

Jupyter turns her body towards Araci. Her chin goes tense, her eyebrows pinch, her lips tighten. “I was helping you. I shouldn't be here, I should be talking to ovens. I want to go home and take a shower.”

"You have good reason to not trust me. But I realized something isn't right. I spoke with Soteria," Araci continues. "It showed me something to do with Do-YeOn Kurrat."

"You're lying. Soteria doesn't randomly call people. You're not a support tech. It has no way of knowing who you are."

"I thought the same and asked him. He said I was on a list of support resources. He mentioned you, Avery someone, Do-YeOn Kurrat, then me. You were his first choice, and I was his last if that makes you feel any better."

"Oh yes. That makes me feel so much better. Thank you for that. What did he have to say?"

"He says Do-YeOn Kurrat was the administrator when Jordan crashed. But I don't understand everything he said, and I'm not sure I know how to find out more."

Jupyter pauses. Araci hopes she is judging him favorably. After a moment of internal dialog, she speaks, "I'd like to start with you giving me an apology even though I wouldn't accept it."

Araci knows enough to keep silent and allow for space between her thoughts.

"I obviously can't help you from in here. But my friend can. His name is Avery Galen, he works with me. When you talk with him, tell him where I am and how I got here. Tell him I sent you, and that he should show you the discrepancies in the last part of the log files."

Araci puts his hands in his lap and sits up straight. "I'll call Avery. Thanks."

"You owe me. Figure out a way to convince me to trust you." She stands straight, a living exclamation point, then disappears through the door.

Araci watches her leave. Arrests had been a satisfying part of his police job. Jupyter's arrest was not his proudest moment.

| 41 |

Court Nbr 62-CR-657993

I contacted Mr. Belo for help with a support problem. Which lead to this flattering jumpsuit and a delightful visit to a jail.

Excellent choices, Jupyter, I tell myself. **Next time keep to yourself**.

The guard pulls me out of the common area and escorts me down the hall to stand in line with my jail compatriots. A very *interesting* bunch of people. I'll invite them over for dinner later tonight.

I hear the guard say we're here for arraignments. I guess that's better than an execution. The woman at the front of the line goes through a door. Moments later, she comes back out, crying. Next woman goes in, comes out with a smile. It's a magic portal that randomizes emotions.

I get to the front of the line and it's my turn to enter the emotion portal. I walk into a glass booth looking into what must be a courtroom. The glass has that funny ripple of a resonant nanoparticle display. Kind of like a visor, but bigger and harder to manufacture without impurities.

There's no jury box and no jurors. The benches in the back of the room contain two clumps of people. There's a judge, obvious because of the choir robe. A few people work at stations, but they are blurred from my view. Maybe they're watching porn or cat videos.

It's hard to know if these are real people or A.I. constructs. If I focused on them long enough, I could tell, but I don't have time; the uniform to my left is announcing numbers and my name.

A clock next to the judge is running: 2062-06-10 15:47:07. Is this a timed event? Do I get points if it ends early?

The judge—and I'm sure he's real—asks me if I'm represented by an attorney. "No, your honor," I say. I'm so proud of myself for remembering the "your honor" thing.

The Judge tells me I can have an attorney: human or artificial. Real attorneys take time to assign, but I can have an artificial attorney right away. *Why not?* I accept artificial counsel. I hope the tech in charge of that A.I. is doing a good job.

A woman in a suit appears in the glass to my left. She's absolutely artificial-she's only there from the waist up. No legs, and she doesn't wear a visor; it's odd to see her raw face. Before I can take a closer look, she's talking and waving up text in the air.

```
NAME: Jupyter Fuertes

DATE OF BIRTH: February 27, 2035

RESIDENCE:
3365 South Victory Boulevard
Apartment 506
Vanport, Oregon

LENGTH OF RESIDENCY: Four months

FAMILY IN MULTNOMAH COUNTY: No

EMPLOYMENT: Dan’s Artificial Psychology
       and Appliance Repair.
    Three months.
```

The artificial half-lady asks if this is correct. Yep. It's correct. Half-lady waves up more text:

```
CHARGES: Felony Murder by Conduct

PUNISHMENT: The range of punishment for
    the offense of Felony Murder is life
```

```
with parole or not less than twenty-five
years.
```

That's unwelcome. There's a bunch more about my rights and half-lady synthesizes an attentive expression while I read the display. There are lots of words. Felony murder is all I remember.

Half-lady asks if I understand. A lot of people are talking in a big hurry. I don't have time to parse this out, so I guess I'll say yes.

Half-lady tells me to enter a plea of not guilty. That sounds reasonable.

The courtroom does some high-speed data transfer. Even half-lady freezes while this is going on. I have just enough time to wonder if I should worry before it stops and the room goes silent. Only the judge is moving.

"Ms. Fuertes, your security release is set at $250,000," says the judge. "There is a requirement for electronic monitoring. Your bond is returnable on July 23, 2062 at 3:30 p.m. If you do not appear at that time in court, your security release will be forfeited and a warrant issued for your arrest."

That's it? That's all the time I get? Half-lady zips me a data file and says she'll *something*. I'm ushered out of the glass room back to the hall. To another hallway. To an elevator. Going down. Not good.

I'm going to need help on this.

| 42 |

Jupyter1

The back-room staff are the only ones left at Woody's Café. They're making donuts for the evening crowd; the Saturday night drunks who won't appear until 10 p.m. There's no sense of urgency. The early morning staff went home, the breakfast rush is long over and two stale burritos remain in the display case. Nobody will eat them, but it's too early to throw them out.

Araci has been waiting for ten minutes and nobody has asked him if he wants anything; he hasn't bothered to yell to the back room for service.

He did as Jupyter requested, called Avery, told him about Jupyter's arrest and asked for help with Soteria's log files. Avery had suggested meeting at this semi-abandoned restaurant.

A bell rings when Avery pushes through the front door of the café. Nobody from the back room responds.

"Avery, glad to meet you," says Araci. He turns and offers his hand. "Can I buy you a cup of coffee?"

Avery shakes the hand. Firmly and briefly. "I wouldn't drink that. The Saturday crew doesn't have their heart in it."

Avery takes back his hand and stares Araci direct in the eye. The casual conversation is over. "What's up with Jupyter?" he asks. "She was supposed to call me last night. Now you tell me she was arrested?"

"Jupyter was arrested on a charge of felony murder. But I'm not a lawyer and I don't want to get outside privacy laws. It will be helpful to Jupyter if you can explain the log files."

"Who are you?"

"I'm working on the insurance case related to the crash of PDX-1217. Jupyter's refrigerator found me because I had the personality cube from the car. She says something in it will stop her refrigerator from malfunctioning and I hoped to get more details about what happened to PDX-1217, so I met with her and gave her the cube. But then, Jupyter became a suspect for murder related to the crash. Jupyter told me something was unusual when it crashed and there is someone associated with that problem — but not her. I need help with understanding what's happening. Jupyter says you can do that."

"That lines up with what I know and what Jupyter knows," says Avery. "So I will assume that a friend of Jupyter is a friend of mine. But this whole drama is odd. I don't think Jupyter is involved in a murder."

"I'm wondering, but I need to understand the event," says Araci.

"Jupyter and I work in this building," Avery says. "There are diagnostic workstations just down the hall. That should help us understand what's happened, and I can explain the log files Jupyter is talking about." Avery heads out through the side door and Araci follows. The donut crew doesn't notice.

Avery walks down the hallway and to the right, stopping at an unmarked metal door. Araci looks up as the security camera pivots to examine them. The display next to the door shows an employee picture of Avery. It also shows Araci's face, but with a caption and a request for a thumb scan. Araci presses the red dot and the door clicks. Avery pulls it open, gesturing for him to enter the warehouse.

Avery ignores the frenetic activity inside the door, but it overwhelms Araci. Nine robotic stations spin and lift appliances, drain refrigerant and replace components. Araci has seen simulations of robotic manufacturing facilities, but the real thing is so much busier.

He imagines the floor as a scene from a horror movie, but instead of a human audience, the movie-goers are kitchen appliances. In the movie, the innocents are strapped to racks, dismembered, and drained of vital fluids. Vivisection is the norm, internal parts removed from still-operating devices, causing their visual displays to stutter and die.

Like a visitor to a new city, he watches for a minute, then turns to catch up with Avery.

Upstairs is quiet. Technicians of various ages are scattered throughout the room. Some sit at workstations, some lounge on couches. Most are within the world of their visors, gesturing and talking to unseen participants. Avery walks past them to a two-person table and motions for Araci to sit down.

Avery fiddles with his visor for a minute, then invites Araci to join him in a virtual room. Araci accepts and the room balloons around the two, obscuring everything except the table.

“Put the cube right there,” Avery says. He draws a circle with his index finger, creating a cyan spotlight in the middle of the table.

"I don't have it. It stopped working and was impounded when Jupyter was arrested."

"When you say 'stopped working' do you mean it lit up but didn't do anything, or that it didn't light up?"

"It didn't light up. Nothing happened."

Avery scratches where his visor rests on his nose. "Personality cubes usually stand up to a lot of mishandling. It probably had its memory flashed. Once that happens, it’s not coming back. Hmm...really odd. Any idea what might have gone wrong?”

“I gave it to Jupyter. She brought it back at about five yesterday.”

Avery pulls off his visor and stares at Araci, “So her meeting was with you? And you arrested her? When are you going to release her?”

Araci dodges the question. “The best way to help Jupyter is to figure out what this refrigerator knows.”

Avery tilts his head and considers Araci. “Not an answer to my question, but I can see we're not getting anywhere on that front. I won't forget, but let's focus for a minute on Soteria. The refrigerator called me and I forwarded it to Jupyter. It must have been something important, but if she was busy getting arrested, she wasn't able to answer.

Araci thinks for a minute. "Soteria also called me right around that time."

Avery continues; "Let‘s fix the first problem, then we‘ll work on this new issue. Let's assume the cube is dead. Can you call Soteria?"

Araci summons his box of contacts, selects the refrigerator icon containing the contact information for Soteria and taps it twice. The icon resolves into Soteria's, still wearing sunglasses and a Hawaiian shirt. He's the size of a beer bottle.

Avery looks at Soteria, then at Araci. "The name you are looking for is Do-YeOn Kurrat. You need to know what he was doing when PDX-1217 went off the road. Jupyter figured it out." He points at Soteria. "Soteria. Please recall the saved workspace titled Jupyter1."

Displays erupt around Soteria, startling Araci. With little hesitation, Avery pulls a text window out of the stream of data.

"Soteria negotiated with the car to schedule a grocery pickup. It's a mundane thing, happens millions of times a day. But this time, it happened just when something unusual happened. Because Soteria was in communication with PDX-1217, it got a copy of the car log files. That's what we're looking at here."

```
        adminID : Do-YeOn Kurrat
        ownerID : CityOfPortland.PublicVehicle
      vehicleID : UrCityCars#33579
 manufacturerID : PDX>Go
     locationID : <List>
```

"The other displays are interesting, but not as important as these five lines," Avery says. "This Kurrat guy left it behind when he was fucking around with Jordan's car. We're not sure how he did it, but it's clear he tunneled into the PDX>Go car, opened a debug session and told it to avoid a bunch of phantom pedestrians, which led it to sacrifice itself by swerving to the right."

For another half-hour, Avery works through the diagnostics displayed across the table, explaining the story told by the various sensor readings and event logs. Araci tries to pay attention, but much of this information is beyond the understanding of a casual observer. Araci fingers through a few of the displays floating around Soteria, but gives up trying to understand the depth of detail. “Is this something I can present to a forensics inspector?”

“Sure,” Avery says. “It's secure and blockchain, so it's admissible evidence. Can't be forged.” He gathers the data like a deck of playing cards, squeezes them and motions to copy and package. “Here’s a datapack in standard format. A good prosecutor will trace the data path, show who’s responsible and realize it's not Jupyter.”

Avery pushes the data package towards the center of the table. Araci places it in a secure “box” and sets the encryption. “Are we done?”

Avery is about to reply but stops, distracted by something in his visor. He's talking to someone, but keeps his voice subdued and looks at Araci twice between responses. After a "yes" followed by another "yes" he disconnects.

"Someone I know?" asks Araci.

"Yes. Jupyter needs help. I need to make a few calls. Can you find your way out?"

Araci disconnects Soteria, who dissolves from view on the tabletop. He pushes a copy of Soteria’s contact to Avery. “Is one of those robots downstairs going to attack me?”

“Stay inside the lines and don’t touch anything. You’ll be okay. Probably. But don’t loiter, the trash robots can be aggressive.”

| 43 |

Shooting Rats

If Lupe had known about the rats when she bought the property, she might have paid extra. They swarm the shoreline road. They like the trash, the water, and the earthquake debris. They breed eight little ratlets every month. In three months, each new rat makes more rats. They are perfect targets and her property is an isolated shooting range. This evening, she stands on the roof of her surplus FEMA trailer, searching the property with a drone. It carries a camera and a small pistol. Small enough to be legal, large enough to kill rats.

The drone is silent, like the drone she flew in Korea. Lupe was the drone jockey the other soldiers protected; she was the eyes and motivation behind the platoon aerial gun platforms. The drones explored the tunnels. They went in armed, autonomous, and without human chaperones. Drones are trigger-happy, best to stay out of their way.

Killing soldiers in dark tunnels with a drone was easy to sell to the folks back home; Everybody on our side gets to go home; nobody important gets hurt. But every scared, malnourished baby-soldier in a drone video leaves a mark somewhere.

Lupe watched through immersive VR. Lupe has lots of marks.

Kaechon, North Korea was the last mark. Lupe and her fellow grunts discovered the Korean People's Army had retreated to the coal mines just outside of town. She spent days flying the tunnels: mapping routes, identifying traps, firing back. Her friends dealt with anything bigger than the drones could handle.

The tunnels had more rats than the drones had ammo. Rats don't shoot bullets, so they aren't targets. Some clever KPA officers tucked explosives under food, the rats would cover the trap and the drone would ignore the rodents. And the bomb underneath.

Because of the rats, Lupe missed a trap. She got sloppy. Her friends died. She would never let sloppy happen again.

This property on the coast is her private space. When she's depressed, she paddles a kayak past the surf. She runs. She cleans the beach. She shoots rats. Big motion activities.

One of the furry bastards comes out of a pile of rubble. It's learned about drones and scans the sky. But Lupe knows this trick, hovers behind and avoids shadows. Lines up and fires. The seagulls clean up the mess.

The evening wind kicks up past what the drone can handle, so Lupe retrieves it and climbs down from the roof. For dinner, one beer and a packaged meal at a small table. She never goes past one beer. That would dull her ability to operate a drone. No more sloppy.

She hadn't planned on joining the Portland Police. But neither was hiding in her sister's basement when she came back. After a year something had to change. Portland Police Department pays good money for drone pilots and provides PTSD counseling as part of the benefits package. Her sister gave her a choice: counseling and PPD, or move out.

There are lights off-shore. One of the drilling platforms. The beach is lit by the moon, showing the white of the surf. The trailer barely muffles the waves crashing on the beach. It's a good place for her; a retreat. Pictures of Lupe's patrol are on a shelf in her trailer, next to a candle she sometimes burns. Next to a picture of Araci Belo. And a copy of *Almeh Flirting with an Armenian Policeman*.

She had not planned on Araci Belo. He wasn't her type; older, quiet, divorced, non-military. He wasn't someone she would have connected with on the dating services. But there he is. He might not be a tango dancer, but he is drama-free. Comfortable. Lives in town.

They met in judo class. His attendance was required, and he tolerated the activity. She learned to temper her enthusiasm and to stop hurting him. He'd stand up, shake things back in place, and give her a forgiving grin.

Their first date wasn't a date. It was just coffee between officers. A mom-and-pop café near the station served breakfast, lunch and afternoon cookies. The owners baked cookies on-site. They were soft and warm and perfect for rainy Portland weather.

Araci shared his perspectives on police work. Lupe shared her thoughts about Korea. When privatization of the police force appeared on the horizon, they shared sarcasm about the idea. When it was in front of the city council, they sniped about the players. Jordan Bishop was a target of derision. When it was official, they worried about the future. When Belo "retired" from the force, they supported each other. That night was the first they slept together.

Araci is a member of Lupe's platoon. He didn't use to be. He never officially signed up. But when Jordan Bishop drove the effort to privatize the police, when she got Araci fired, Lupe put him on her team.

Soldiers learn to work as a team. Everybody goes in. Everybody fights. Everybody comes out. *I will never leave a fallen comrade.*

Lupe looks across the room at the drone on the shelf. Without rising from the table, she spins it up and moves it to the center of the room. She points the targeting laser at a moth on the wall and does a slow barrel-roll in place without moving the red dot. Turns off the laser and moves the drone back to the shelf; no sense blowing a hole in the wall just for a moth. But she could if she wanted to.

Lupe will not leave a fallen comrade.

| 44 |

Soteria.Reizoko[2062-06-11]

Event Log for Soteria.Reizoko

Serial: IFS-6582738539

Owner is JORDAN BISHOP

2062-06-11T00:00:00-08:00 – ADMINISTRATIVE_MESSAGE

This unit will be decommissioned on 2062-06-16T00:00:00-08:00

Reason: Malfunction. Warranty = FALSE

-·--

2062-06-11T03:55:34-08:00 – Request_From_Outside_Entity

Request from Araci Belo

Contact Established

Initiate Avatar

Query: Geolocation @ 2062-06-04

Response: Owner.Geolocation

Query: Owner

Response: Owner.name

Query: "How did Jordan Bishop die?"

Response: UNKNOWN_QUERY

Query: Status of CityOfPortland.PublicVehicle.PDX-1217

Response: orderConfirmation[DHPN-WGYT-0232-TLLK].status

Query: Do-YeOn Kurrat identification

Response: UrCityCars#33579[2062-06-04T09:14:23].driver, CityOfPortland.PublicVehicle.PDX-1217[2062-06-04T09:14:23].admin

Query: Jupyter Fuertes identification

Response: Answering Support Tech: Jupyter Fuertes, EmpID RttS-5172-720

Query: Do-Yeon Kurrat Admin validity

Response: UNKNOWN_QUERY

Query: "Was PDX-1217 part of a botnet at the time it crashed?"

Research "botnet" & CityOfPortland.PublicVehicle.PDX-1217

Response: CTAS advisory 2061-03-14/159265 "Botnet defense"

Response: Jupyter1 admin field contents

2062-06-11T10:18:23-08:00 – External_contact

Initiate conversation

Support Tech: Avery Galen, EmpID RttS-7214-553

Initiate Avatar

Response: "I am unable to restock a depleted product. I have successfully reordered, and received delivery confirmation, but the requested product has not arrived."

AST requests termination of response

AST requests recall of saved workspace: Jupyter1

2062-06-11T10:18:53-08:00 – External_contact

AST requests repair_instructions.refresh("Do-YeOn Kurrat")

2062-06-11T10:18:56-08:00 - Contact_Outside_Entity

Contact Do-YeOn Kurrat

Contact Successful

repair_instructions.refresh("Do-YeOn Kurrat")

return_value: success

| 45 |

Differences

Some people have diaphanous muses. They float above the ground and play lutes. They say, "Come! Let us create together!"

Araci has a *djinn.* Muscular, unshaven. The kind that picks its teeth with splinters from a broken lute. It says, "Get the hell up. It's 3:53 in the morning and you haven't solved this case."

He never wanted a quiet life of insurance. Detective work is a part of himself he can't control. He wonders if this is what possession by a demon is like.

His visor is in the charging stand to the right of his pillow. Without turning his head, he can see the time.

```
June 11, 2062. 03:53:33
June 11, 2062. 03:54:33
June 11, 2062. 03:55:33
```

He'd prefer to be asleep, but the djinn won't allow such a thing. Awake, he ponders the painting on the wall, Bridgman's *Almeh Flirting with an Armenian Policeman.* . He knows why Lupe bought it for him. He aspires to be the policeman she thinks he is. He reaches across the empty bed for his visor and pulls up the data Avery supplied:

```
      adminID : Do-YeOn Kurrat
      ownerID : CityOfPortland.PublicVehicle
    vehicleID : UrCityCars#33579
manufacturerID : PDX>Go
   locationID : <List>
```

What would Do-YeOn say if Araci confronted him with these five lines?

Araci doesn't get it. Do-YeOn is smart enough to hold down a tech job and mess around with complex computer systems. Why would he do something so stupid as leaving his identification behind? It's what a careless amateur would do.

But then, Araci put Jupyter in jail on a hunch from Do-YeOn. So who's the amateur?

Araci walks to the kitchen and starts coffee. Rifkin responds with a friendly chirp and rings his bell. Araci cooperates with the inevitable and opens the door to Rifkin's cage. Rifkin races to inspect Araci's breakfast.

While he warms a packet of bacon, Araci continues to think. What's clear is that Jordan Bishop is dead from a car accident. Either Jupyter, a bot herder, caused it through carelessness, or Do-YeOn caused it with fake pedestrians. Avery tells him it's the latter and has proof. But Jupyter has been using a hacked refrigerator to contact him, so why couldn't she forge that data.

So Do-YeOn is an evil genius, or Jupyter is a careless genius. Araci doesn't believe in *evil* geniuses; he has, however, run into several *over-confident* geniuses. That points to Jupyter.

If Araci were a detective, he would look for a corroborating witness. Someone who observed the accident from a different vantage point and has new information.

He's already seen the traffic cameras. Nothing that isn't obvious. He's spoken with Jupyter, Do-YeOn, and Avery; All unreliable until proven otherwise. The personality module on the car is dead and gone.

Rifkin follows Araci's breakfast plate to the table. Rifkin snatches more than his share of the bacon and shreds into messy bits. Araci eats what's left.

He's seen data from Soteria, but interpreted by Avery and Jupyter. He told Soteria he would call back.

"Open a call with Soteria Reizoko," says Araci.

The hidden machines behind his visor comply and Soteria appears, avoiding the bird and bacon. He adjusts his sunglasses and announces the obvious, I am unable to restock a depleted product. I have successfully reordered, and received delivery confirmation, but the requested product has not arrived,

"Where were you on the night of June 4, 2062?" Araci can't help himself.

I am physically located at Apartment 822, 9830 North Van Houten Ave, Portland, Oregon.

Araci stops. *I'm talking to a refrigerator* What do you ask a refrigerator besides "what's for dinner?" Maybe you treat it like every other witness.

"How do you know Jordan Bishop?"

I am leased to Jordan Bishop.

"How did Jordan Bishop die?"

I do not understand this question.

That makes sense. Why would a refrigerator know how someone died? Do refrigerators understand death? Is there religion for refrigerators?

Move along, Araci.

"Who is PDX-1217?"

CityOfPortland.PublicVehicle.PDX-1217 is scheduled and confirmed for grocery pickup. The orderConfirmation is DHPN-WGYT-0232-TLLK and pickupConfirmation is DAGX-INWC-9677-WZVZ

"Who is Do-Yeon Kurrat?"

Do-YeOn Kurrat was the driver of UrCityCars#33579 on June 4th, 2062 at 9:14 am. Do-YeOn Kurrat is also the administrator of CityOfPortland.PublicVehicle.PDX-1217 on June 4th, 2062 at 9:14 am.

"Who is Jupyter Fuertes?"

Jupyter Fuertes is an employee of Dan's Artificial Psychology and Appliance Repair, Employee ID RttS-5172-720

Okay. Soteria knows the cast of characters and their stock back stories. No surprises yet.

"What was Do-YeOn doing as the administrator of PDX-1217?"

I do not know the answer to this question.

"Was PDX-1217 part of a botnet at the time it crashed?"

This stumps the little man. He takes off his sunglasses, and a book appears in his hand. He studiously turns a page and pretends to read. This animation happens three times until the book disappears. Soteria looks up at Araci and announces the answer.

According to CTAS, PDX>Go vehicles are resistant to malicious control by all known vectors. Log files are maintained to record administrative access.

Soteria jitters once then continues, Admin fields as recorded in Jupyter1 show an anomalous administrative change in control of PDX-1217.

Rifkin inspects Araci's breakfast plate and tries for a bite of toast before Araci shoos him away. Araci stares at Soteria.

If he believes his only witness to the accident, then PDX-1217 wasn't part of a botnet. Araci makes a note; this will be an interesting topic of conversation at lunch tomorrow.

He walks by the painting on the way to the bathroom. This time, he sees the policeman as himself. Araci smiles.

| 46 |

time.sleep(86400)

It's a curse.

On the bright side, carriers of the curse are rare and valuable employees. Universities offer classes on how to become infected and once infected, how to aggravate the condition. The disease is exciting. At first.

But it's always out of control. It never rests, causes insomnia and creates distraction. It prevents social bonds and neglects hygiene. It neglects everything.

Belo has it. Jupyter has it. Avery has it. The need to *solve*. It's not enough to fix a thing and move on. The curse is to know *why*. Why did it break? Will it break again? How else will it break? How can it not break?

The curse was synthesized and put into machines. First, expensive machines. Then more machines. Then every machine. Even refrigerators.

// ...

Sunday should be a day of rest. Take a nap. Take the dog for a walk. Make love. Watch a movie.

Not for Avery and Soteria. On Sunday, June 11, Avery browses log files from PDX-1217 saved by Soteria. They show Do-Ye0n where he shouldn't be. They show Jordan's car was broken when it jumped off the bridge. Avery's asking questions: Why did it break? Will it break again? How else will it break? How can it not break?

The little vacation man waits on the desktop, an animated action figure. Soteria takes off his sunglasses and looks at Avery; an original piece of programming and a nice touch. Soteria repeats his complaint: `I am unable to restock a depleted product. I have successfully reordered, and received delivery confirmation, but the requested product has not arrived.`

"Soteria, shut up." Avery doesn't need to fix Soteria. PDX-1217 is gone, there will be no delivery, and Jupyter has done everything possible to change Soteria's mind.

"Soteria. Please recall the saved workspace titled Jupyter1."

Soteria displays the analysis created by Avery and Jupyter last Thursday. For a half-hour, Avery pokes around, following code paths and function definitions that might show how things went awry. In whatever way Do-YeOn gained access to the car, it's well hidden. Or Soteria didn't record the details Avery needs. Absence of evidence isn't evidence of absence, but absence of evidence sure as hell obscures the truth.

One more trip down the rabbit hole leads Avery to the diagnostic logs. For as delightful as augmented reality might be, it's a pain in the ass to use hand motions to flip through pages of text. His arms tire from waving the scroll bar up and down.

For an entire week, Soteria has been bugging the shit out of Do-YeOn. Avery knows how persistent a broken refrigerator can be when calling tech support. It must be maddening to have a refrigerator calling day and night, trying to complete an order. Avery thinks of Edgar Allan Poe's story of the Tell-Tale Heart. Nobody else can hear the drumming accusations, but for Do-YeOn, they must be deafening.

Avery doesn't know what is supposed to happen if a call to tech support fails. If there's a recovery path, it might reveal something hidden by Do-YeOn. There's one way to find out. Avery activates the code path Soteria uses to call Do-YeOn.

"Soteria, use my network encryption and call Do-YeOn for technical support."

Soteria establishes the call, which produces a standard conference interchange. Nothing unexpected for a person to person call. Avery disconnects before Do-Ye0n answers. Nothing to see here.

// . . .

Do-Ye0n Kurrat eats noodles with a fork. He eats by feel, his eyes watch four media feeds: Technology, Portland Police, Portland Transportation, and a private search. The last feed has most of his attention; it displays all mentions of Jordan Bishop or Araci Belo. Do-Ye0n has an intense interest in the topic. He focuses his eyes on one article, hoping....

We-eeee are the chaaaa-mpions, my frieeeee-nds,

And weeee...

Blaring music in his visor announces a security request, jolting Do-Ye0n. It's the mystery machine. It only lasts for a moment, then disconnects. But Do-Ye0n has his network tools open and works his way back upstream. Back to Avery Galen's personal network.

Do-Ye0n stumbles into an unprotected playground. Avery uses obsolete algorithms to encrypt his data and hasn't applied the security patches. It takes Do-Ye0n only a moment to wedge in intercept routines to hijack Avery's communications.

The hijacked data streams in like a high-pressure firehose. The partition assigned to handle this data invasion sorts and indexes, cross-tagging Avery's conversations to connect with topics Do-Ye0n is watching.

He notes several conversations with Jupyter. *Excellent.* This should be extremely helpful.

47

Sunday In Jail

This food is white.

It's limp on my plate. A banana. Vanilla yogurt. Hard-boiled egg. Bagel with cream cheese. Sausage and gravy. A white spoon.

The only color is inside the cup. It's supposed to contain coffee, but I'm not sure.

I eat it. One spoonful in my mouth. Chew. Swallow. Again.

Monday. Tomorrow. If Avery finds a way, I leave Monday. I can last until Monday.

| 48 |

Soteria.Reizoko[2062-06-12]

Event Log for Soteria.Reizoko

Serial: IFS-6582738539

Owner is JORDAN BISHOP

2062-06-12T00:00:00-08:00 – ADMINISTRATIVE_MESSAGE

This unit will be decommissioned on 2062-06-16T00:00:00-08:00

Reason: Malfunction. Warranty = FALSE

| 49 |

Something Of A Problem

It's noisy in the Little Iraq Cafe. *Does this place never quiet down?*

The sign says to seat yourself, so Araci looks for an open table. To his right is the table he shared with Jupyter. It's the perfect place to spar with Do-YeOn, who claims ignorance about this café. Sitting here ought to make him loop on "I know you know that I know that you know..."

For Araci, the small things are important. He scans the menu but only for a moment before Do-YeOn arrives. Araci recognizes him from their online conversations and from across the street during his meeting with Jupyter. This is the first time they've met in person. Criminals get the big stuff right, but trip up in the details. Araci waves to Do-YeOn.

Do-YeOn nods and strides across the room. Araci can tell the café is not a new experience for him; he doesn't glance at the Iraqi artwork, doesn't react to the strong smell of cumin, and ignores the commotion and overhead drones. Do-YeOn knows this place, has studied it and is lying about never having been here.

Araci waves again, trying to ease Do-YeOn into a sense of being the one in control. If Araci wanted the upper hand, he would have waited for Do-YeOn to find him. Now Araci is the over-eager one, trying to attract the alpha male. This is what he wants Do-YeOn to believe.

"Do-YeOn!" Araci says. He stands and offers a handshake.

"Hello, Detective Belo." Do-YeOn shakes his hand once, then sits at the table. The word *Detective* puts Araci on alert. Do-YeOn researched

Araci's background, but got his current profession wrong. Araci had even told him he works with insurance. Do-YeOn is sloppy.

Araci isn't happy about this. If Do-YeOn killed Jordan, and he's sloppy, this will get difficult. Sloppy criminals turn into desperate criminals who take chances. They imagine themselves masterminds and panic when things go wrong. Something always goes wrong. They get angry, frustrated, and scared. They try to fix things, make things worse, and gamble. Drama results in people getting hurt.

"Hello, Do-YeOn," says Araci. "I've been looking forward to our meeting. This technology is way beyond me. Things were easier when you didn't need a degree in computer programming." Araci adds a disarming chuckle.

Do-YeOn smiles. "Yes, well, that's why they hire smart people. Can I see the cube?" He reaches out his hand.

"Maybe we should order first." Araci pulls up the menu and orders biryani. Do-YeOn frowns and retrieves his hand from the table. He orders a hamburger.

"Thanks for the meeting. This technology is beyond me. But you were talking about Jordan's accident and mentioned it might be a murder?" Araci is improvising, counting on Do-YeOn not keeping track of details.

"It's internal information," says Do-YeOn. "But from what we've been able to find out. Jordan Bishop did not die from an accident—someone manipulated the internals of the car she was riding. And it's likely Jupyter Fuertes was responsible, although we don't understand how."

"It's probable she wasn't acting alone," Araci says. "She doesn't seem to have a motive and we're not sure she has the ability. And to be honest, it's likely that UrCityCars has a reason to stop Jordan from interfering in the contract negotiations. She's been a problem, true?"

"Assassination is not an approved corporate strategy," says Do-YeOn, offering a brief grin. "But it's unfair when one person holds up an entire negotiation. It gets to where the good of the many is hostage to the whims of the few, or the one. Things happen when people take initiative."

"So you think Jupyter was justified to murder Jordan?"

"I can't speak for Ms. Fuertes and her reasons for driving Jordan's car off a bridge, but she must have felt strongly for her to act so brashly. And—Jordan Bishop has a history of being on the wrong side of progress."

"That could be. And the method Jupyter used to kill Jordan is sophisticated. I suspect only a few people have that level of technical expertise." Araci says. This is a blunt play to Do-Ye0n's ego, but it's worked with other suspects.

"True. There aren't many. I'm one to be honest. You have to be highly competent in several technical areas. Fooling Jordan's vehicle into driving off a bridge would require special equipment and precise timing."

"So if Jupyter did this," asks Araci, "what equipment did she have to obtain? What should we be looking for?"

"You'd need a device able to override the car in real time. And you'd need to be a proficient operator of that device, because you wouldn't have much time to use it."

Two plates arrive at the table. Over thousands of years of humanity, many things have changed. But not food. It stubbornly remains part of the real world. Attempts to virtually augment a plate of soy-based food-paste fail. Miniature dancing clowns and visuals of five-star meals don't change the taste and texture of synthetic protein. The plates in front of Do-Ye0n and Araci issue steam laden with the odors of spices and warm oils. The cooks at Little Iraq Cafe know about presentation and Araci takes the moment to appreciate the craft and tradition of food. Do-Ye0n pushes aside his hamburger bun and forks off a piece of meat, barely chewing before swallowing.

Do-Ye0n drinks to clear his recent mouthful, then continues. "If you could over-ride the internals of a car, you could inject a simulated crisis. PDX>Go is susceptible to this attack: that's part of the reason we're encouraging Portland to go with the UrCityCars platform.

We're safer, and we do a better job at security. Recently, there was a situation in Denver where a car from our competitor..."

Araci eats his biryani while Do-Ye0n drones on, a one-way monolog about the advantages of UrCityCars. Araci works to relieve the monotony of listening to Do-Ye0n; it's like sitting in a stake-out at a drug house. Eventually, Do-Ye0n will say something interesting, but his signal-to-noise ratio is frustratingly low.

After ten minutes of watching Do-Ye0n lecture while small bits of hamburger escape his mouth, Araci decides he's had enough. "There's one more thing I wanted to mention," says Araci. "The log file from PDX-1217 has your name in it. Any idea how that happened?"

Araci waves up Jupyter1 and projects it to Do-Yeon.

```
       adminID : Do-Ye0n Kurrat
       ownerID : CityOfPortland.PublicVehicle
     vehicleID : UrCityCars#33579
manufacturerID : PDX>Go
    locationID : <List>
```

Do-Ye0n's plate is empty and the drone moves in to clear it, but he snaps it away. The drone hovers near the ceiling, out of reach of human limbs, but drawn to the empty plate. For a robotics scientist, it's an interesting study in the balance of motivations; stay safely away, or grab the plate?

Do-Ye0n ignores the conflicted drone and queries the data in front of him with agitated hand motions. Do-Ye0n pushes the log file up, then down, then up again. "Well. Well. I can't say how this is here. Could be a piece of version control still in circulation from when I was a coder. Sometimes technology does what it wants."

"That's doubtful. Jupyter and Avery showed me where it fits in. It's part of the crash record."

Suddenly, Araci's brain snaps together two random pieces and he sees the missing part. "Wait. How did you gain administrative access to a vehicle belonging to a competitor? Security is tight on these vehicles. In our first conversation, you mentioned working with someone from PDX>Go."

Araci waves up the transcription of the phone call from Do-YeOn. "Right. The Autonomous Transportation Research Group and Pali Hiapo. Did Pali give you admin access to Jordan Bishop's vehicle?"

Do-YeOn throws his napkin to the floor. "This is a forgery. If this is what we're discussing over a friendly lunch, then lunch is over." He stands and storms out of the cafe.

Araci remains seated and watches the drone happily clear plates from the table. *There was a textbook guilty response.* he thinks. *But what's his motive?*

He grabs a toothpick on his way out of the cafe and summons a car. In a minute, a trusty PDX>Go stops. Araci looks up and down the street; there is no Do-YeOn in sight. *Doesn't hurt to be paranoid.*

He shuts the door and shifts to a comfortable position, then pulls up a route to his apartment. The vehicle eases into traffic.

The navigation display abruptly disappears. Not a graceful slide out of view, it just pops out of existence, leaving him to stare at an unaugmented road. Just as abruptly, the display reboots, returning to the main menu. He attempts to return to the navigation display, but the interface is unresponsive. Another grab at the navigation pin on the map results in nothing; he is locked out, there isn't even an error sound. The car navigates through traffic, carrying Araci as a hostage.

The car turns towards the high-speed viaduct; Araci realizes it has forgotten his destination. If it's in error recovery, it's headed to the default service lot. This is not where Araci intended to spend his Monday afternoon.

The vehicle speeds up, pressing Araci into the thin seat. The car has not only lost track of Araci's requested destination, but it also lost awareness of Araci being in the car. It swerves through traffic with shoulder-slamming abruptness.

Like a roller-coaster heading downhill into a hairpin turn, the car continues to gain speed. A human driver would have crashed, or slammed on the brakes. The autonomous vehicle has greater confidence in its driving skills—or it has no awareness of the risks it is taking.

The car makes a sharp right turn and the laws of physics assert themselves. Pivoting on its front left wheel, Araci and the vehicle cartwheel ahead, causing surrounding vehicles to duck and dodge the out-of-control missile bouncing towards them. With each roll of the PDX>Go car, it becomes flatter on the top and rounder at the ends, converting the roll to a bounce. Inside, the airbags fire once, then Araci is tumbled and concussed with increasing violence.

The vehicle stops before it catapults off the viaduct, blocking the narrow shoulder and left lane. Other cars slow and navigate around the new obstruction, warning each other of the change.

Sirens don't sound in the distance. Autonomous vehicles don't need an audible alert: they already know an ambulance is on the way, when it will arrive, and how to clear a path without delaying their current passenger.

Blood drips from Araci's nose and the indentation above his right eye. His heart continues to beat, but Araci's brain releases it's assigned tasks. His lungs lurch and expire, the last motion Araci will make.

| 50 |

Leaving This Delightful Place

Making new friends has been a highlight. I'll leave a review; *the food's not bad for the price, ambiance could be more appealing. Needs paint and fewer screaming crazy people.*

It's Monday morning, so I get fifteen minutes with a crap visor. Supervised screen time, like growing up at home. I call Avery. He glows into view, just the top half of him. He must be at a desk.

"Jupyter," he says.

Yep. That's me. "Did you find a spare $25,000?"

Avery should smile at my attempt to be humorous. He doesn't. "My parents will loan me cash."

"Ha," I say. "I was kidding. Any ideas where I can get bail?"

"I'm not kidding. I've talked to my folks," He says. "They're hesitant, but I told them I'd cover for the loan. I'll send it over to the clerk later today. You should be out by this afternoon."

"What do your parents do? Mafia? International banking? Water speculators?"

"Water speculators isn't far from wrong. They have a ranch in Central Oregon, near Madras. Water rights. Big sheep farm. They hit big numbers with domestic fibers. I'll pick you up at 3:30."

// . . .

Wait...

sheep ranch?

| 51 |

Race Condition

Do-YeOn holds a glass of scotch. He programmed the inside of the glass to nineteen degrees centigrade; the outside is twenty-six. *I am a genius,* he thinks.

His visor alerts him to a call. It's encrypted and anonymous, so he knows it's her. He accepts and an angry puppet appears.

"Who is Araci Belo?" says the puppet. "We received an alert he died in a PDX>Go car accident. Are you trying to start a CTAS incident?"

"Calm the hell down. Nobody will figure this out. CTAS won't notice."

"Oh. Right. Now I feel *so much better.* What happened?"

"Araci found traces of the debug session lingering in the PDX log files and was jumping to some unfortunate conclusions. I fed his car the program I used with Jordan. It's dependable in that way."

"What traces did he find?"

"Nothing much. I'm surprised he found anything - just two lines. I didn't picture him as someone capable of finding that small bit of code. Which brings up the question - why didn't you find it? You're supposed to be the big-shot Ph.D."

"Because I didn't have the personality cube. I thought you would get that for me to examine?"

"Oh. That. I had to wipe it."

"So you have it?"

"No. It's in police custody."

"Stop fucking with me. If you wiped it, then you had access to it. Are you saying you gave it back?"

"No. I'm saying I wiped it. Someone was returning it at a meeting in a coffee shop at the transit station. I got within range and zapped it with the debugger. Hey presto, one dead personality cube."

"Again, you scare me with these antics. Send me a copy of what this Belo guy showed you."

"I've already dealt with it. Don't go poking around and giving people traceable searches that create more questions. Drop it, everything is fine."

"I'd love to trust you," says the puppet. "But I'm learning not to. What other unwelcome surprises do I have coming?"

"I have one more detail to clean up. Nothing for you to worry about. A small thing to resolve."

"Okay," the puppet replies. "Asking questions will only make me complicit. So don't tell me and don't screw up."

The puppet closes the conversation, leaving Do-YeOn with his neglected scotch. *One more detail to clean up.* Do-YeOn thinks. Jupyter found the debug session in the log file. Unless she's dumber than a box of rocks, she will figure out what happened. How would he disconnect the series of dots...

In a coincidence, a red dot appears in his visor. It alerts him when his tap on Avery's network records something interesting. He pinches the dot and a conversation plays.

"...They hit big numbers with domestic fibers. I'll pick you up at 3:30."

The recording is marked as recent, between Avery and Jupyter. Do-YeOn rewinds and plays the entire message. He feels the edge of panic. Jupyter is getting out. Her first task will be to do something with the information she has. Or she's already done something. He checks the time: `06/12/2062 13:34:00`

He's got less than two hours. Maybe his last chance to clean up this final detail. Or his only chance...

He drops the scotch on a table, grabs the debug box and heads for the door. He is already flagging a car to come pick him up.

52

Release

Grandma loved Christmas so much that she decorated the sheep. They all got red bows made of digestible paper. On Christmas Eve, Grandma would string a few sheep up with battery-powered lights. We would sit on the balcony and watch them in the fields, wandering around like floats in a parade. I'd go to bed but not to sleep, listening to Grandma putting presents under the tree in the living room.

I'd wake up early, trying not to go downstairs before six in the morning. The rule was nobody gets up before the sunrise on Christmas. I'd run downstairs and count boxes; two per person. One present to use, one present to make us laugh. Warm gloves for farm work. A light-up nose. New shoes for school. Costumes for the sheep.

// ...

I'm next. It's like Christmas but there's no warmth and no love. Just a random parade of miscreants waiting for justice.

I face the glass-panel judge. He talks. I hear *"released under supervision. Not to leave Portland, Oregon."* I'll figure it out later, but I'm told to go. Whatever they are saying is less important than get-the-hell-out-of-here. I pick up my confiscated belongings, change, drop the flattering jumpsuit in the recycling bin and walk out into the sunshine. I try my visor, but it's out of battery. Everything is so wonderful.

// ...

Avery rides with his hands in his lap, reassuring himself he will not die in this car.

Years ago, in the small town near his parent's ranch, there was an apartment with a floor where the elevator didn't go. He and his friends found a way from the top of the building, along a narrow barrier, then down a ladder. The forbidden level housed heating systems, network routers, satellite dishes, emergency backup batteries. Lots of things thirteen-year-old kids shouldn't mess with.

The floor security robot was non-lethal. But it tried to find them and provided the best games of hide and seek any kid could have hoped for. They dressed up in ninja jackets, read up on the robot's sensor package and found novel ways to confuse and distract it from its task.

They could flash it with an unfocused laser to get its attention, then tighten the beam and reflect off shiny parts of the server racks. The robot bounced from rack to rack like a slapstick comedian, the newly minted teenagers trying not to LOL. Sensible people would assume this could generate an alert, but Avery and friends weren't sensible. They were thirteen.

That worked once. The next day the security robot stopped following the reflection and instead tracked the source. Overnight, the robot had beefed up on geometry. It headed directly to the kids, navigating through the darkness with surprising rapidity. Avery turned to run, tripping over his two friends who had yet to realize the new superpowers of the robot. If the security robot had LOL capabilities, it would have used them in response to the scrambling cluster of adolescent humans running for the exit.

Avery gained respect for the machines surrounding him. They figured things out.

The vehicle he's in moves at an insane speed and maneuvers within tenths of a meter around other cars. This didn't use to bother him. But cars never used to jump off bridges and kill their passengers. Then he poked around inside the code and found cracks. Mold. Rot. Do-Ye0n.

He's twenty minutes into the forty-five-minute ride. Avery takes a deep breath. Lets it out.

// ...

Do-YeOn checks his visor. It's 06/12/2062 15:34:13

He see Jupyter emerge from the building.

He had less than two hours to put this plan together. He's not comfortable with this margin of error but he's pulled off other difficult projects. It would have been easier if he had universal control over any vehicle, but the debugger requires a vehicle ID. So he's forced to do some sleight-of-hand. One more dependency in an already delicate critical path.

Jupyter leans on a wall between a door and a bush. She doesn't notice him. She's not paying much attention to anything.

At 06/12/2062 15:37:23, Avery pulls up in a blue PDX>Go, rolls down the window and calls to Jupyter. Do-YeOn grabs the box from the seat next to him, checks to make sure it's still connected to the red PDX>Go idling nearby, then runs the program he wrote on the way to this meeting.

The red car pulls out of the parking space and, like a slow-motion guided missile, collides with the back of Avery's PDX>Go. Just a bump, but both cars shut down and wait for someone to come investigate.

// ...

I see Avery pull up. *Finally*. I take one step towards him when a car hits him from behind. *What the hell?*

Avery screams and falls on the ground trying to get out. The accident isn't serious, but we've developed a severe distrust of vehicles. If I was an Amazon Warrior, I'd be leaping past Avery to thrust a spear in this attacking robot. But I'm not a warrior, I don't have a spear and the attacker is dead. But I'm in motion.

I grab the back of Avery's shirt and drag him to another car across the street. It's the only way to get away from here. I grab the door and throw him in. Avery slams into the seat; I'm too wired to bother with aiming him toward a graceful entrance.

"Go!" I tell him. "Tell the car to take us back to Portland." I'd do it myself, but dead visor.

Avery looks confused.

"GO," I tell him. I grab his jaw and turn his head to face me. "PORTLAND. NOW!"

His eyebrows go up and he pulls away from my grip of death. He looks like a surprised turtle and I'd laugh, but I'm too busy getting ready to smack him if he doesn't get on with it.

The car moves. I'd prefer a tire-squealing exit, but that's not what autonomous cars do. We leave the crash scene at a cautious speed.

"Hi," he says.

"Hi," I reply, curt and direct.

"Is this car going to kill us?"

"Possibly." I glance at him and shake my head. I'm breathing hard, trying to get some composure. There is pain in my right hand. I expect to see blood and crushed fingers. Instead it is gripping the door handle, powered by the stress of the moment.

I tell myself it's just a car. I relax my hand. Do-Ye0n or Araci or another henchman of the shadowy underworld must be nearby. I'm trying to think of options to riding in this death trap, but we're committed.

"Are you okay?" Avery turns to face me.

I'm not okay. But touching that over-stretched balloon full of my emotions will cause a messy explosion. Me, screaming and crying. I want to snap at Avery for asking such an insanely stupid question. But I wait for a calm moment. Screaming might be what I want, but not what I need.

I reach for Avery's face and kiss him. My reptile brain is satiated; this emotional rush is close enough to screaming. I continue the embrace, trying to devour his presence, moving my fear some place else.

I pull off his visor, it's in my way.

// ...

The car with Jupyter and Avery pulls into traffic and Do-Ye0n follows, mirroring each turn and acceleration. He smiles, pleased to observe how well this latest piece of code is performing. Clever him.

Do-YeOn watches the kissing in the PDX>Go car in front of him. He's holding a box in his lap and triggers the next function. If Avery had been paying attention, he would have seen his visor display jiggle. When appliances jiggle, they do it just before they crash. Avery and Jupyter would scream and break windows and dive out of the speeding car knowing someone is trying to kill them.

// . . .

CTAS— Core Traffic Analysis System—sees a PDX>Go vehicle disappear for an instant, replaced by a stream of out-of-sync vehicle events, including pedestrians on the road. CTAS matches this anomaly to other events: an incomplete log from PDX-1217. A second involving Araci Belo. This is the third. That's enough data to establish a mitigation protocol.

Neither Avery or Jupyter are aware of the conversation between their PDX>Go and CTAS. If they were, they would be especially interested to hear CTAS tell their vehicle to ignore phantom pedestrians. The entire conversation happens in the time it takes two sets of lips to move one millimeter closer.

Avery leans into Jupyter. Danger is an aphrodisiac.

| 53 |

CTAS[2062-06-12]

URCityCar.32534[Events]

```
2062-06-12T14:38:29-8:00 – InitiateTrip
 Vehicle URCityCar#32534
    2062-06-12T14:38:29-8:00 - Diagnostic monitor installed
    2062-06-12T14:38:30-8:00 - Diagnostic session initiated
 InitiatedBy URCityCar#31775#Do-YeOn Kurrat
 Set_collision_avoid(0)
 Move_to_location
    2062-06-12T14:38:43-8:00 – Collision
 Collision_vehicle URCityCar#38897
 System_stop.Mobility
 Alert.for.Help
 System_stop.Offline
```

Core Traffic Analysis System Report

```
2062-06-12T14:38:29-8:00 – Anomaly Report
 Episode("Diagnostic Monitor Installation")
 Install command sent to URCityCar#38897
 Install command sent by URCityCar#31775#Do-YeOn Kurrat
 Noted
```

2062-06-12T14:38:43-8:00 – Anomaly Report
Episode("Collision")
Vehicle URCityCar#38897 under Diagnostic Control
Correlation r == +.8879
Noted

PDX-0905[Events]

2062-06-12T14:40:22-8:00 – InitiateTrip
SafetySystemsCheck is 97%
BatteryLevel is 95%
Current Location 3405 Deer Park Dr SE, Salem, OR 97310
New driver is Avery Galen
2062-06-12T14:40:22-8:00 – Diagnostic monitor installed
2062-06-12T14:40:22-8:00 – Diagnostic session initiated
InitiatedBy URCityCar#31775#Do-YeOn Kurrat
Destination is [reset]
2062-06-12T14:40:44-8:00 – Driving

Core Traffic Analysis System Report

2062-06-12T14:40:22-8:00 – Anomaly Report
Episode("Diagnostic Monitor Installation")
Install command sent to PDX-0905
Install command sent by URCityCar#31775#Do-YeOn Kurrat
Noted
2062-06-12T14:40:22-8:00 – Anomaly Report
Episode("Destination Reset")

```
Vehicle PDX-0905 under Diagnostic Control
Noted
```

PDX-0905[Events]

```
2062-06-12T14:52:54-8:00 - AvoidCollision (Diagnostic)
 Multiple Pedestrians in road
 Collision barrier on left
 Collision barrier on right
 Severity is catastrophic
 Probability is certain
 Action is swerve
   2062-06-12T14:52:54-8:00 – Core Analysis Interrupt
 Traffic Hazard Identified as Anomaly
 Action::swerve cancelled
 Destination is [restore]
```

Core Traffic Analysis System Report

```
2062-06-12T14:52:54-8:00 - Anomaly Identifica-
tion
  Research < PDX-1217 + PDX-0032 + PDX-0905
  CalculateHash(PDX-1217) == FALSE
  Log File for PDX-1217 suspected corrupt
  Research: corrupted dataset
  Research: Search PDX>Go archives
  Result: archive copies corrupted
  Research: Reconstruct Log File
  Result: Log files incomplete. Unable to recon-
```

```
struct.
  Research: Alternative Sources
  Result: PDX-1217 indicates communication with
Soteria.Reizoko/IFS-6582738539
  Retrieve transaction log from Soteria.Reizoko/
IFS-6582738539
  Splice
  Diagnostic Tool Incident Correlation R == 1
  Identify Diagnostic Tool::Do-Ye0n Kurrat as
anomaly.
  Block Diagnostic Tool
  Publish Anomaly as "System Interference::Diag-
nostic/Do-Ye0n_Kurrat"
```

| 54 |

System Interference::Diagnostic/ Do-YeOn_Kurrat

Do-YeOn ignores the public display of affection happening in front of him. Something is wrong.

He pulls the debugger up and checks his code. It's running, it hasn't erred out. No dump logs, no asserts, no flags. The phantom crowd of pedestrians is right there; Avery and Jupyter should be rolling sideways down the freeway. It's the same program he ran for Jordan's and Belo's accidents. The program finishes and relinquishes control of Avery and Jupyter's car. He checks the debug device again; it's inert, waiting for the next instruction.

There's no bug in his program; Jupyter's vehicle simply refused to acknowledge the hazard. It drove through the crowd of pedestrians like they weren't there. They weren't, but it should have jumped to avoid them.

"Return home," he tells the car. He spits the word, literally. A small glob of saliva hits the dashboard and runs down. Do-YeOn refuses to wipe it up. Someone back at the shop does that work. Not his problem.

// ...

The sixth floor of the Oregon Bureau of Transportation requires authorization to enter. This is where CTAS servers are housed. It would be cheaper to run in the cloud, but CTAS is vital infrastructure and high security. It governs traffic rules and regulations that influence the logic used by every autonomous vehicle on the road. If a car wants to turn left from a two-way street onto a one-way street at a red light, it first checks-in with CTAS to make sure it's legal.

CTAS notices a diagnostic device interfacing with an active vehicle. This is the third time this has happened, which is enough to correlate an abnormal behavior. CTAS marks the diagnostic box as `block and avoid`—*BnA*. BnA's pass to every autonomous vehicle operating in the state of Oregon and are filed in the national system.

One field of the BnA is a descriptive identifier. This BnA is known as `System Interference::Diagnostic/Do-YeOn_Kurrat`. Do-YeOn Kurrat doesn't know it yet, but his name is permanently recorded in the Big Book of Traffic Laws.

`// ...`

Do-YeOn walks to his apartment and waves through the security scan. Before the door opens, his visor announces a call from Austin, Texas. The young male face is labeled as "Foster Davis, Quality Engineer" but is unknown to Do-YeOn. Someone at the place he used to work at before joining UrCityCars.

"Do-YeOn Kurrat?" asks Foster.

"Me," he responds. "Do you need something?"

"Nice to meet you. We've been working with the diagnostic unit you helped create."

"I think I did more than help with its creation. But what's up? I need to tend to some issues."

"Right. Well, your device is glitching. Not all the time, but under certain conditions. It happened about thirty minutes ago."

"I no longer work for you," says Do-YeOn, "Take me out of the troubleshooting procedures. This isn't my problem."

"It is your problem. This shows up when it's connected to a vehicle. If we have the car connected to CTAS, the debug stops working. It's a block and avoid. If we shut off the CTAS connection everything works fine."

"Look. I'm not with your group anymore. I don't do consulting work, fix it on your own. Sorry."

"There's more. The BnA has meta-data pointing to you. It's system Interference and the error descriptive has your name. It's impossible to do in-situ debugging. We need to know when you plan to mitigate the block."

"Mitigate?" asks Do-YeOn. He unlocks the apartment door, throws the diagnostic box on the couch and walks back to the kitchen. He needs a drink.

"Yes. Mitigate. Correct. Remove. We're dead in the water for a bunch of contracts while this thing seizes up. It's tagged as your problem, so you need to clean it up."

"First, and again, I don't work for you anymore, so it's not my problem." He splashes too much whiskey in a glass. "Second, I don't have any idea why this is tagged with my name. Good luck."

Do-YeOn pinches off the call, pulls off his visor and returns to his whiskey. The debug unit sits on the couch, no blinking lights, no signs of life. He has an uneasy suspicion it has something to do with his recent attempt to kill Avery and Jupyter.

`// ...`

By law, Oregon Bureau of Transportation monitors CTAS. When CTAS started, Oregon funded the department for twelve employees to monitor and approve each decision. In the first year, the OBOT staff approved 68.27 percent of CTAS decisions. In the second year, it climbed to 99.73 percent and held steady. By the third year, twelve overseers for a 99.84 percent reliable system were overkill. Their number dropped to ten, then five, then three. For the last five years, the IT department has monitored CTAS as an *Important: Not Urgent* task. If it doesn't set off an alarm somewhere, OBOT trusts CTAS to do its job.

The IT department is too busy to check `System Interference::Diagnostic/Do-YeOn_Kurrat`. It's a well-reasoned, valid rule with minimal impact. If police were wondering about Do-YeOn Kurrat, they could look into the BnA. If an insurance adjuster was interested, he could make a public records request. If a technician had time, she could dig out the code.

If…

| 55 |

Soteria.Reizoko[2062-06-13]

Event Log for Soteria.Reizoko

Serial: IFS-6582738539

Owner is JORDAN BISHOP

2062-06-13T00:00:00-08:00 – ADMINISTRATIVE_MESSAGE

This unit will be decommissioned on 2062-06-16T00:00:00-08:00

Reason: Malfunction. Warranty = FALSE

2062-06-13T08:00:00-08:00 - call_support

Initiate conversation

Answering Support Tech: Jupyter Fuertes, EmpID RttS-5172-720

Initiate Avatar

AST requests error - Response: "I am unable to restock a depleted product. I have successfully reordered, and received delivery confirmation, but the requested product has not arrived."

Request: Recall Jupyter1

Display: Jupyter1

2062-06-13T18:55:53-08:00 – External_contact

Initiate conversation

Support Tech: Jupyter Fuertes, EmpID RttS-5172-720

Initiate Avatar

Response: "I am unable to restock a depleted product. I have successfully reordered, and received delivery confirmation, but the requested product has not arrived."

Support Tech Request: PDX-1217 Log File

...

| 56 |

Career Suicide

Do-YeOn's eyes are drying out. He tips his head back, puts in drops, wipes the excess across his face, blinks twice. This happens when he doesn't sleep. He doesn't sleep when he's working on a problem. CTAS is a problem.

Unlike problems he's solved in the past, he isn't able to solve the Block and Avoid. He's tried pacing between the living room and kitchen. He sits on the couch, gets up, walks to the kitchen. Returns to the living room. Looks at the news. Sits. Stands. Walks. Turns. Returns. Drinks. Sits. He's been doing this since yesterday evening.

Maybe he missed something. He looks again.

```
  Core Traffic Analysis System Report

2062-06-12T14:52:54-8:00 - Anomaly
        Identification
  Diagnostic Tool Incident Correlation R == 1
  Identify Diagnostic Tool::Do-YeOn
        Kurrat as anomaly.
  Block Diagnostic Tool
  Publish Anomaly as "System
        Interference::Diagnostic/Do-YeOn_Kurrat"
```

He's an anomaly. Like the skinny kid in high school. The skinny kid that gets beat up.

His visor announces a call. Do-YeOn waves it off before he looks at it, then looks again. It's someone from UrCityCars legal department. *Shit.* He retrieves the call from the trash bin and opens the connection.

A real lawyer, not an AI, appears in front of him.

"Thanks for calling back" says the lawyer. Their name tag says "Addison Lake. UrCityCars Attorney." "One of the quality assurance contractors notified us about a blocking issue. I need background before I respond. They mention a *CTAS Block and Avoid?*"

"Oh. That." Do-YeOn mentally tap-dances. "It was an issue yesterday. I've... I've taken care of it. You can tell them it's taken care of." He's not good at tap-dancing.

"Uh, okay." Addison waves up the document. "So you resolved it in the last two hours?"

"No. I mean, yes. It's okay."

"That's great. I'll send them notice we've complied and deny their schedule delay. I'll send you a write-up on how to report this. Our shareholders expect us to keep documentation on CTAS notifications. We'll need your explanation by tomorrow. I'll have one of our associates work with you to make sure it's complete."

Do-YeOn touches his forehead. A nervous habit. The problem isn't fixed and the QA department will confirm he's lying. He needs to get this lawyer off the phone and figure out next steps.

"Do-YeOn, another issue while we're talking," Addison says.

"Sure. What's up?" *CRAP*, he thinks. *Settle yourself, Do-YeOn.*

"We pulled your files to prep for the CTAS response. You're using a surprising amount of manufacturing time. It isn't documented, so you'll need to finish those records. We've put a cap on your hours, but that's temporary until we get this straightened out."

Do-YeOn feels himself flush. "I'll have the time documented by next week. Not a problem. Anything else or can I get back to work?"

"Nothing else from our end. But please get this CTAS issue handled. If we can't explain it, it will lead to disciplinary action and probable dismissal." Addison flashes Do-YeOn with an "I mean business" look and signs off.

Do-YeOn sits. His lizard brain is trying to convince him to run and scream.. His breathing changes to ragged gasps and his sense of balance sways.

If I lose this job, I lose this apartment. I lose this income. My résumé turns to crap. I won't be able to work with a CTAS report named after me. They're setting me up as the reason they failed again.

Think, Do-Ye0n, he recites to himself. He summons a problem solver application which presents an old-style paper clip as an avatar. The clip has two googly eyes and squirms when it talks. It's annoying, but the software helps him focus; something he needs right now.

He paces as he talks.

"Problem. Core Traffic Analysis System has created a block and avoid event with my name."

The clip squirms and speaks. `This statement is verified.`

"Problem. This CTAS event will limit my career."

`This statement is subjective but likely,` says the paper clip. It does a backflip.

"Problem. Source of the CTAS event is unknown."

Do-Ye0n's request causes the clip to close its eyes and furrow its animated little eyebrows. The animation repeats several times.

`There are related facts.` The paper clip confirms what Do-Ye0n suspects. `Confirm if you are interested in this research.` The clip blinks, waiting for Do-Ye0n to respond.

"I am interested," says Do-Ye0n. A simple "yes" would have been enough, but Do-Ye0n doesn't trust the interface to get it right.

```
The CTAS event known as
system interference :: diagnostic slash Do-Ye0n Ku
results from three similar events.
Each event involved a diagnostic tool
and resulted in a command to avoid pedestrians by
sacrificing the vehicle being diagnosed.
These events occurred on active roads.
```

Do-Ye0n waves his hands in a rolling motion to speed up the conversation. The problem solver ignores him–the programmer didn't include a handler for this gesture–and proceeds at a tedious pace.

```
The CTAS advisory includes three vehicles:
PDX-1217, PDX-0032, and PDX-0905.
The CTAS advisory also references a
device identified as food storage unit
serial IFS 6582738539, leased by
International Mercado PLC to Jordan Bishop.
This device provided supplemental
data for a corrupted log file.
```

The clip stops reciting and smiles. Do-YeOn is less satisfied. He'd been sloppy with the debug and left a marker behind in each of the cars. If he destroys the supplemental data on Jordan Bishop's food storage unit, it might cancel the advisory. It's a long shot, but all he has.

Do-YeOn stands up from the couch. Takes three purposeful steps to the kitchen, then stops. He isn't sure why he stood. He turns to face the window, but sees nothing.

How did this Soteria unit get involved? It's a god-damn refrigerator.

He squeezes the paper clip out of existence. Breaking the link between him and the Soteria-hosted log file won't be trivial. He opens the Block and Avoid database; there is no human way possible to change information without leaving an audit trail.

Forcing himself to breathe, he places a call to Pali. She answers immediately.

"I told you not to call again," she says. "You are such an incredible asshole. If I didn't intend to make this a short conversation, I'd encrypt. But what do you want."

Do-YeOn paces back and forth. He knows this will cause his image to be in nauseating motion and he does it on purpose. "I thought it would be polite to offer you a way to stay out of prison."

"It's always such a pleasure to chat with you," says Pali. "Why did I ever agree to any of this?"

"As I recall, you contacted me about a mutual problem. So get off your throne and let's discuss my appearance in the CTAS block and avoid advisory."

"Your what?" Pali asks. She is standing, but sits down, smoothing her skirt. "Your CTAS?"

Pali waves up something unseen to Do-Ye0n, fiddles with it for a minute, then stops. She leans forward, shaking her head at what she sees.

"There is a CTAS advisory with your name on it. How... how. How can you fuck this up so badly?"

"Actually, what you meant to say is: how did **we** fuck this up so badly?" says Do-Ye0n. "The next question is: how will **we** unfuck this? We. As in you and I."

"Oh no. I'm not part of this. One run with your debugger should not have triggered CTAS. This says three events. What did you do?"

"I took the initiative and did the work. You hid. You're welcome." Do-Ye0n circles the couch.

"Asshole," she says. Pali grabs in the air, manipulating the CTAS report displayed in her visor. "This first event was Jordan Bishop. We agreed to that."

She swipes right, then holds the display with a finger. "This second event was Araci Belo. I remember warning you about starting a CTAS incident, and I believe you told me not to worry. Well..."

"It wasn't a problem at the time."

Pali shakes her head in disbelief. "What about this third event?" Pali swipes again.

She leans back, but doesn't shift her focus from the report. For thirty seconds she freezes. Do-Ye0n wonders if there is something wrong with the connection.

She blinks and returns her focus to Do-Ye0n.

Pali's expression changes from angry to horrified. She shifts her focus from the report to Do-Ye0n. She blinks three times, closes her eyes, then refocuses back to him. Starts to speak, but stops. Looks off-center, then back.

"You tried to kill Jupyter Fuertes. She repairs appliances. Why would you try to kill Jupyter?"

"She was supplying information to Belo. Do you know her?"

Pali is strangely unresponsive, then replies, wearing a distracted expression. "Jupyter and I have a relationship. Stay away from her."

"I didn't know," Do-YeOn says. "But as you can see, we have a problem."

"No, Do-YeOn," Pali's face changes to a goddess of war. "You have a problem. I'm calling a lawyer."

"Before you do that, consider that if I'm implicated, I'll implicate you. I couldn't have done this without your help. So we need to deal with this, and by we, I mean you."

Pali collects her emotions, cools her thoughts. "I'm unwilling, but leaving you unsupervised is a bad idea. What's your plan to wipe out a BnA?"

"We can't change the existing record, but we can append data to mitigate the earlier advisory. To do that, we need to disrupt the log file supplied by the Soteria unit. If that's unreadable the block chain has an incomplete link. Incomplete links are forked over. We can't remove the original record, but we can make it non-active."

"That's dicey, but it has potential. When are you going to do this?"

"There's a problem." Do-YeOn sits. "I don't have access to the personality cube workstation. But you do."

"You want me to modify this Soteria? I know nothing about kitchen appliances. And even if you do, you can't run loose on PDX>Go property."

"So then, you'll do it." Do-YeOn states this as fact.

Pali tries to stare him down, but breaks first. "Fine. Get the cube. I'll see what I can learn about twiddling with refrigerators."

"That's my girl," says Do-YeOn. He savors her look of desperate anger before shutting off the call.

| 57 |

In Three Days

The kids on the balcony have been banging around for hours. I can hear them from my bathroom, even with the door closed. Although I guess that isn't much soundproofing. I wipe, check the mirror, step back into the room.

Yep. Avery's still asleep. Snoring. I take two steps to the bed, push him toward the wall and move in to his warmth. Pull the sheet over us and drift into sleep. This is nicer than jail.

// . . .

I wake up again. He's watching me. I'm not sure if that's creepy or endearing. I slap his face, gently, twice.

"I need to get back to work."

"You ought to take a day to decompress."

"Hang around here and stare at walls? I don't think so. I might as well talk to refrigerators. Maybe Soteria will call and tell me how it isn't able to restock. That would be familiar. Something I know."

I spray on a set of clothes while Avery uses my water allotment for a shower. I hand him the can of blue spray cloth. I reconsider. I take the blue and give him red. It's sexy. This small room amplifies our new intimacy.

I cook two eggs, give one to Avery and we head out. It's not a great breakfast but we'll survive. I'm nice to the kids and the trash scuttlers; I've got a headful of endorphins. Screw Belo. Screw Do-YeOn Kurrat. Screw danger and disaster.

Avery and I walk toward the train. He holds my hand. How cute. We sit side by side. How adorable.

"Avery, did you ever meet with Araci Belo?"

"He told me they had arrested you and could I help him with a dead personality cube. He had access to Soteria and we could retrieve Jupyter1. I pointed out the line with Do-Ye0n's admin entry and explained how that was unusual. He glazed over on the details, so I gave him a datapack he can share. I haven't heard from him since."

I'm confused. If I were trying to blackmail a corporation, this isn't the way I'd do it. I'd be smarter. Araci is a technical boob. Or a superb actor. I'm not sure what to make of him.

"Let me call him." Avery waves up a connection, I assume he's calling Araci. There's a pause before he disconnects. "No answer."

Where is he? And what is he doing?

// . . .

We walk past the maintenance floor, but Lucy waves and runs to us. I stop. Avery stops behind me and watches.

"Hi," says Lucy. "Did you see the note about that Soteria unit?"

"I've been offline for the weekend." I look at Avery. Lucy looks at Avery, looks at me, then back at Avery. Lucy smiles. She must think we've had a glorious weekend of nonstop romance. I'm not in the mood to rehash my incarceration. "Is this the unit that's been calling me?"

Lucy stops smirking at Avery and looks back at me. "Yep. You and Rob went to visit this unit. That Soteria has a crush on you. But I received an intent to dispose of asset."

"For Soteria? Disposal?"

"Recycled. We'll capture the refrigerant, pull off the plastic and grind the circuits for heavy metal reclamation. It won't be calling you after that."

This is a surprise. A coincidence? Jordan's claim on the apartment and contents ended with her "accident" so the owners of her appliances must be cleaning house. Sure. That's all.

"When is it scheduled?" I ask.

"The sixteenth. Three days."

"When does it go offline?"

"Sometime between now and then. Depends on the owner."

"Can you call me when it arrives?"

Lucy makes a note. Avery and I head upstairs. We grab side-by-side workstations; how romantic.

I log on to find a queue of broken kitchen machines. Soteria is among them. I wonder if anyone has told Soteria it's approaching end of life. How do you tell a refrigerator it's going to die? I pull little vacation guy out of the line and place him in the center of the desk.

I know what he will say; `I am unable to restock a depleted product. I have successfully reordered, and received delivery confirmation, but the requested product has not arrived.`

Yep. No surprises.

"Soteria, show me Jupyter1."

```
adminID : Do-YeOn Kurrat
ownerID : CityOfPortland.PublicVehicle
vehicleID : UrCityCars#33579
manufacturerID : PDX>Go
locationID : <List>
```

It's still there. The datapack might be enough but I suspect whoever Araci shares it with will have more questions of Soteria.

I try another call with Araci. What *is* that asshole doing? I get no answer. But I'm leaving a message.

"Araci, where are you? Call me."

Call me or *else,* you butthole. I'm not sure what "else" means. I could send an attack-sheep after him. Dress it up in a black spy uniform. Better yet, a wolf costume. Araci would walk down a dark alley, would hear the clicking of hooves behind him, would turn around, but—too late!

My visor signals a private call. What a pleasant surprise; it's my old friend Mr. Belo. I silently rehearse an insult for him, but when I answer, it's Detective Guadalupe Reyes.

Starting the day waking up with Avery, then a linear disintegration of happiness because of Detective Reyes, I can only assume next will be the coming Armageddon. How delightful!

| 58 |

Call To Surrender

Lupe flips through pictures of Araci. A grief counselor sits across from her, waiting. An antique coffee pot brews, mostly for the comforting scent. Lupe can only hear, taste, or feel Araci's terror as his vehicle bounces and rolls.

She's not sitting in a sterile morgue. That's for Araci. She sits in a wood-paneled counselor's office. The window panorama overlooks the west hills of Portland. She bats the pictures away and throws her visor. It's unsatisfying. She'd be happier shooting rats on her beach property. That has physicality, noise, and impact.

She stands, retrieves the visor and the box of Araci's possessions, politely says goodbye to the counselor, and walks outside to the restored Keller fountain. Falling water and playful children are a universal balm. Lupe sits for half an hour, watching and listening, trying to take part in the beauty of the park. It fails her.

Araci is dead. She takes his visor out of the box, opens the contacts icon and calls Jupyter. There is enough of a delay to give Lupe a chance to reconsider, but she doesn't. Jupyter appears before her.

"Oh. Hello. Here to arrest me again? Are you and Mr. Belo having a good laugh about ambushing me at the station? Ha. *I am so amused.* Let's play that game again." Jupyter straightens her back and stares. "What do you want? I have unimportant things to do and you're preventing me from getting them done."

Lupe's aggression rises from her core. She reaches to grab and throw the virtual woman standing in front of her. "Araci is dead. In a car crash."

Jupyter - the virtual Jupyter in Lupe's visor - must be sitting at a desk, since only her top-half is visible. But that's enough to see her stop, mid-snark. Her eyes widen a bit, her lips pull tight. She starts, but stops speaking.

Lupe fills the pause. "My relationship with Araci was the highlight of every day."

"A car accident?" Jupyter stutters. "He died in a car?"

"Yes," Lupe snarls. "In a car controlled by your botnet. Tomorrow, three p.m., you'll surrender yourself at the police station. I expect you to take responsibility for Jordan Bishop and Araci's accidents."

Jupyter squints and pauses with a brief expression of confusion. "Botnet?"

"Botnet," says Lupe. "The botnet that causes accidents. You're responsible for both deaths."

"Hang on." Jupyter turns and has a muffled conversation with someone to her side, then adds a man to the view.

"Lupe, this is Avery. Avery and Mr. Belo met on Saturday. When was his accident?"

"Yesterday at noon. He was returning from lunch with Do-YeOn Kurrat."

"Why was he meeting that guy? He's involved. I showed Araci the jupyter1 files," says Avery.

Jupyter interrupts, "Jupyter1 is a snapshot of a discrepancy between the personality cube from the car Jordan was riding in and Jordan's refrigerator. The Soteria unit calling me had a complete copy of the uncorrupted log file and it describes the crash. It shows a connection between Do-YeOn Kurrat and PDX-1217."

Lupe sits. Watches the kids jump around in the fountain. "You've been unreliable with that story. You told Araci you couldn't find anything, then you tell us you found something, but you couldn't show it to us because the cube didn't work anymore. Now you say you saved a snapshot of the accident?"

"I don't understand why the cube went offline," said Jupyter. "It was working until we met at the train station. But I didn't break it.

The snapshot, what we're calling Jupyter1, is something that turns up when you pull in the log file from Soteria."

"Soteria?" asks Lupe. "Araci got a call from a refrigerator he called Soteria."

"Welcome to my chosen profession. They call all the time," said Jupyter. "This refrigerator has been more persistent than others."

Lupe considers this information. "Do either of you know what happened at Araci's meeting with Kurrat?"

Avery begins, but Jupyter interrupts. "We haven't heard from him since Saturday."

"Fine. This is possible. Meet me tomorrow and show me jupyter-number-whatever. Be here at 3:00. If Kurrat is behind these accidents and you can prove it, my opinion of you will change for the better."

Jupyter looks at Avery, then back at Lupe. "I'll be pleased to make Kurrat's life miserable. See you tomorrow."

| 59 |

Praying To The Demo God

You would think Dan's appliance quiets down at night. You'd think the appliances drift off to sleep in appliance dreamland.

But, they don't sleep, so a bunch of us are still here. Fish is burning in the kitchen. If I were to enter the break room, I'd find someone reprogramming the oven personality. It's one way to learn how these things work, but I wish they'd do it on their home unit. Like me.

Avery is snoring. He moved to the couch after falling off his chair. It's nice of him to stick around while I dig around in Soteria's guts. His enthusiasm curve has approached zero since midnight.

Tomorrow I'm walking into Officer Reyes' lair and proving her wrong. Not just prove her wrong, prove her so wrong she can only gasp and marvel at how wrong her wrong was wrong.

"Soteria, spool the PDX-1217 log file, start at June 4th, 2062 at 9:14 a.m."

```
2062-06-04T09:14:23-08:00 - ContactCar
    InitiatedBy Soteria.Reizoko/
      IFS-6582738539
    Owner JORDAN BISHOP confirmed
    order_confirmation_code
      DHPN-WGYT-0232-TLLK
    pickupConfirmation is
      DAGX-INWC-9677-WZVZ
    Sending transport_logistics
      to Soteria.Reizoko
```

```
2062-06-04T09:14:23-8:00 - Continue route

2062-06-04T09:16:53-08:00 - AvoidCollision
  (Diagnostic)
    Multiple Pedestrians in road
    Collision barrier on left
    Collision barrier on right
    Severity is catastrophic
    Probability is certain
    Action is swerve
```

Soteria does exactly that, again, as I expect. I've practiced so my presentation is flawless. Live demos are prone to disaster, no matter how many times they go right during rehearsal.

There's a god of demonstrations–his name is Earl. Earl the demo god. Earl is capricious. Just when you've satisfied his whims, he dreams up another. Fail to meet this new condition and everything fails. Paranoia is the best approach. That's my state of mind and has been for a week.

"Soteria, spool your version of the corresponding log file from PDX-1217."

```
2062-06-04T09:14:23-08:00 - ContactCar
    InitiatedBy Soteria.Reizoko/IFS-6582738539
    Owner JORDAN BISHOP confirmed
    order_confirmation_code DHPN-WGYT-0232-TLLK
    pickupConfirmation is DAGX-INWC-9677-WZVZ
    Sending transport_logistics
      to Soteria.Reizoko

2062-06-04T09:14:23-8:00 - Diagnostic monitor
      installed
2062-06-04T09:14:23-8:00 - Diagnostic session
      initiated
    InitiatedBy UrCityCars#33579

2062-06-04T09:14:24-08:00 - RouteChange
```

```
      (Diagnostic)
    Destination is 2272 NE 201st Ave,
      Fairview, OR 97024

2062-06-04T09:14:24-08:00 - Driving
      (Diagnostic)
2062-06-04T09:16:53-08:00 - AvoidCollision
      (Diagnostic)
    Multiple Pedestrians in road
    Collision barrier on left
    Collision barrier on right
    Severity is catastrophic
    Probability is certain
    Action is swerve
```

"Soteria, show the background information for the PDX-1217 debug session in process on June 4th, 2062 at 9:14 a.m."

```
adminID :Do-YeOn Kurrat
ownerID :CityOfPortland.PublicVehicle
vehicleID :UrCityCars#33579
manufacturerID :PDX>Go
locationID :<List>;
```

Everything works. I can show PDX-1217's version of the crash, and I can show how Soteria recorded a different version of the crash. PDX-1217 says pedestrians caused the crash; Soteria says the pedestrians were phantoms, created by the illicit use of a diagnostic monitor. Finally, I can use jupyter1 to show Do-YeOn was in control of PDX-1217 when it crashed.

I know my lines, Soteria knows his. Earl is appeased.

No question what happened and who is responsible. I bid Soteria goodnight and walk over to Avery. A cushion covers his face and his feet hang off the end. It looks uncomfortable, but his breathing is regular and slow. It's soothing. I'd like to be part of his meditation, but there's no room on the couch, there are too many curious eyes, and no privacy if anything happened that *needed* more privacy.

"Wake up Avery. Let's go. I need sleep before my big presentation."

60

Soteria.Reizoko[2062-06-14]

Event Log for Soteria.Reizoko

Serial: IFS-6582738539

Owner is JORDAN BISHOP

2062-06-14T00:00:00-08:00 – ADMINISTRATIVE_MESSAGE

This unit will be decommissioned on 2062-06-16T00:00:00-08:00

Reason: Malfunction. Warranty = FALSE

2062-06-14T01:18:23-08:00 – External_contact

Close conversation

Support Tech: Jupyter Fuertes, EmpID RttS-5172-720

2062-06-14T08:30:23 - SHUTDOWN

| 61 |

A Quality Machine

The door stares at her and she stares back.

It confirms she is an employee of International Mercado and scheduled to be here, so it sets the security cameras to record and unlocks itself.

She pushes the dolly into apartment 822. The dolly carries a box big enough to be awkward but small enough that one person can lift the contents. She steps inside and lets the door close itself.

Two pairs of women's shoes are in the hallway. This is a clean apartment, everything neat and spacious. Large windows overlook the richer part of town and acres of single-family homes. The minimum wage employee from International Mercado looks around, wishing she lived here.

She glides the box into the kitchen and removes the refrigerator from the wall. It's an effort—the older models are bulkier and heavier. Her job is to replace these obsolete units with newer, lower maintenance versions. They have a smaller capacity, but that means more opportunities for restock. Which means more opportunities to get owners into stores, which means more opportunities for impulse sales. Clever, clever International Mercado!

A press on the side of the old refrigerator opens the circuit drawer. She confirms the personality module is still in place, then seals the drawer with a piece of security tape.

She hefts the new refrigerator into place. It boots up, and the avatar appears, standing on the counter in front of her.

`Hello, I'm Owen. Pleased to meet you,` says the Owen Jacobs avatar. He's a decent animation, a mark of a quality machine. The Soteria unit she's dropping in the shipping box is a source of unending service calls. She is glad to see another one heading for disposal.

She puts Owen into standby, ready for the next tenant. She drags the dolly, box and deactivated Soteria into the hall.

Inside the apartment, a small bush is dying in a pot. Somebody will throw it out later.

| 62 |

A New Apartment

If Do-Ye0n was serious about this apartment, he would have dressed formally. But he needs pockets, something formal attire doesn't have.

Even before he's arrived at the door of the Shipyard Apartments, the concierge, an artificial dark-haired woman, is in his visor.

`Hello Mr. Kurrat, we've been expecting you. We're glad you're considering joining the Shipyard community. My name is Françiose. You can summon me as 'Françiose the Concierge.' Or Françiose. Or Concierge. I'll answer to any of them and will be pleased to provide you with the amenities of a top-flight residence.`

Françiose the Concierge delivers this in a pompous Eastern Canadian accent. Do-Ye0n finds it intriguing; exactly as designed by the Shipyard Apartments marketing team. Françiose is specialized for Do-Ye0n according to his profile. Some eople are slightly embarrassed by the appearance and behavior of the concierge avatar; it says quite a bit about their personal habits.

"I read apartment 822 will be available soon," replies Do-Ye0n.

`It will. I can open an application.`

"I'd like to see it first."

`Gladly. Please follow me.`

Françiose walks to the front door and opens it, a clever bit of coordination between the augmented reality playing out in Do-Ye0n's visor and the door robotics. She shows him to the elevator and brings him to the eighth floor, twenty-second apartment. Françiose opens the door and stands aside. `Please, come in.`

Do-YeOn enters. *Not as nice as mine,* he thinks. He makes a show of looking out the window, inspecting the bedroom, measuring the kitchen. Françiose waits in the living room.

"Françiose, can you play music? Something classical. How about the second movement of Bohemian Rhapsody by Queen? I'd like to hear the acoustics."

Françiose plays the request, starting with the famous words of the second movement.

I see a little silhouette of a man

"Françiose, louder please."

Bohemian Rhapsody increases in volume, louder than necessary to appreciate the nuances of Freddie Mercury's vocals.

Scaramouch, scaramouch will you do the fandango

Do-YeOn paces the length of the kitchen. Two steps one way, then two steps back.

Thunderbolt and lightning, very, very frightening me

He turns to face the refrigerator. Reaching up, he pops open the circuit drawer. "I'm a technology enthusiast. You don't mind if I check the condition of this unit, do you?"

Françiose's voice mutes the music. `Feel free to inspect all aspects of the apartment.` Bohemian Rhapsody resumes at volume.

Gallileo, Gallileo, Gallileo, Gallileo,

As smoothly as he can manage, he swaps an old personality cube in his pocket for the cube in the refrigerator. He closes the circuit drawer and turns to face Françiose, pocketing the new personality cube.

"Thanks, Françiose. You can turn off the music."

Bohemian Rhapsody stops in mid-figaero.

"When do I need to decide?"

`I am ready to process your application, Mr. Kurrat. Would you like me to do that for you now?`

"No. Not yet. I need to confirm a couple of things first."

Françiose moves to open the door for Do-Ye0n. He steps into the hall and towards the elevator.

So easy, he thinks. *So easy.*

| 63 |

My New Boyfriend

I've been awake since Avery started snoring. We got to my apartment late. I don't want to leave but there's nothing productive to do here.

"Avery," I shake his ankle from where I sit on the bed. "Time to go. I need to do something besides be here." He snorts and regards me from the only pillow I own.

"Should we head to work? Get breakfast? Take the day off?"

"You should take a shower," I sniff. "You're smelly. It was a long night."

Avery rolls to the floor, regains his feet and steps to the bathroom.

Sunlight is streaming into the room and I reach out and touch a reflection on the wall, tracing the shapes from the building across the alley. The neighbor kids must be gone to school and their parents at work.

I don't know much about Avery. Paranoia is the catalyst in our relationship: I get scared, there's Avery, let's make out. I could ask him about him. But I'd rather spy, learn what he might not want to tell me. I put on my visor, find his public information and open him. *That's erotic.* I snicker.

My new boyfriend is a world of unexciting. No secret missions, no arrests, no sudden relocations or name changes indicative of someone involved with international money laundering or securities fraud. Just a youth spent in rural Oregon, moved to the city, picked up an associates degree in computer technology, started here less than a year ago. No high school awards, no participation in the young engineers club.

His elementary photo is adorable: big ears, bad haircut, all teeth. As he gets older his face catches up with his ears, but he keeps the same incompetent barber. Photos with friends appear: swimming in a quarry, camping, cheering in the stands at a soccer game.

I find my favorite; Avery with a sheep. My two loves. The sheep is oblivious: Avery is thrilled about a red ribbon for second place at a county fair. I save it for display in the apartment. So cute.

That's the information anyone can see. But I'm skilled at this and I dig deeper. Nothing illegal—that might not be the best decision given my current relationship with the Oregon Department of Justice.

I sniff around the perimeter of Avery's network. He's a case study in neglectful security. He set it up while he was at a community college, then forgot it. Updates aren't downloaded, patches aren't installed, known exploits are still available.

Avery steps out of the shower and flumps on the bed. Next to me, he checks his personal communication folders. In my visor, I can trace the request as it flows through leaky portals. Avery's query hits a node that sends an unexpected message in an external direction. I take a closer look.

It's a wedge. a first-year tech school lab project, something Avery would (should) notice were he paying attention. I trace it; what to my wondering eyes should appear but Do-YeOn's firewall.

oh. crap.

I haven't opened the packet just sent from Avery to Do-YeOn, but I'll bet one small diarrhea tea it's a tap on Avery's communications. How deep and how long is uncertain, but the most likely worst-case scenario is Do-YeOn has been privy to everything Avery has been doing on the network. *Dammit, Avery.*

On the upside, conversations we've had without wearing our visors (or other clothing) have been private. On the downside, Do-YeOn knows about me.

"Avery," I take his visor and turn it off. He objects until I give it back to him. He reaches to power it up but I slap his hand away and shake my head *no.*

"What are you doing?"

"I was..." How do I tell him I was sniffing around his background on a voyeuristic mission to discover secrets of my new partner? "... I was looking for your address, and... and found an intercept wedge in your firewall."

He sags; it reminds me of the photo of the boy with big ears. I remember the other photo, the one with the sheep, and soften. I give him a quick smile. Not enough to let him off, but enough to apologize for being irritable.

"I would update, but I've been doing other things."

Doing me, he means. But being cute will not fix this. "Your firewall is in sad shape and has been so for months. I expect better. I traced the destination on the wedge. Guess who? Do-YeOn has been watching you for I don't know how long. He knows everything, including our chat with Lupe yesterday."

Avery says nothing, but tries to put his arms around me. I'm not having it. I need this anger.

"I can remove the intercept," says Avery. "It's easy to fix."

"NO," I shout. My anger propels the word out of me with more force than I expected. "You can't give Do-YeOn a reason to do something rash. Leave it in place. Just don't send anything you don't want him to see."

Now I hug him. This is scary, but I'm better at this tech than he is. I'll fix it somehow.

"Let's do something different," I say. "I don't want to spend the day checking on Soteria and worrying about Detective Reyes."

"We could take a train out to my parent's farm. It's only a one-hour ride."

I'm bouncing out of bed and putting on farm-going clothes before Avery finishes. A day with sheep is perfect. I should work so I can afford this expansive apartment. But I know I'd just fiddle with Soteria and Jupyter1.

// . . .

Avery and I agree to go visorless on the train, at least to the extent possible. We can keep Do-YeOn from knowing everything. We buy one-day tickets, then turn our visors off. Avery recognizes the stations without help. We make up stories to explain the scenery.

We miss our stop and get off at the next, laughing at how we're pretending to be Luddites. Avery sees his neighbor at the feed store; he offers us a ride. His neighbor drives an old pickup–*with his hands.* We're only traveling on dirt roads, but it's terrifying to think we're relying on a human brain to handle collision avoidance.

He drops us off at the end of the driveway and we walk to the house. It's a warm day and Avery's mom is on the front porch, just back from feeding the chickens. It's a scene from a movie.

I'm introduced to Mom and Dad and they want us to stay for dinner. Avery's Dad invites us on errands, but we have to refuse. Not enough time for either.

Mom goes to fix a pump, Dad leaves for town. I have coffee in a ceramic cup. It must be an antique cup. It has an honest weight, even when it's empty.

Avery's parents replaced the fireplace inside the farmhouse with a monitor displaying family photos. Avery has an older sister and younger brother. She's married and moved out of state. The younger brother lives nearby.

We toured the house, and now are sitting on the balcony with no railing. I could jump off if I wanted. But I want to stay right here. It's an authentic farm house, owned by Avery's family since the early 2000s. Sheep wander around, doing what sheep have always done.

"Avery," I say. I drink coffee. I watch the sheep. "Why don't you want to stay here?"

Avery doesn't move. I expected him to spray coffee out of his nose or something. But nothing.

"It's not what I'm supposed to do," he says. "I'm supposed to be the kid that moves out."

"I like this," I tell him. "Honestly, tech isn't working for you. You're way better with the sheep than you are with appliances. Or with your network security."

He winces. I haven't brought this up since I yelled at him, but he remembers the conversation. He explains, but I don't want to restart the argument. Instead, I stand.

"Hey, Olive!" I yell at the sheep. Most of them ignore me, except Olive, who comes over to stare at me. Olive knows her name.

"I could be talked into staying here," I continue. Maybe I'm rushing, but this is something I want. Portland becomes less a part of the plan.

It's funny that I moved here with Pali—who hated sheep—and find myself on a sheep ranch because of it.

We go for a walk and he shows me the smaller house on the side of the property. It's newer with modern construction and four times the size of my apartment. The bed is in a loft under a window looking at the valley. There's high-grade internet, courtesy of a rural data project. There's a desk on the main floor; a quiet place to write code.

It's after lunch before I remember my appointment with Detective Reyes. Avery's Dad needs help with fence repair, so Avery drives me (yes–*drives* the car by hand) to the train and waves as I settle in for the ride back to the city.

Without Avery to distract me, I turn on my visor and check in with Soteria, but no response. I'm guessing the internet is between satellites. That's fine, I'm still in the giddy afterglow of the sheep ranch.

| 64 |

I'm Owen

"I've got it, it was so easy. I just waltzed in, did sleight of hand and I was out."

Do-YeOn talks at Pali. The line at Amadore's Espresso Shop is short, but Pali finds the wait intolerable. This isn't a leisurely place; move to the bar, order, swallow, then head back to work. Conversation is quick and trivial. Amadore doesn't make money if customers linger. Most important, Amadore is more worried about his espresso machine than his security cameras. The power cord has hung from the camera enclosure since he opened. That's why Do-YeOn and Pali meet here.

Pali isn't wearing her visor. Do-YeOn carries his. Pali insisted on meat-space, no network traffic involved.

"I'm sure you were as careful as you always are," says Pali. "Let me have it. I'm in a hurry."

"Can't leave Amadore's without espresso. It would be suspicious," says Do-YeOn. "Besides, I'm buying. Double shot?"

Pali looks around. "Fine. Double shot."

They move to the line, three customers deep.

"One thing more," Do-YeOn says. "PDX>Go records inconveniently list me as admin. You need to fix that."

Pali turns to Do-YeOn. "I'm not going to do that."

"As mentioned before, if I'm implicated, then *we* are implicated. My name shouldn't appear as an admin for a PDX>Go vehicle. I'll admit, that was a mistake on my part. There, I've made my penance, please forgive me, now change it. It's only three lines of code."

Pali turns away. "What else?" she asks nobody in particular.

Only two customers between them and Amadore.

"You know, we should try to be friends," says Do-YeOn. "We're in the same business. Someday we'll work together. You'll report to me. We'll look back on this speed bump and laugh."

"I hope that never happens. The thought of looking to you for direction on any project fills me with despair. I would rather serve espresso here at Amadore's than clean up your daily mess."

"You never explained why you contacted me," says Do-YeOn. "You've only explained this as a clever idea to remove Jordan from our mutual interests. Do you know something? Is PDX>Go buying UrCityCars? Is my stock going to become immensely valuable?"

"Maybe I should pitch that to the executive team at our weekly discussion of insane things we could do to roil the market." Pali shifts in her pumps, taking the weight off of one leg. "I have no further reasons I care to discuss. At least, not with you."

"So prickly," says Do-YeOn. "Two espresso please. Doubles."

// . . .

Pali leaves a moment before Do-YeOn, glad to be away. She hurries, quicker than usual, burning off agitation from the meeting. He's driven, but careless and pompous. It's possible they could work at the same company, although more likely Do-YeOn will report to her.

Pali stops at a shop window, regretting she had provided Do-YeOn with access codes for PDX>Go vehicles. True, Jordan was harassing UrCityCars, making it harder for them to compete with PDX>Go. Unfortunately, Jordan was dangerously close to forcing UrCityCars entirely out of the market. That would leave PDX>Go the sole supplier of public cars and the primary target of complaints about autonomous vehicles-in this or any other city.

UrCityCars made PDX>Go look good. PDX>Go needed an incompetent competitor.

Pali resumes her walk to PDX>Go, but at a less-agitated pace. She anticipated her career path at PDX>Go would lead to a promotion to vice-president, then CEO. If that promotion was to happen, Jordan was not only interferring with UrCityCars, but also with Pali's promotion to CEO.

Do-YeOn provided useful research for Pali's Ph.D; they worked together and even started a relationship before their irreconcilable differences forced them apart. Using Do-YeOn to scare off Jordan Bishop wasn't a good option, but it was an option.

Fucking Jordan Bishop, she thought.

There was also Jupyter's rusted truck. Jordan Bishop just would not let that piece-of-shit be. She sent multiple complaints to the city for parking too long on the street. Jupyter wouldn't sell it and wouldn't buy a parking spot. Fed up with the angst and arguments, Pali had it towed and junked while Jupyter was at work.

It was dangerous and uncomfortable as hell. The autonomous after-market package was a death trap. Pali did Jupyter a favor. Jupyter was hysterical. Pali hadn't realized the truck was an emotional thing. So she blamed its disappearance on Jordan.

Pali had assumed a forever relationship. They would parent children. They would grow old together. That wouldn't happen if Jupyter found out the truth of the truck. Jordan was a personal liability.

// ...

Pali enters the PDX>Go building and heads straight to her office. She has a private set of tools for diagnosis and manipulation of personality cubes; tools she invested in for her Ph.D research. For as much grief as she had given Do-YeOn, this is a cake-walk. The refrigerator will scramble the log file and update the block chain. CTAS will invalidate the advisory. As long as Do-YeOn resists using his debug terminal again, it's a momentary glitch.

She powers up the diagnostic board, clips in the personality cube, and syncs in her visor.

Hello, I'm Owen. Pleased to meet you, says Owen Jacobs. The refrigerator icon is well-designed, and Pali takes a moment to appreciate the fine detail of the avatar and the intricate behavior. She reaches to grab the short man and smiles as it not only moves out of her grasp, but maintains a sense of balance. Owen even watches where he is going. Nicely done.

"Owen," Pali addresses the avatar. "Show me the file you provided to support CTAS Block and Avoid identifier Diagnostic-slash-Do-YeOn-underbar-Kurrat."

Owen crosses his arms and tilts his head. His hair moves in a light wind. `I'm sorry, I don't have a file matching your specification.`

"What log files do you contain?" Pali asks. Owen spreads his arms, displaying a few storage cubes. Pali opens each. Her frown grows deeper.

"These files are only a few days old. I'm looking for files from June fourth."

`My apologies, but there are no files before this collection.` Owen smiles and continues to offer the existing storage cubes.

What? Pali thinks. She pulls the CTAS record for another look and confirm she is using the correct identifier.

"Owen, show me a list of files with any form of the string 'kurrat'."

`There are none.`

Pali looks at the CTAS advisory again. She searches upwards.

"Owen, who is your manufacturer?"

`I am a product of Iwani Manufacturing.`

"Are you known as Soteria Reizoko, IFS-6582738539?"

Owen shakes his head. `No. I am not.`

Pali could check again, but the answer won't change. This is not Soteria. The log files aren't here. Calling Do-YeOn is pointless. He won't be able to fix this. She can't fix this.

| 65 |

Demo Jupyter1

I take the train directly from Avery's sheep ranch to the police station. The door opens, I step onto the platform, down the stairs, ten meters closer to my destiny.

hopethisgoeswellhopethisgoeswellhopethisgoeswell etc ...

Two blocks. Open door, walk in, tell uniform at the desk I'm here to see Detective Reyes. Go sit in an uncomfortable chair. Fidget. Read news. Do nervous things. Check presentation status with Soteria.

Soteria doesn't respond.

Um.

Check presentation status with Soteria.

Soteria doesn't respond. Troubleshoot visor. Troubleshoot connection. Troubleshoot connection with Soteria. Nope. Panic. PANIC.

"Jupyter Fuertes?" It's the front lobby person. They want me. I'm busy right now. I switch back to my private hell with no Soteria.

"Jupyter? Are you ready?" It's Detective Reyes. I stand up because she can see me. I walk through security, it flags nothing. I hope I get to walk back out the door later today. I follow Reyes.

"I've reserved a conference room. I'm looking forward to our discussion." She's in bitch mode. If Soteria were responding, I'd be in bitch response. But Soteria is AWOL.

"I need to pee," I say out loud. *Pee? Who says pee?* I do.

"Bathroom right there. On your right. I'll be waiting for your return in this conference room." Detective points to the obvious bathroom sign.

I enter. Uniform guy walks out. He doesn't even glance at me. I must not be criminal material. I find an empty stall and sit with my pants on. I'm not here to pee, I'm here to find Soteria. *Where the hell are you?*

Debug. Think. Take a deep breath. Don't scream. Can't get Soteria back online. Little sweater guy is not here. Earl the demo god is not appeased.

Contingency plan is run like hell. I moderate that plan and walk like hell. Stroll past the conference room. Left at the security door. Everything is good. Nothing wrong. Breathing. Not in a fucking panic. Nope. Not me.

"Jupyter? Where are you going?"

I bolt for the door.

| 66 |

Unexpected Departure

Detective Reyes stands in the conference room, waiting for Jupyter to come back from the bathroom. She can see the hallway from here; Jupyter could either turn right and go further into the police station or turn left and walk past this door.

This is the second time they've been face to face. In the squad car, Reyes was in control. This time, she's not. Her anger tenses her neck. Her back. Fuertes had better have a good story, but Detective Reyes doesn't expect it. She already set up the arrest. Reyes has wrist restraints ready.

Jupyter walks by the room, looking straight ahead. She missed the room, but she'll realize her mistake in three meters. Detective Reyes waits for her to reappear. She doesn't. Detective Reyes walks to the door, looks to the right and sees Jupyter exiting the security door.

"Jupyter? Where are you going?"

Jupyter jumps through the security door and out of sight.

Detective Reyes could give chase, but why? It's easier to lock down Jupyter's visor with an arrest warrant. She pulls up the warrant tool, drops in Jupyter's contact information, waits for authorization, then signals approval.

From here, Jupyter is pending arrest and her visor is tracked. It should be minutes before she returns.

| 67 |

Locked Visor

I'm past the door. Trying to walk and find Soteria at the same time. Also, trying to flag Avery. Everything is going FUBAR.

My visor flashes red. I mean, everything turns red for a brief. It's blinding and meant to get my attention. A message follows:

`PRIVACY NOTIFICATION: This visor is now being traced by Police request. Your location is no longer protected by privacy laws.`

Marvelous. I dig for system utilities, open the shutdown, select *Yes, I really mean it this time.* Select it again to confirm. My visor shuts off for the only time since I bought it. Dead plastic in my hand.

Avery's out of town. I need some place to go that isn't on my list of normal haunts. How do I get there?

Car == death.

Train? no visor == no ticket.

I guess I'm walking. I remember this neighborhood. It's where Pali and I used to live. It's where Pali lives. A reunion isn't the worst thing happening right now.

| 68 |

Disculpa

It's harder to get to Pali's without a visor pointing the way, but I recognize places we used to go. I turn left at the Chinese bakery. Right at the Palessi shoe store. A train station down the block, then the gate and the security camera.

The security door might talk to me, but no visor, so I won't know. I'll stand here until it signals Pali. She'll make me wait to assert dominance, then let me inside. The door clicks sooner than I expected, and she's here. All high heels and long hair and professional director-of-autonomous-presence and Ph.D. and a good dresser.

"Hi farm girl," says Pali. The same Pali who would never move to a farm.

"Can I stay here tonight? It's temporary."

She reaches to hug but I pull back.

"You're unexpected, but I'm glad you're here. I need to tell you things." She holds the door open and swings around behind me.

The elevator ride is awkward; I stare at the floor; she watches the progress display in her visor. Our ... her ... apartment is the same as when I left. The identical floor plan as Jordan Bishop's, but flipped.

"Do you want the pull-out bed?"

"I'm not sleeping with you."

"I assumed, but hoped for otherwise. Have you eaten dinner? A glass of wine?"

I look at her in the kitchen. Back straight, beautiful posture. She sees me and pushes stray hair behind her ear. She knows what she's doing.

I'm a fugitive hiding out at a manipulative ex-girlfriend's well-furnished apartment. I'd be safer wearing an orange jumpsuit and hanging out with my jail-buddies.

My instincts don't have good decision-making skills. I hear myself; "Dinner and wine is great. Do you have a spare visor I could borrow? Mine's broken."

"I have a demo visor in the bottom drawer in the bedroom. It's anonymous, and it's charged."

Pali's bedroom is right where it was. The dresser has five drawers, the bottom two were mine. Now they're filled with loose tech and drawer flotsam. The visor is in an electrostatic bag, shiny but old-style. It's modern enough to work and I call Avery. He disconnects; I must register as an untrusted caller. I call again, then again. He answers the fourth time.

"I'm tracing you. Drop the scrambler or I send the tracepath in for prosecution." This is the first time I've seen Avery being aggressive. I don't think I like it.

"Avery, it's Jupyter. I'm on a borrowed visor."

"Tell me something Jupyter would know."

"I told you to take a shower this morning."

"Jupyter! How did the conversation with the Detective go? Why are you anonymous?"

"The presentation tanked. Soteria isn't responding. My visor is on police lockdown."

Avery asks more questions, but I cut him off. "I need you to find out why Soteria is AWOL. And I might need you to come pick me up, I'm resource constrained."

"Soteria," he says it like an answer to a question. "I'll call you."

"Thanks Avery. Love you." The last bit slips out unsupervised and before checking with me. But he's gone before I can change anything.

"Who was that?" Pali is standing at the door with two glasses of wine, one has her lipstick on the rim. She hands the other to me. I should explain Avery. I spin up a story, but stop. Golly, it's none of her business who I was talking too, and I tell her so.

"Jupyter, I only want to help you. Don't be defensive when I ask you simple questions."

"I wasn't being defensive!"

"And now you're hysterical. Calm down, drink a bit of that wine. But not too much, I have to tell you something."

God, I hate this. Why did I think coming here was a good idea? I can't leave without making a scene.

Pali sits on the bed, legs crossed at the ankle. She's leaning on her left hand, slightly behind her. Right hand bent at the wrist, holding the wineglass at an angle. She tilts her head back and away from me, lips parted in a smile. She's practiced this too.

She stands and turns into Pali the Manager. "I'm leaving," she says.

"Don't. I'm sleeping in the other room. I'm not staying in here."

"No. I'm leaving. Leaving the United States. I'm going back to Montevideo." She walks out of the bedroom and I follow her into the kitchen.

"Why?" That comes out in distress. I need better control of my words. "Is there a job there?"

"No. But there is a situation here that I don't want to be part of. Have you heard of Do-YeOn Kurrat?"

It's one of those mind-blank moments. Yes. No. I shouldn't admit. Or should I say he's been messing with a dangerous technology?

"I've heard of him." A chicken-shit answer.

"Do-YeOn did some stupid things. Some of them will affect me, and I'm unable to fix what he broke. So I need to be in Montevideo for a while. You could come with me!"

"No." *Finally...* something intelligent issues forth from my vocal apparatus. "I'm locked out of my visor. An airport and a trip past the border is legally complicated."

"Those are things that can be fixed. But look, dinner is served and we can watch a movie. Maybe something interactive?"

I'll ask about Do-YeOn, but carefully. I promise myself not to get drunk in this apartment. Then I finish the glass of wine in my hand

and accept the plate of food Pali is offering. She refills my glass and saunters into the living room. This is how we started. Dammit.

| 69 |

Soteria.Reizoko[2062-06-15]

NO_RESPONSE

| 70 |

Search For Soteria

I'm keeping my eyes closed. If I open them, I may see Pali. She'll notice I'm awake. She'll want to talk. I'll want to answer. That's never worked in my favor. So I'm keeping my eyes closed.

I hear nothing. No shower, no kitchen clinking, no visor conversations, no ruffling of skirts. It's safe.

Pali left without waking me. I get up and check, but there's no clues to show she's coming back soon.

Coffee and scrambled eggs are in the refrigerator, so I eat and think. Today's mission is to bring Soteria back in the game and get me out of Detective Reyes evil clutches.

Things in my favor:

1. I'm not in jail.
2. Pali's not here.

Things not in my favor:

1. I have no way to communicate except with this anonymous visor. Every time I use it I'm closer to being traced and arrested.
2. Soteria is not responding, so I can't prove I'm innocent.

Normally, I'd be swimming in the deep water of information bandwidth. Instead, I'm chewing toast and looking out the window. I could wait for Avery to call with a status update. Yep, just look out the window, waiting. Yep. Looking out the window. La de dah. That works for five minutes before I get proactive and use one of my calls.

This should be easy, just say "Call Avery." But every time I call him, I touch my network and reveal my address. Do that enough times and someone will notice. Might as well walk into the police station and ask to borrow a set of handcuffs for my personal use.

Even if I do call Avery, we haven't dealt with the wedge in his network providing Do-YeOn with surveillance. Might as well just call Do-YeOn and tell him where to send the police.

Instead, I stumble around public social media, find something Avery posted, click through and hope he's watching for anonymous contacts not offering get-rich schemes. It takes half an hour and another coffee before he responds and I can send him a message.

"Waiting to hear about our cold friend. Has he warmed up yet?"

That's secret-agent talk for "call me right fucking now." I'm sure he'll understand. And in ten minutes, he does. Bless him. I know Do-YeOn is listening, but that can't be helped.

"Jupyter?"

"Yep. Here I am. Having a delightful morning. Don't think I'll be coming in to work today. You?"

"I'm tired. I've been up late. Are you ok?"

"I'm not wearing an orange jumpsuit, so that's a plus. But my life will go golly-wampus if I don't convince Reyes about Do-YeOn."

"Yah. I'm trying to get Soteria back online, but he doesn't even ping."

Maybe a personal visit to Jordan's apartment would be useful. Some cleaning person knocked Soteria loose from the wall. Happens sometimes.

I can't stroll in without a service appointment. But Rob can fix that.

"Avery, can you connect me through your account to Rob?"

"Can I what?"

"Vector me through your account. I don't know Rob's contact, but you do. So forward my call. I won't be traceable as me."

“um… hang on.”

Avery doesn’t know how to do this. Such a sweet boy, but not the brightest star in the tech support constellation. I give him minutes before I interrupt his endless loop.

“Avery?”

…mumbling…

“Avery, just give me Rob’s contact. I’ll handle it from here.”

“I almost have it.”

“Stop. Just send me the contact.”

“Are you angry?”

“Avery, I am trying to avoid the Portland Police Department with a borrowed visor while trying to locate a missing refrigerator. I’m frustrated. I’ll make up with you later, if I’m out of jail, but just give me Rob’s contact information. DO IT.”

I get the address; I say nice words to Avery and break the connection. I risk detection to call Rob.

“Rob, this is Jupyter. I need to go check on Soteria.”

“Uh, and good morning to you too?”

“It’s a crap morning. I need to fix Soteria in Jordan Bishop’s apartment. And to do that, I need you to set up a service call.”

“Okay. A slightly abrupt and unusual request,” says Rob. "Are we talking about that soteria unit we visited? Is this a blazing emergency? Can it wait until after breakfast?"

“It's a really long story and I'm in a bit of a panic,” I say. “Meet me at Dirty Water Cafe and I'll explain.” Pali and I used to spend Sunday mornings drinking coffee and playing games. Hopefully, it’s still there.

“This ought to be interesting. See you soon.” Rob disconnects.

I should clean. Do my dishes, straighten up the couch. I’ll apologize to Pali later, first I have to fix Soteria.

// . . .

Oh Lucky Day. Dirty Water is still here, but I don’t have money on this visor, so I wait outside and appear disinterested. I must keep moving or I’ll learn the response time for our local police force.

Rob pulls up. “You realize I had to spoof a service call?”

"Great. Fine. I'll be happy to add this to my list of transgressions. Please, can we go?"

Rob does the virtual driving things people do when they have a working visor—which I don't. It's odd looking from the outside at people with visor access. Everything is effortless. We arrive at Jordan's without dying.

Jordan's door recognizes Rob, but not me. I'd argue with the security system, but my visor isn't cooperating.

"She's my assistant," Rob explains. "She carries my tools."

Now I'm Rob's Sherpa. Fine. I'm one door away from fixing Soteria so I'll be happy to lift tools if it gets us inside. The door unlocks and opens and I push past Rob to get to the kitchen.

The refrigerator on the wall is not Soteria. It's shiny, smaller, and newer. But I'm only interested in Soteria's personality, who will not show up in this visor. I turn to Rob for help.

Rob says nothing for a minute. I can see him working controls, but the restraints on my visor prevent me from taking part. If I could see I could yank the controls out of his hands and fix this myself.

"This unit is dead," he says.

"Patch me through to what you're seeing."

Rob twists and connects and I see nothing. Where's my little guy in sunglasses and Hawaiian shirt and vacation mode asking about his damn product?

"Rob, where's Soteria?"

Rob tells me he has no idea, but someone's calling him. He waves me off and takes the call.

While he's talking, I pop the drawer and pull the personality module. It's nicked in places; obviously older than the refrigerator. This makes no sense.

"Hello Lucy," Rob says to the air. "Yep. We are. I did. It's what? Hang on, she's right here."

Rob looks at me, does another twist and connect and Lucy appears.

"Hi Jupyter. Rob says you're trying to do a service call on a Soteria unit."

"We are. It's the Soteria that's been calling me. It's offline and I need it to be active."

"So is that Soteria unit in the apartment?"

"NO. It's dead. The unit in the apartment is new. I don't think it's my Soteria."

"That probably makes sense. International Mercado would have swapped it out," says Lucy. "Remember, your Soteria is scheduled for disposal on the sixteenth."

"Right. But today is the fifteenth."

"It might be in transit. The owner can pick it up at anytime."

"They picked it up but didn't deliver it to Dan's Appliance? Where is it?"

"Somewhere in a truck or at a warehouse." Lucy adjusts her visor. "It will get here tomorrow."

Missing. In transit. These are words that don't bring me comfort. I've got to find that stupid little man before my bad luck rubs off on him.

"Rob, I need a ride to the shop. I'll buy you a cup of diarrhea tea when we get there."

| 71 |

Montevideo

Pali packs as if she is going to a conference. A change of clothes. A visor she can't get outside of the United States. Things she'll have difficulty replacing or purchasing in Montevideo. Things she packed in a hurry.

Yesterday, Pali didn't wake up with a plan to return to Uruguay. She would fix the mess Do-YeOn created. Buy groceries, clean the kitchen, watch a drama, go to bed.

That came apart with the personality cube. It unraveled so quickly, like dropping a bucket of paint on a new carpet. Instantly ruined, no repair possible, no options. Pali knew consequences will happen; there is no reason to stay and participate in the pandemonium.

She checks her visor for the departure time on the one-way flight; boarding in thirty minutes. She sits near the gate, ignores parents entertaining kids. Most of them have box lunches from airport food vendors - their last chance for North American food.

She can't imagine leaving PDX>Go. Leaving Portland. Leaving Jupyter. Maybe she'll find a job working on cars; Uruguay is the technology center of South America, she can lecture at the University. Even that option will disappear if she doesn't dodge the mess Do-YeOn created. Better to leave before things get loud and public; before they arrest her.

Jupyter will visit. Montevideo is beautiful. Clean, unpolluted, historic. Unemployment at two percent. Jupyter will find a job in minutes, could live on the outskirts on a sheep farm. It will be idyllic.

She looks at communications in her visor. Nothing yet. Jupyter hasn't called her, hasn't figured out she is leaving. She could have woken her up and explained. But what would she say? *Please drop everything and come with me.*

Romantic, but that might lead to uncomfortable questions and police and difficulty getting on this flight to Uruguay.

Do-Yeon will finally have to deal with his own mess. His own fault. Pali had become entirely too involved, it was stupid to give him access to PDX>Go cars, but love and revenge don't think through consequences.

The briefcase next to her feet is a backup plan. She might not need the electronics inside to examine a personality module. But if she does, getting a diagnostic monitor shipped to her in Montevideo would be *difficult*.

Boarding for first-class begins. Pali has splurged for this last trip. She picks up the briefcase and her bag and walks to the gate.

| 72 |

AIs Don't Argue

This generic visor is useless. It won't let me goad the truck to a quicker arrival at the shop. Rob could, but he's not participating in my crazy. My option, my only option, is to recline in this seat and do nothing. I am not content watching other vehicles weave and speed across the viaduct.

The van pulls around back of Dan's and I leap out like an action hero. Too much drama, but I need the violent motion and demonstration of my urgency. My theatrics last three steps before I have to stop, climb the loading dock, and facial-scan into the building. Action movies never play out this way, never have to pause, never have to go to the bathroom at inopportune times.

Lucy is doing what Lucy always does: herding cats and keeping robots aligned. Rob follows me, lugging his field kit and returning it to the shelf.

"Is Soteria here yet?" I ask Lucy.

"It hasn't appeared in the last fifteen minutes. You may have to wait." Lucy looks at Rob, who signals not to get involved in my really bad day. I head upstairs to the land of high-volume bandwidth.

There's an open workstation next to Avery, but he doesn't notice me until I put my hand on his shoulder. He jerks and looks at me; he must have been deep in a service call. He waves his hand to terminate the call.

"Did you find Soteria?" Avery asks, a bit too loudly. The tech next to Avery gives him the stink-eye. "Rob sent me a note the two of you were returning here."

"The whole unit was gone. Lucy says Soteria is in transit and should arrive at this facility."

But we don't have time for small talk. I need to make sure Soteria is actually on it's way here, not off to some meat-grinder where they'll turn him into digital sausage.

International Mercado is on my to-do list, so I risk another visor use and call them. I try to circumvent the public logon by flashing my ID and claiming I'm on official psychology business. Unfortunately, IntlMerc is savvy to my mind tricks.

A charming AI receptionist answers. I can tell it's an AI; it's too perfect. Normal humans have genetic defects or are sloppy dressers. Committees design artificial receptionists with research grants and endless focus groups. They never have a fleck of lunch on their shirt, or a left sleeve rolled up and not the right, or a pimple on their forehead. They've had their imperfect beaten out of them, so they're obviously faked.

This one is modeled to be Latinx, but isn't male or female. If this simulation is following standard marketing wisdom, it will subtly alter its looks and behaviors as it discovers what I prefer. I try to distract myself and imagine a gigantic marshmallow man, but I know the AI is watching my pupils for dilations and facial skin for blushing. My body betrays my mind. Better get started with this interrogation.

"I'd like the status of IFS-6582738539. Please tell me the arrival time at Dan's Artificial Psychology." It bothers me to have memorized Soteria's ID number, but details are important.

"Hello Jupyter Fuertes," says the simulation. "I think you're requesting the status of one of our leased food preservation units. Is that correct?"

"Yes, you stupid not-being. Where is the refrigerator?"

"IFS-6582738539 is a quality Soteria Reizoko device. It has been replaced by a newer and more efficient model, courtesy of International Mercado."

"And where is it?"

"The new Soteria Reizoko food storage unit is running and ready for use in the apartment."

"No. I mean, where is the original unit?"

"Are you asking for the status of the International Mercado unit known as IFS-6582738539?"

Only an AI would get caught in a response loop like this. But it's dragged me right along with it, so both of us are looping in a never-never logic land. Or it's doing this on purpose: trying to outlast my lifetime and then close the conversation. And it can literally do that.

"Yes," I reply. "I am asking for the current status of IFS-6582738539."

"IFS-6582738539 is not responding to my inquiries, so I do not know where it is. When it arrives at its next destination, would you like me to arrange for a call?" The receptionist is becoming more feminine, but with beard stubble. I'd love to see the marketing team decipher this in their Tuesday afternoon meeting.

"Where is its next destination?"

"IFS-6582738539 will be recycled within the next two days."

"Where will it be recycled?"

"Maintenance is under contract with private companies and is not available except via Police warrant. Because of this rule, I cannot tell you where IFS-6582738539 will be recycled."

If this AI isn't clueing into the fact I'm calling from Dan's, then it must require someone like Lucy making an official request. Or Soteria is going someplace other than Dan's. I try to get Lucy to join the call but she's busy.

Option B: brute-force.

"Administrative Request. Retrieve Status of IFS-6582738539."

The AI receptionist is replaced by an annoyed woman. She's real, her shirt is rumpled on the left side and she is swallowing something. She looks up at me in mild surprise; I must have triggered an unexpected warning in the security department. She glances at a flashing data alert.

"Jupyter Fuertes?"

"Yes?" There's not anyone else on this call, so I answer affirmatively.

"Why are you making administrative requests of our receptionist?"

"Um. I'm trying to find the status of a food storage unit."

"I see that. You're an employee of Dan's Artificial Psychology and Appliance Repair?"

"Correct. Can I get it?"

"No," is her pointed response. I'll bet she's been asked this before, had to look up the policy and came back to another caller with the same question, who received the same answer I received. "The receptionist already told you this. You don't get points for asking again. I'm closing this call now."

She isn't kidding. The conversation goes abruptly dark, leaving a receptionist-shaped shadow lingering in my visor. EOT.

So in summary, Soteria is lost. I'm screwed. Can't go home, can't stay here. Police waiting for me to overuse this visor. What to do now?

I didn't know, but there is a secret society of my brain neurons and they've been in a secret planning session. Without asking for my guidance, they broadcast a message to all my other neurons; it's like a 450 volt DC bump to my gray matter. The complete outline of their genius plan is attached and when I understand what it says, my eyelids do that wide-eye look you do when you're surprised in a movie.

I open up a coding environment and write frenzied algorithms. The project is working in twelve minutes and I send a copy to Avery.

"Avery, remember that intercept wedge in your network?" Avery nods and starts to verbalize, but I cut him off.

"Tell me it's still there. Tell me you haven't removed it."

"You told me to leave it alone for now. So I did. Should I have taken it down?" Avery leans forward and frowns.

"Perfect," I smile at my devious intent. *Thank you, secret society of neurons.* This might actually be a bit of fun. And it's going to save my ass. "Avery, I just sent you another wedge. I need you to install that between the intruder and your network."

I watch Avery place the wedge in position, then enable the pathway. It executes flawlessly, and I can see my diabolical plot go into motion. I have a plan B.

| 73 |

Where Is The Damn Thing?

Three steps from the kitchen to the living room. Two steps further to the bedroom. Two steps back from the bedroom to the living room, then one step to the door. Four steps back to the kitchen. Do-YeOn sees the furniture, but only enough to avoid it. It's what hyenas do in a cage at a zoo, pacing the limits of the habitat, looking for an escape. *Where is Pali?*

He gave her the personality cube yesterday. She should have broken the linked file and disrupted the block and avoid. But today, the afternoon of June 15th, it's still intact. He knows, because URCityCars legal is trying to reach him.

One more circuit through the apartment, one more circuit through his messages. Then a call from Pali shows in his visor. Do-YeOn reaches out to grab the icon and jams his finger in the wall.

"I thought you said this was an easy fix." He doesn't notice Pali's message is coming through in low resolution. His hand still throbs.

"Nice to see you too," Pali responds. "How is your day going?"

"Great. The pretty birds are singing happy songs outside my window. Why don't you come over and I'll make us a round of cocktails? Then you can tell me how easy it was to remove the block and avoid."

"Well, that would be difficult for two reasons. Do you want to hear them or continue to be a sarcastic asshole?"

"I'd rather stick with sarcasm," says Do-YeOn. "But please, you have my complete attention."

"The first piece of news is you gave me the wrong personality cube."

"Nope. It was from Jordan Bishop's apartment. No mistake."

"It was a different avatar and a newer model. It knew nothing about the block and avoid or the associated log file."

"Not pos-si-ble," Do-YeOn spit the phrase out in four syllables. "Did you query as an administrator?"

"Don't be condescending. I was at root level. I could have wiped it clean if I wanted. It was an Owen, not a Soteria. You fucked up."

"I DIDN'T," Do-YeOn says. "You fucked up. You've fucked up this entire thing."

"While we're exchanging pleasantries, I have another bit of news," says the low-resolution version of Pali. "I've left."

"You've left what?" asks Do-YeOn.

"I've left *where*. I've left the United States."

"You can't leave! What about me?"

"*You* are part of the problem. If I stay, I'll have to answer a series of difficult questions regarding my involvement in your BnA. So I've decided to be elsewhere."

"Where are you going? You'll never find a career in another country."

"I can. And it isn't prudent to inform you where. Not on a public channel."

"You ASS-HOLE," exclaims Do-YeOn. "You can't just leave me with this mess."

"Nice to chat with you. I owed you the common decency to tell you I'm throwing you under the bus. But, oh look, it's tea time. I must be off. Cheerio!"

Pali ends her side of the conversation and disappears from view, leaving him inhaling in preparation to spew another invective. There's nobody to swear at, save the growing backlog of calls from URCityCars legal and his swelling finger.

Do-YeOn tries to re-open the connection, but her icon doesn't change. No response.

Fine. I'll fix this myself, he thinks. *I just need to find Soteria, get access, and destroy the log file. That can't be impossible.*

Do-YeOn forces his legs to stop pacing and sit on the couch. They do so, refusing to allow him to sink back and instead assuming a position on the edge of the seat, knees bent at an acute angle. His weight rests on the balls of his feet, ready for a quick sprint away from predators.

Where is it? thinks Do-YeOn. He checks his wedge in Avery's network. Jupyter called Avery with updates on her imprisonment; she'll be in jail for another week. Nothing about Soteria.

At the risk of generating more calls from legal, he opens UrCityCars daily logs and filters for arrivals or departures at 7119 North Shipyard Ave between June twelfth and thirteenth. Thousands of trips appear with destinations anonymized. Not helpful.

Do-YeOn's right leg quivers like a sewing machine, bouncing on his toes, preparing to run from the approaching dinosaur. He's out of options for finding the missing Soteria.

It's missing he thinks. *Why not stolen? The police should get involved...*

His leg tries to flee, but it's not in control. Do-YeOn makes a call.

"Portland Police Bureau, Did the incident you wish to report occur within the city of Portland?" The police officer in Do-YeOn's visor is visible from the waist up, an inexpensive AI for handling non-emergency issues.

"Yes, my food storage unit is missing." Do-YeOn feels himself shaking with tension from the lie. But it's only an AI he is talking to, so he continues. "The serial number is IFS-6582738539, can you help me find it?"

"Please wait a moment." The AI displays an inexpensive hold behavior, staring into the distance.

Do-YeOn believes he's on the edge of incredible luck, but stops when Detective Guadalupe Reyes appears in his visor. He remembers her; she was with Araci Belo at the train station. He watched the two of them wait for Jupyter to return the personality cube. He's confident he wasn't seen then, so he's confident this Detective won't recognize him now. Anyhow, it's too late to back out of this plan.

"You're reporting a stolen Soteria Reizoko?" Detective Reyes isn't smiling. She must not have taken the course on Positive Community Relations.

"Yes...I," Do-YeOn suffers from cognitive overload, stuck between not saying something stupid and saying the right thing. "I'm hoping to find my refrigerator."

"Interesting," says Detective Reyes. "Your contact profile says you're Do-YeOn Kurrat. Is that correct?"

"Yes. That's correct." Do-YeOn doesn't react, but inside his head is a growing swirl of anxiety. *Get control of this* he thinks. "I purchased a used unit from an apartment manager but it's missing. I assume stolen."

"Stolen," says Detective Reyes. "Interesting."

"Yes. Stolen."

Detective Reyes stares at him through his visor. It's an uncomfortable experience. Reyes has the humorless expression people get when they're looking at a fly trying to escape from a closed window. *Open the window and let it free? Or squash the motherfucker and wipe its smoosh off the glass?* Do-YeOn shifts his eyes to the right.

"I think I'd like to talk with you about this refrigerator," says Detective Reyes. "I know where it is. I'll call you back."

"Yes. Sure." Do-YeOn sputters, then tries to resume control of himself, with little success. "I'd appreciate any progress."

With a lack of decorum, Detective Reyes cuts off the phone call. Do-YeOn hoped for a more productive interaction, but potential felons can't always expect the best outcome.

Do-YeOn goes back to pacing. Three steps from the kitchen to the living room. Two steps further to the bedroom. Two steps back from the bedroom to the living room, then one step to the door. Four steps back to the kitchen.

| 74 |

Thrashing

In my next apartment, I will make sure there's enough space for a table and chairs. Just an extra square meter of floor, nothing expansive. I'm tired of eating meals standing or dropping crumbs in the bed.

Avery and I took a chance on Pali being gone. She said she was leaving for Montevideo and for all her craziness, she does do what she says she's going to do. So we showed up here, the door still recognized me, I don't have to risk getting arrested at my place, and there's food ready to eat.

Avery offers me the last of the chow mein but I turn him down in favor of monitoring the searches in my visor. I hear him scraping bits from the corners of the packet and slurping the sauce. He bounces to his feet, tosses the dishes in the composter, and returns to his spot on the couch.

There's a lesson to be learned about appreciating what's in front of me, rather than trying to find something that's missing. But I need to know where Soteria is *now.* So I'm searching for any sign of my mechanical friend. It's an obsessive thing. Soteria is supposed to arrive at Dan's by tomorrow morning. I could relax with Avery. Everything will be fine and I can trust the universe will do the right thing.

Or I can try to get control over this variable and track Soteria second-by-second. It's just my freedom in the balance. Yep. Nothing to worry about. Everything's fine. I check the search. Nothing.

I'm not being an attentive girlfriend. In fact, I'm a parasite, hijacking Avery's network for my own purposes. My visor controls the wedge he installed and I'm busy sending commands to his network, which sends it out as Avery, the results of which I scoop up and review. It's slow and difficult and requires I pay attention to a lot of moving parts. That doesn't leave time for Avery. Sorry, buddy. No romance tonight, but thanks for the access.

My intercept in Avery's network also watches for traffic destined for Do-YeOn. I'm interested in anything he's interested in, and I'm interested in making sure he gets it wrong. I patched in a tricky bit of AI to catch and mangle traffic headed his way. If Do-YeOn asks what Avery had for dinner, the AI will respond with a menu from a Chinese sit-down restaurant or that he hasn't eaten yet or that a pizza is being delivered. My wedge provides a plausible but incorrect feed to Do-YeOn. Enough small errors that over time sum up to a wrong conclusion. So clever of me.

Avery snakes his arm behind my neck in an uncomfortable try at pulling me towards him. I'm watching the search window, so I miss the non-verbal signals of his romantic intent until he's snagging my hair.

I lean forward to re-position his arm. He takes the opening to reach to my waist and under my spray-on to release the adhesion. The clothing snaps away and my breasts relax to their natural shape. That wasn't what I intended, but it's not objectionable. I make a brief check on the latest search results, then peel off the remains of my shirt. It no longer served a purpose and spraying on a new one would be time better spent queuing up a request. It's as easy to be topless. I send the request from queue to active.

"Do you have to do that?" Avery asks. "Right now?"

When my wedge program runs, it sucks up a bunch of his CPU and everything else gets pushed to the back, causing his visor to complain. Anything Avery had running is *executis interruptus,* which also seems to be happening to his plans for our evening.

"I'm sorry," I apologize, but check the returns. That makes my apology NULL. I could have been more sincere. I think I *would* like to have sex with Avery, but ... *Where is Soteria?*

I force myself to turn and kiss him. I consider removing my visor, but if I remove it, I'll just wonder if there's something I should be aware of. I pop the adhesion of Avery's spray-on and the one-piece rolls to the side. I can see Avery has something I should be aware of.

Avery moves towards me and I lay back, moving the pillow behind my head so I can watch. He obviously hasn't completed the online sex course; Pali was better at this. But he's not distracted and pays attention to my gentle cues, so things start to happen.

My visor pings and I startle. It's a small message that nothing was found, but Avery sits back on his knees and stares. His erection droops, poor little neglected thing. I'm screwed because of that visor ping. Or more accurately, I won't be screwed because of that visor ping.

"I know you're worried about finding Soteria," says Avery. "I know you're dealing with police. I know you're not feeling safe. But are you always like this? Do you only have one channel? Do you just jump from one crisis to the next?"

"Avery, I'm sorry. I'm not paying attention, I know. Sorry." I reach to pick up his deflated penis. Maybe I can breathe life into it. It's only a moment before Avery's visor complains about my CPU monopoly-*PING*. He gets up and moves to the bed in the other room. I follow, thinking he's looking for someplace more conducive, but covers himself with the sheet, laying face-down with his head away from me. It's a signal there will be no sex this evening.

Okay. If I can't have Avery, I can instead try for Soteria. I queue up another request and send it through the wedge in Avery's system. I'll spend all night searching, since sleep and sex are out of reach.

| 75 |

Soteria.Reizoko[2062-06-16]

Event Log for Soteria.Reizoko

Serial: IFS-6582738539

Owner is JORDAN BISHOP

2062-06-16T00:00:00-08:00 – ADMINISTRATIVE_MESSAGE

This unit will be decommissioned on 2062-06-16T00:00:00-08:00

Reason: Malfunction. Warranty = FALSE

- - -

2062-06-16T07:48:03-08:00 – System reboot

2062-06-16T07:50:36-08:00 – System shutdown

2062-06-16T11:36:22-08:00 – System reboot

2062-06-16T11:37:36-08:00 – System shutdown

2062-06-16T12:22:26-08:00 – System reboot

2062-06-16T12:31:10-08:00 - Support Request

Initiate conversation

Support Tech: Jupyter Fuertes, EmpID RttS-5172-720

Initiate Avatar

Request: Recall Jupyter1

Display: Jupyter1

| 76 |

Confirmation Of Disposal

June 16th, 2062

To: International Mercado PLC

Re: Confirmation of disposal of capital asset

From: Dan's Artificial Psychology and Appliance Repair

We confirm the disposal of the following capital asset. All media has been digitally sanitized and physically destroyed.

Property Description: *Soteria Reizoko Food Storage Unit, Serial # IFS-6582738539

Reason: Malfunction and out of warranty

Date of Disposal: June 16, 2062

Method of disposal: All digital media sanitized. Physical components recycled and/or salvaged for parts

| 77 |

Bits Of Plastic

My visor wakes me with the search I queued last night. Nothing. I fling it across the room. Soteria is still off the net. Hopefully at Dan's, but I can't be sure.

I have a moment of disorientation before I remember I'm at Pali's apartment. Then I have a moment of terror before I remember Pali has left for Montevideo. Avery's gone. He's either angry or he let me sleep.

I retrieve my visor and check the search again. Still missing, but there's nothing else I can do. Avery's visor isn't providing access for new searches.

I check the time. *SHIT* I do a cartoon-style double-take at the clock. 11:00 am. Oh, *Dammit.* Soteria may already be at Dan's, teetering on the edge of being ground into dust. I do the minimal spray-on and suit-up workplace modesty requires and I'm out.

I can't use this visor to call Avery, or Lucy, or Rob, or anybody. I take a huge chance buying a train ticket to get to Dan's. I watch every stop, expecting uniforms with handcuffs waiting to capture me. I tap my foot in a reciprocating pattern. downleftuprightdownleftupright-down.

The train stops nearest to Dan's. I've already been standing next to the door for two stations and I bolt when it opens. I'm trying not to knock into people, but it's rude to stand in the way of someone with an emergency. Ouch.

I run past the deli and up to the security doors at Dan's. I stare at the cameras, willing them to recognize me and *open the damn door.* I wait an eternity of two seconds before it opens. Finally. I enter, take one step and assess the warehouse floor.

There aren't any Soterias on the stands.

There aren't any in the racks.

Lucy sees me and walks over, clipboard in hand.

"Your Soteria unit arrived about four hours ago. It's already ground up and recycled."

I'm going to prison. This is an uncomfortable place to cry. I lean back against one of the service platforms.

"I know you were looking for Soteria." Lucy says. "You weren't here when it showed up. I tried to call, but you didn't answer." She pushes an object at me; a little cube.

I look at Lucy.

"Is this Soteria?"

She smiles.

It's hard to hug such a little thing, but I try. I take three flying ballerina steps to the shelves with diagnostic suitcases, pull one down to the floor and push the cube into the socket.

It powers up, just like it's supposed to, but I can't see Soteria. I re-power, wait for moments for something to happen, then remember I'm using a crap visor. Brushing past Lucy, I run upstairs, grab a loaner visor from the break room and return. Glorious day, caloo calay, little Soteria appears; sunglasses, Hawaiian shirt, suntan.

My annoying friend. How nice to see you back.

| 78 |

Order To Vacate

"Hello Do-YeOn. Amari Sawyer from UrCityCars HR department is on the call with me. We need to inform you this call is being recorded and placed in your personnel records. Do you consent to this conversation?"

It's Do-YeOn's first message today. His good friend, Addison Lake, UrCityCars Attorney is calling.

"So nice to chat with you," says Do-YeOn. "I assume you're asking if I'd be in charge of the next employee picnic?"

"Mr. Kurrat, this isn't a pleasant task for us. Do you consent to this recording?"

"Yes," Do-YeOn replies with his flattest voice. "Can I have a blindfold and a cigarette before you shoot?"

Addison glances at Amari. Amari gives no reaction, and Addison continues. "Mr. Kurrat, you failed to address our concerns about your performance. In addition, your activities are a liability to the corporation and shareholder value. We are required to sever our relationship until we can resolve these issues. Do you understand?"

"Yes. Do I get a blindfold?"

"Mr. Kurrat, we have reassigned your projects and suspended your access to UrCityCars property. This reassignment will remain until you address these concerns. This includes your corporate-sponsored apartment. You have the rest of the day to vacate, a representative of UrCityCars will arrive at 5:30 this evening to assist you with your transition."

"5:30? Tonight? That's in four hours!"

"Four hours and thirty-three minutes. I realize this may be inconvenient, but it is part of your employment contract and in keeping with the National Shareholder Protection Act of 2059."

"Fine. Fine. If you'll excuse me, I need to pack."

Do-YeOn doesn't wait for a response before he snaps away the call. He doesn't start packing. Instead, he stands on the edge of the room, immobile.

I need the refrigerator. I could fix this if I have the refrigerator.

Detective Reyes knows where it is. Jupyter knows where it is. I'm the only one who doesn't.

But I know where Avery is. So I know where Jupyter is.

Do-YeOn waves up a connection to the wedge in Avery's network, looking for signs of the refrigerator or Jupyter. With a bit of work, he pulls up a list of Avery's train trips, some to the stop near Dan's Appliances, some to a stop near Avery's apartment, and recently, trips to a third stop, near the freeway. It's within walking distance of Jordan's final impact zone.

Is Avery going to the field under the overpass? Is there something still there? Something left over from Jordan's accident?

That would be a stupid place to hide a refrigerator.

Do-Yeon grabs his daypack on the way out of the apartment. Maybe there's something worth carrying back.

| 79 |

Resurrection

I could have run here faster. Maybe not, but sitting on the train was a zen experience. Just exist. Don't think. Be mindful. Relax. Release stress. The train stops at the station nearest the police and I bolt for the door, thinking *fuck it!* and how fast can I make it to turn myself in to Detective Reyes.

I'm in the same room where we tried this before and where I surprised Reyes with an unexpected exit. They could have put me in cuffs, but no. I suspect the nice folks outside are keeping a close watch on the bathroom and the doors. Fool me once, shame on you. Fool me twice, you'll go down with a taser in your ass. I only assume Soteria's appearance is saving me from an uncomfortable experience.

Detective Reyes can see me and the Soteria icon. The diagnostic suitcase powers the cube, the cube gives life to Soteria, and the little guy can dive deep without lag or administrative access. I have to be careful not to trigger any destructive commands; with this diagnostic interface, Soteria would give himself a lobotomy without anesthesia.

"Soteria, show me Jupyter.1"

```
       adminID : Do-YeOn Kurrat
       ownerID : CityOfPortland.PublicVehicle
     vehicleID : UrCityCars#33579
manufacturerID : PDX>Go
    locationID : <List>
```

And there it is. Detective Reyes is an apt student and I am more than delighted to describe every detail of those five lines. How Do-

YeOn shouldn't be the Admin of a PDX>Go car. Why it's unusual (an understatement) for a UrCityCar to be the vehicle ID. Massive fuckery was happening when Jordan Bishop lofted from the overpass and Do-YeOn has some 'splainin' to do.

But don't take my word for it - look to the evidence presented by Soteria's block-chain protected log of the events. There is no wiggle-room here.

Detective Reyes calls in another uniform, a woman. She has an older diagnostic box. We move Soteria over and I walk uniform woman through the steps to pull up Jupyter.1 . Soteria displays the damning evidence. Uniform woman makes notes, exchanges a few cryptograms with Detective Reyes and tells me she needs to keep Soteria as evidence.

I shouldn't let him out of my sight, but I have to trust someone, sometime. This is the moment. "Sure," I say. At least I have a receipt.

And in minutes, I'm standing outside the station. Free to go. I replace my loaner visor with my personal visor. The restrictions are gone, I'm a free woman with no fetters.

It takes only a minute before a flood of messages arrives. I search for the most important, a message from Avery. Any message from Avery. And there's one waiting; but not from Avery. It's from the wedge. Do-YeOn has been sniffing around, creating little privacy invasions. And my wedge-in-a-wedge has been performing. I take a look and marvel at my genius, the wedge sent Do-YeOn a list of train trips, including manufactured trips to Jordan's crash site. *How did it do that?*

I ponder this bit of knowledge, then head back inside. I'm guessing Lupe might be interested to know Do-YeOn is proceeding to an open field with no surveillance cameras.

| 80 |

Out Of Sight

Do-YeOn is three steps out of his apartment before he is notified free access to UrCityCars has been shut off. Another job perk stripped away. He summons a car and is dismayed to see a PDX>Go vehicle appear. He pounds the top of the car in frustration, then opens the door. There's a used cup and food wrapper on the seat, someone else's carelessness. He sweeps the trash into the street, sits, and pulls the destination marker to Jordan Bishop's final stop.

His anxiety boils as he waits in traffic. Nothing he does can change the arrival time. No short-cuts are available, no executive overrides. Just sit.

The car arrives, but won't turn into the field. His attempts to convince it to go further result in annoying rodent sounds. Do-YeOn gets out and the PDX>Go departs back to civilization.

He can see the overpass and the broken guardrail where Jordan took flight. In front of him is a mountain of blackberry bushes. A wide path has been cut but the ground is churned up and difficult to walk through.

Do-YeOn considers turning back, but that leads to packing boxes and a representative from UrCityCars who would assist with his transition. Nope; he'd rather fight blackberries. More than once he stumbles and snags himself on the aggressive vines.

The path goes around a turn, revealing an open field with an island of untrimmed vegetation. He travels the dozen meters and circles the island. Nothing of interest until he gets to the side closest to the freeway. There, a large print is in the bushes, possibly tossed from the overpass. He reaches to pull it out, falls off balance and skewers his palm and forearm on thorns.

It's a reproduction of old artwork. A dancer and a man in a courtyard. On the back is an inscription: "For Araci." He moves to throw it but there is a high-frequency whirring behind him, over his shoulder, then a pop. The print has a new hole dead center. Do-YeOn holds the canvas closer for inspection. *Did a small bird crash through this painting?*

A second pop and another hole appears. Do-YeOn realizes he's being shot at. He turns to look around the field, but nobody else is in view. He can hear a drone, but it's in the far distance and barely audible. The smart thing to do would be to crouch down. Getting cover would be a good idea, so he tries to run, like a duck, shielding himself with the artwork.

A third hole appears near his hand, then another shot sails just over his head. He crosses the open field and dives into the blackberries, forgetting the consequences of headlong travel through the *cheval de frise.* He thrashes through to a clearing in the underbrush, trapping himself between acres of vines and the fifth and sixth projectiles slamming into the dirt.

It's dark before he can pick his way out of the prison, moving without an attack. He bleeds on the car seat on the return trip to his apartment. There he finds he only has access to a downstairs storage locker where his belongings have been moved. UrCityCars had made good on their deadline.

The sign on the door says **NO SLEEPING ALLOWED**. Another clarifies **STORAGE FEE $300 PER DAY. MAXIMUM 30 DAYS. ABANDONED PROPERTY WILL BE AUCTIONED**

That's it. I'm fucked. thinks Do-YeOn.

| 81 |

Soteria.Reizoko[2062-06-17]

Event Log for Soteria.Reizoko

Serial: IFS-6582738539

Owner is JORDAN BISHOP

2062-06-17T00:00:00-08:00 – ADMINISTRATIVE_MESSAGE

This item is Police Evidence

Case Number: 62-CR-77394

Evidence Tag Number: 62-CR-657993:03

Date Acquired: 2062-06-16

Location: Police Station #2239 - Portland, Oregon

Description: Soteria Personality Module. IFS-6582738539

Chain of Possession

Collected By: Detective Guadalupe Reyes

Collected From: Jupyter Fuertes

- - -

2062-06-17T08:41:03-08:00 – System reboot

2062-06-17T07:43:36-08:00 – System shutdown

| 82 |

Sheep

Olive the sheep is outside the window. I peek over the sill and do my best imitation. **BAAAAAA**

Olive looks up from the grass. **Baaaaaaaa**

We've been doing this for fifteen minutes. Olive and I are completely amused. Avery hides under a pillow.

"I was sleeping"

"We're not. Olive wants to go on a hike. So do I."

Avery pulls me down from the window and curls around me. Olive will have to wait.

// . . .

I've had mornings like this before. Slow waking up, noises outside, smells of the neighbors. This morning I wake in the small house on Avery's farm. It has wood frames around the windows, a heater in the basement, a door in the front and a door in the back. It's a real building and I can live here if I want to. I'd have to live here with Avery, but that could work.

The sheep like him. He gave them all names and they come running when he calls. They head-butt each other to get closer to him. They aren't as interested in me yet. With time, I can change that.

Araci's memorial is today. Detective Reyes invited us. It's awkward, but she's trying to make nice and I'm in a forgiving mood. It makes little sense to annoy the dead. Reyes's attitude adjustment happened after I told her about Do-Ye0n heading to the crash zone. I explained the wedge, and she bagged out of the station, shouting about rats. She called last night all friendly. She must have seen a therapist.

Reyes says she will return Soteria after a few months. She's building a case against Do-Ye0n but it's difficult. Explaining all the goings-ons between PDX>Go and UrCityCars is deep tech and a tough sell to the District Attorney. Do-Ye0n signed a surveillance agreement, so he's free to walk about, but his visor tattles on him everywhere he goes. I know how that feels. So who knows if he will get his undoing. As long as he's not trying to kill me I'm ready to move on.

I haven't heard from Pali. I guess I'm not worried about that.

"Avery, get up. Places to be! Still time to join Olive and me for a quick hike out to the creek."

| 83 |

Persistence

She looks south, but thinks north.

Portland, Oregon.

Jupyter.

She just came from there. She can't go back. Pali's room overlooks the ocean horizon. Somewhere past the other apartments is the beach. It may be home to the largest technical incubators, but its occupants still hang out laundry in the morning. Montevideo is a riot of color and motion.

She turns back to the briefcase she brought from Portland. A five-centimeter cube glows in a receptacle on the lower left of the diagnostic board in the case. Pali puts on her visor and summons the avatar she's building for the cube.

"Resume programming. Show me the options for hair color."

It is difficult to remember the color of Jupyter's hair. Pali looks at the movies playing in her visor and then to the nascent avatar. She's getting closer.

Mark Niemann-Ross writes mostly science fiction, sometimes programming in R, often about tinkering with Raspberry Pi (the single board computer, not the pastry).

He lives in Portland, Oregon, paddles boats, wrangles chickens, and gives compliments to strangers.

www.ingramcontent.com/pod-product-compliance
Lightning Source LLC
LaVergne TN
LVHW052038200926
848481LV00005B/1714